Praise for *Restrung* . . .

"An engaging memoir about fathers, sons and how the things we never say are louder than the things we hear, this is powerful and unreasonably brilliant work."

—ALEX GREEN, host of Stereo Embers the Podcast

"A compelling memoir of a young urban music fan diving headlong into the passion and pathos of rock 'n' roll."

—JIM WHITE, Pushcart Prize–winning author and musician

"Underneath the memoir's twinned reflections on Fogelson's discovery of the rock scene and his young fatherhood, *Restrung* throbs with the bassline of what it means to become a man."

—HILARY ZAID, author of *Paper is White* and *Forget I Told You This*

RESTRUNG

RESTRUNG

FATHERHOOD IN A DIFFERENT KEY

MATT FOGELSON

spark press

Published in 2026 by
SparkPress, an imprint of The Stable Book Group

32 Court Street, Suite 2109
Brooklyn, NY 11201
https://shewritespress.com
Library of Congress Control Number: 2025916868
ISBN: 978-1-68463-342-5
eISBN: 978-1-68463-343-2

Interior Designer: Kiran Spees

Printed in the United States
Names and identifying characteristics have been changed to protect the privacy of certain individuals.

For my mother. Your boundless love for me has made everything and anything possible.

CONTENTS

OAKLAND, CALIFORNIA

2005

River gonna take me, sing me sweet and sleepy
Sing me sweet and sleepy all the way back home.

Those were the words I sang that finally cracked the code, that finally nudged my two-day-old son Jed off to sleep his first night home. It was like a magic trick. All my prior efforts to get the boy to stop crying and for the love of God just close his eyes had failed. Reasoning with him—telling him he'd had a strenuous couple of days, that he needed his rest, both in the short term to brace for meeting his maternal grandparents in the morning and in the long term to prepare for the protracted, arduous journey that is life—hadn't worked. Neither had politely shushing him. Trying to barter with him by asking him to do me this one solid and I'd have his back forever was equally fruitless. Bouncing with him on a huge yoga ball only agitated him more, as if he wanted to bust out of his blanket swaddle and heave the yoga ball at me. And feeding him only took the decibel level down from ear splitting to can't-hear-myself-think.

Out of options as I held the boy like some incredibly fragile over-inflated football, I retreated to the same wooden rocking chair in which my mother had rocked me, and I sang to him. It was an odd turn because I'm not the singing type. Never have been. Not in the shower, not while strumming my guitar, not in the car (okay, sometimes alone in the car—I'm only human). But honestly, I didn't know what else to do.

As strange as it was to hear myself singing to Jed, perhaps even more puzzling was my song choice. For some reason, it didn't occur to me to go with a tried-and-true bedtime staple like "Rock-A-Bye Baby" or "Twinkle, Twinkle, Little Star." No, I sang "Brokedown Palace" by the Grateful Dead. I gave absolutely no thought to the choice; it just flowed out of me like a breath. Luckily, it turned out to be the perfect lullaby, full of imagery of flowing rivers, sleep, and the peace that comes with being home.

As I began the second verse, the furious howling bundle unclenched and started to relax. The eyes got a little narrower, the body went a touch limp. Peace and harmony were restored. I was amazed. Thank you, Jerry Garcia! A memory of myself as a little kid home sick from school flashed through my mind, my mother taking me in her arms and spinning me around in front of the large mirror in the hallway, me watching us laughing until I became dizzy and my mother put me down. Perhaps not the best home remedy, but I felt comforted and loved, as I hoped Jed did now.

As I watched Jed's tiny chest move up and down almost imperceptibly, I realized that not only is "Brokedown Palace" the perfect lullaby, it's also a statement of the transcendent: "Lovers come and go, the river roll, roll, roll." It was plain to me that first night at home with Jed that he and I are forever joined no matter what lies ahead for each of us. We are stones in each other's river, carried along in the other's current. I am his father. He is my son.

I rose from the rocking chair, gently placed Jed in his crib, and kissed him softly on the forehead, a bit anxious the kiss might wake him but unable to stop myself. Then I stood and gazed down at him, wondering who he might become and thinking of my own father who died when I was in college, wishing he was there beside me, the two of us trying to acclimate to our new roles—his as grandfather, mine as father—and wishing he could watch Jed grow, that he could see his own son become a father, that I could tell him I loved him.

In that moment I felt my father's absence as I had so many times over the prior fourteen years as I morphed from boy to man, a feeling like I was flailing in quicksand, struggling not to be sucked under. But the truth is, I felt my father's absence long before he died, the presence of an absence—his absence—gnawing at me always. My father dedicated himself to his career as a high-powered corporate lawyer and was rarely around as I grew up. Even when it was painfully clear that he was very near the end of his life, he had work papers delivered to his hospital room. His family came a distant second—I came a distant second. It's a realization I struggled with for a long time, wondering if the person I became was truly me or the person I thought my father wanted me to become, if perhaps I'd succumbed to the pull of loyalty as a stand-in for closeness.

I didn't know much yet about being a father, but I knew I didn't want Jed to ever feel that same absence, that same kind of ache. A song by Bruce Springsteen, one of my all-time favorite artists, hummed in my ears, a plea that the sins of the son be his own, not handed down from the prior generation, that the cycle of emotional neglect be broken. And I committed to Jed then and there that I would be present for him as much as he wished and for as long as I was around.

I gazed down at my son, just now embarking on a life-long adventure full of possibilities, and I wondered, had my father lived long enough to become a grandfather, might *that* have broken the spell of work, might he have at least occasionally left his corner office early to catch his grandson's basketball games? Would he have felt excited to cheer from the stands for Jed even if he'd never shown up to cheer for his son? I smiled at the thought of my father watching Jed drain three-pointers in some imaginary dream world. And then a memory of my father bubbled up in my mind. He and I were with my mother somewhere in Colorado sitting at an outdoor table with a panoramic view of the Rocky Mountains. The cancer that eventually destroyed my father had started to manifest itself in his thinning frame and bald head. He stared out at those majestic mountains and said, "Well, I'd have done a lot of things differently if I'd known." What did he mean by that? Did he mean he would've spent less time working and more time with his family? With me? Did he ultimately find his work soulless and deadening? Did he wish he hadn't built his life around it? Is that what he meant? Is that what killed him? His work? His regret?

I didn't know the answers to those questions then and I still don't. But I do know this: before Jed arrived, I was on a path heading straight to that same place, a place of deep regret. And I was headed down that dark, dead-end road in the name of trying to keep my father close. But that first night with Jed started me on a different path, a path to freedom from the constraints I'd placed on myself. And as was the case at so many turns in my life, I have music to thank for showing me the way.

Looking back at that night singing "Brokedown Palace," I realize my impromptu rendition was the manifestation of a deeply-held wish to share my passion for music with my son. But even more than that, to stake a claim to a part of myself I'd held in check my entire life, that had lain dormant as I tried to fill the hole created by my father's absence. Singing to Jed started me on a journey toward recognizing the indispensable role music has played in sustaining me and it allowed me to begin to embrace that part of myself, to know that the hole cannot be filled by suppressing my passion, that in fact the hole is of a type that can never be filled but must instead be acknowledged, honored, and somehow, someway, transcended.

Satisfied that Jed was down for the count, I turned on the baby monitor and tiptoed to the door. My wife was standing in the hallway outside Jed's room. "That was incredible," she said, giving my hand a squeeze. "Was that 'Brokedown Palace'?"

I nodded and squeezed her hand. She pressed her head against my chest and hugged me close. I felt my head gently drop and come to rest on top of hers.

"He's lucky to have you for a father."

I tunneled my nose into her hair and breathed deeply. Hearing her refer to me as Jed's father made me feel proud. I sensed my father passing me the paternal torch for safekeeping. And I hoped that his absence wouldn't dim its glow.

My wife looked up at me and sighed. "That song really saved us," she whispered as we embraced in the blissful quiet.

I smiled. Music as succor, music as sustenance—music as savior.

1

DON'T SPEAK OF IT

I was a sophomore in college when my father told me he had lung cancer. He was forty-six. I was nineteen. He broke the news during our family's Christmas vacation. My older brother Rob and I were throwing a football on a white, crescent-shaped beach, and from under an umbrella a short distance away my father looked up from the work papers he'd been reading and called to us, "Guys, let's take a walk." Rising from his chaise, he carefully secured the papers under one of the chaise straps, those papers that followed him everywhere as a corporate lawyer, so light they could blow away in a faint breeze but so heavy they could cause his entire body to slump.

We set off down the beach, my father walking slowly between Rob and me, his eyes staring straight ahead. I don't remember the exact words he used to convey that my life, and his, would no longer be recognizable to either one of us. But I distinctly remember the phrase "five years on the high end"—that found purchase in my memory. I still can't shake it. It's always there in moments of absence. I hear it in the backcountry, while hiking in remote, beautiful places. I heard it on my wedding day—before the ceremony as I stood alone at the end of the dock at our summer place on Long Island, closed my eyes, and breathed in the sea. I heard it as my son slept in my arms the day he was born.

I also remember pulling my baseball cap down to keep out the sunshine that was suddenly blinding me, turning everything that was, moments before, carefree—the sailboats anchored offshore, the palm trees, a tray full of umbrella drinks, the toddler dressed in a rainbow bathing suit holding a small plastic shovel—into one giant blur of nothing, a Seurat painting viewed from three inches.

And then just as suddenly, objects regained their form, lines and dimensions were reestablished. I looked at Rob. He stood straight and stiff, his jaw fixed, his eyes boring into my father's. The football floated in the light surf at his feet, bumping into him every few seconds and receding. He looked taller than usual, but that could be because I was slouching, my body having lost some of its structural integrity, like a puppet without a puppet master.

There was a huge disconnect between what my father was saying and his demeanor. We learned they had caught it early, that he was optimistic, that he had no symptoms and was otherwise in great health. "There's a good chance I'll be an outlier," he said, practically upbeat.

"I thought only smokers got lung cancer," I said, stunned.

"Apparently not." My father put his hand on my shoulder. "Look at me, Matt." I'd been staring down at my feet, watching the water bury them deeper with each passing wave. I looked up and met his gaze. "You have to play the hand you're dealt," he said.

We walked back down the beach in silence. I shivered in the searing mid-afternoon heat. My father returned to his work papers and Rob and I retreated to our hotel room, a thatch building on stilts with a view of the ocean and a large ceiling fan that kept the mosquitoes at bay. My mother came in and asked how we were doing.

"I'm feeling okay about it," Rob said. "Sounds like they caught it pretty early so I think he's got a good chance of beating it. I'm not all that worried." I couldn't tell if Rob actually felt that way or was putting on a brave face. My mother's eyes narrowed slightly, as if she was trying to see something in the distance.

She turned to me. "Matt, what about you?"

"I feel like I've been hit in the stomach," I said.

My mother's shoulders dropped a touch. She nodded and took my hands in hers. "It's shocking," she said. "Really shocking." I thought back to when I was a small boy and would climb into my parents' bed to play Old Maid with my mother. We had one of those jumbo card sets with the old maid pictured on her rocking chair knitting a long pink and green scarf, a Dolly Madison pendant around her neck, her glasses riding low on her nose. I remembered my mother's laughter whenever she'd be left at the end with the old maid. "You little stinker!" she'd howl and throw her hands up in the air like it was the worst thing that could possibly happen, and then she'd laugh and laugh as she hugged me tight. I wished I could climb into that bed again, drink in my mother's all-encompassing love, and feel I wasn't alone.

That night after dinner, Rob and I retired to the hotel lounge, a small open-air room with a view out to the black emptiness of the ocean, and sat at the bar drinking vodka-grapefruits. Most of the other vacationers were drinking daquiris of some fruity type or other, strawberry or peach, in large bowl-shaped glasses, but this night called for stronger stuff, something without a whiff of the festive to it.

"I always knew something like this would happen," Rob said staring out at the ocean as he swirled the ice in his highball glass. "Our lives were too good. The other shoe was always going to drop." The comment caught me off-guard, both because I'd never pegged Rob as a philosopher type, but also because I could see his point even though I'd never thought about our family situation in that way. But yeah, now that he'd said it, it made sense. Nothing really bad had ever happened to us. Or maybe I was just grasping for some explanation—any explanation—for what was going down, even if it was some crazy mystical shit. Maybe Rob was too. "But like I told Mom, I think Pops will be okay. They caught it early," he went on, somewhat undermining his newfound philosopher's wisdom.

"Yeah, I'm sure," I said, although I didn't believe it.

After last call, Rob and I staggered back to our room, where Rob caught site of the complimentary bottle of Mount Gay sitting atop the mini bar. "Hate to see that bottle go to waste," he said. "Whaddya say, Dice Man? To the beach?" "Dice man" had become Rob's nickname for me after I developed a habit in grade school of saying "no dice" in any context that a simple "no" would've done.

I wasn't much of a rum drinker. Neither was Rob as far as I knew, but like my father had said, you've got to play the hand you're dealt. "Sounds good," I replied.

As we traded the bottle back and forth, the exhausted late-night waves lapping against the beach with a gentle whoosh and me getting further and further away from myself, I remembered all the times Rob and I had gotten drunk together, my mind eventually settling on one beer-fueled night at the old Nightingale Bar on 13th and 2nd when Rob was home from college and I was a senior in high school. We'd gotten fed up with the house band's boring fare of Steve Miller's "The Joker" and Bob Seger's "Old Time Rock & Roll" and started yelling for them to play "Sweet Jane" by the Velvet Underground.

Rob was a big VU fan. He played their records a ton, and the band's fearlessly aggressive energy, their rawness, penetrated not just the wall separating our rooms but my straightlaced sensibilities. I became transfixed by Lou Reed, the prophet of New York's dirty underbelly who told stories of a world I knew nothing about. He made this tight-assed kid from the Upper East Side feel like I'd boarded some magic, graffiti-laden subway car to an enthralling underworld of social delinquency and unleashed desire.

The band ignored us, but we kept yelling for "Sweet Jane." We nagged the band for a full hour, calling out after every song, the way strung-out but tireless Lynyrd Skynyrd fans clamor for "Freebird." At long last to get us to shut up, the band jokingly said they'd play "Sweet Jane," but only if Rob and I sang it. We were just drunk enough to think they were serious. To their dismay, we jumped up onstage and staggered toward the microphone. There was an awkward pause, then the lead singer stepped back and the bewildered band played those four perfect, crystalline chords. Rob and I lurched at the microphone and had at it, with the kind of gusto only drunk teenagers can muster, our contorted, sweaty faces inches apart as we offered up what surely stands as the worst public performance of "Sweet Jane" in the song's long and glorious history. The band cut us off after the second verse, shaking their collective head. They seemed equal parts incredulous and horrified. But we didn't care, and hell, we even got a few wobbly high fives afterwards from the other drunks in the crowd. "I've taught you well," Rob said as we left in search of a cab. "That's the greatest song ever written." He had—and it is.

Even though our performance at the Nightingale had been only two years earlier, on this drunken beach night it seemed of a different epoch. I wondered if all my memories and everything still to unfold in my life would forever be separated—delineated—by this day. Before or after, AD vs. BC.

Rob took a long pull on the rum bottle and handed it back to me.

"We'll be okay," he said. "Whatever happens, you and me, we'll be okay."

Maybe it was the rum, or maybe it was the immutable steadfastness of the stars twinkling above me, but I almost believed him.

After Christmas break, I returned to college at Duke University. I understood that my father would be dead sooner rather than later and felt the weighty truth of the thing biding its time deep in my gut, surfacing through sudden sensations of tightness in my chest that arose unpredictably during moments of bustle and quiet, of pitch blackness and broad daylight and left me in mute incredulousness every time, prompting me to exhale deeply as if to rid my own lungs of some lurking and deadly toxicity.

Like any proud dad, my father adopted my school as his own, becoming an avid Duke basketball fan and wearing with pride all the shirts and hats I bought for him. I made it a mission to get him to Duke for a game and he actually found the time to come down one weekend that winter. Not only were we treated to a thrilling, two-point Duke win over Georgia Tech, but my father got to witness the Cameron Crazies at their clowning best, throwing twinkies at Tech's slightly corpulent star player during warmups. Although we had physical seats in the "adult" section, we opted to stand for the entire game in the student section. I'd occasionally look over at my father and see him smiling broadly, taking in the wild and deafening scene, exchanging high-fives with some of the Crazies in celebration of a dunk or three-pointer.

As ecstatic as I was to be there with my father, as delicious as it was to drink in his unbridled joy, I still felt that darkness, understanding we'd never go to another game together, never get to do countless other things together, probably never again be as happy as we were in that moment. But I never let on to my father, never showed him my anguish. I put on a brave face, for him as well as for my mother and Rob. But the act collapsed when I was alone and contemplated my life without Pops. Like the protagonist of Cormac McCarthy's *All The Pretty Horses*, I felt the fact of my father's terminal illness enter me like another being, felt it bore down in my gut and carve for itself a deep, dark hole. For short discrete periods, and for the benefit of others, I could pretend it wasn't there. But I couldn't fool myself. I knew it was there and I had no reason to believe it would ever leave.

When I went home for the summer, my father's condition was jarring—the person squirreled away in the study working still strongly resembled my father, but something of him was missing. He'd lost weight and his face was drawn. He'd begun to lose his thick, lustrous hair, his beard was fading from his face, leaving just a permanent shadow. But nobody said anything about it; we all pretended that my father's decline wasn't the terrifying portent it clearly was.

My mother didn't have the luxury of ignoring the truth. In countless doctors' offices and specialty clinics all over the country, some of the world's lung cancer experts described to her the limited treatment options and extremely long odds. But I thought my mother needed me to be strong for her, so I kept up the act even though she was no longer watching the play.

One night that summer, I was standing out at the end of our dock when she came to join me. She was drinking a beer. She never drank beer.

"I don't want to burden you," she said, "but I have nobody else to burden." The tears in her eyes reflected the moon's light. "I think we need to start preparing ourselves."

"I actually think he's doing okay, all things considered," I interrupted her. "He seems to be tolerating the treatments really well." It was as if my mother was falling but I couldn't hold out my arms to catch her.

"Yes, he is," she said and looked up at the moon.

I spent the fall break of my junior year back home in New York. My father kept busy as ever, going to work every day, bringing home reading for the evenings and weekends. He was now completely bald and had bought a set of three wigs, all different lengths and thicknesses to mimic the varied stages between haircuts. I'd never thought of my father as a vain person, and so the three-wig program—the effort of it—shocked me, made me wonder how he was processing things. Not that I ever asked him.

One night after dinner, my father surprised me by suggesting we sit for a minute in the living room. It was a large room with three tall windows facing a busy New York City street. When Jed was an infant and we'd visit my mother, I'd stand him up in the sills of those living room windows and he'd point excitedly at all the yellow taxis whizzing by down below. He could spend hours in those windowsills; it was his favorite place in the world. But we'd rarely use the living room when I lived there. It was more of an entertainment space for company. Two tan, low-back sofas faced each other in the middle of the room separated by a glass coffee table. My father sat down on the sofa facing the windows and I sat on the couch opposite him

"Come sit next to me," he said patting the space next to him. I did as he asked, easing myself down gently, as if on a waterbed I didn't want to set in motion for fear of jostling him.

"The cancer has spread to my brain," he said matter-of-factly. He looked straight into my eyes so I couldn't look away. "But it's not in an area that controls speech or other major cognitive functions, so I'm lucky. The next round of chemo should knock it out."

Even though I never held out much hope my father would beat the cancer, the news that it had now invaded his brain—his *fucking* brain, that it had breached mission control—sent a jolt of electricity through my body. I felt as if a black hole was suddenly swirling around me, trying to suck me in. I put my hands down on the sofa as if to brace myself.

"When's the next round of chemo?" I asked casually.

"Hopefully next week. It was supposed to be last week, but it's taking a little longer for my blood count to return to normal after each treatment. The doctor says that's a good sign, though, that it shows the chemo's working."

That sounded like bullshit to me, but I didn't let on about that. Turned out it was. Still, I never asked any questions, never said anything that might reveal I knew he was dying.

My mother asked me to go with my father to that next chemotherapy treatment. She had something else she needed to do that day. "You'll need to help him into a cab afterwards," she told me outside his earshot. *Wow, this is fucking crazy*, I thought as I involuntarily closed my eyes and shook my head.

"It's so unnecessary," my father protested when I told him I'd go with him. "It takes all day and all I do is read. I'll be fine."

"I'll read, too, Pops. Not a problem."

And we did read, for hours, both unable to conjure any conversation that seemed remotely natural under the circumstances. We sat in a cold, windowless room that seemed more appropriate for interrogating terrorists than dispensing medical care. The room's only discernable feature was the chemotherapy bag slowly dispensing its benevolent poison, drip by drip by drip.

"See, it's no big deal," my father said cheerfully in hour four, looking up briefly from his work papers. "I feel fine."

"That's great, Pops. Glad to hear it." We both returned to our reading. Another three excruciating hours passed in silence. My whole life I'd wished for more time with my father, but not like this.

When the bag had finally drained and my father was disconnected from the machinery, I wheeled him to the front door of the medical building. I wasn't allowed to roll the wheelchair into the street, so I left it at the front door and helped him to his feet. We then left to catch a cab. With each step, he became weaker. It was as if a switch had been flipped and he was flickering off. He put his arm around my shoulders as I eased him into a taxi.

"You okay?" I asked.

He responded with a barely audible grunt.

At our apartment building, I helped him out of the cab, into the lobby, and down the three steps that led to the elevator hallway. "I can get it from here," he said.

He shuffled along, pausing every few feet to catch his breath, leaning against the wall for support and stopping halfway down the hall to sit on a couch I'd never noticed before.

When we got upstairs to the apartment, I helped him into bed, getting all the pillows positioned properly. "You need anything, Pops? Water?"

"No, I'm fine."

I turned away. "Matt," he whispered.

"Yes?"

"Thanks for being there today."

My father closed his eyes and fell asleep almost instantly, his listless body completely worn out. I watched the rise and fall of his chest, unable to leave, needing to watch him breathe, as if to satisfy myself he was still alive.

As I stood there transfixed, feeling in some way as if our lifelong roles had been reversed, I remembered myself as a kid, dragging myself out of bed before dawn to troll for bluefish with my father out on Long Island. He and I would set out for Moriches Inlet in our small fishing boat, which he'd christened *The Wanderer.* We'd charge into the giant swells where the ocean collided with the bay, charting a course miles off the coast. Rob had a weak stomach for all modes of transportation, most of all boats, and my mother wasn't what you'd call "outdoorsy," so I had my father all to myself. Just the two of us. I felt important.

The sun would be blazing bright, the ocean calm with only the occasional swell causing the boat to rock side to side. I'd set two rods with umbrella rigs, metal contraptions with five wires of different lengths, each holding a lure and connected to a single point to simulate a small school of fish darting through the water.

When all the lines were in, the boat would chug through the water, the drone of the engine steady, occasionally revving at the apex of a swell and then decelerating as the boat eased back down. The drone of that engine was like the white noise of the womb, creating not just an audible barrier but a physical one that wrapped itself around me, deflecting danger, as if we weren't bobbing on a vast ocean in a tiny piece of fiberglass, defenseless against the elements.

When it came time for lunch, usually tuna fish sandwiches with a slice of American cheese on white bread, a Welch's grape soda for me and sparkling water for my father, we'd reel the lines in and kill the engine, the stillness, the near perfect silence, interrupted only by the sound of the swells lapping against the side of the boat and the occasional squawk of the radio.

It was in fugitive moments like this, alone with my father, no legal briefs to lure him away, staring out at the endless flat of the horizon, that I felt as if everything in the world made perfect sense, my place in it secure.

But such blissful intervals were short-lived. After a bluefish seized a lure, the spell was broken. The adrenaline rush and excitement I felt as the reel spun wildly was inevitably followed by a pit in my stomach as my father barked orders to steer the boat this way or that to keep the lines from getting tangled. Although I tried as hard as I could not to disappoint him, the lines would occasionally cross and my father would have to cut one, relegating the attached umbrella rig to a long, slow fall to the bottom of the ocean.

Once things were under control, he would pass me the rod, take the wheel, and allow me to reel in the fish. The rod arched like a giant question mark, and the resistance on the line invariably left me feeling like I was fighting a great white shark—I was always surprised when my father would plunge the net into the water and haul out a little bluefish, usually no bigger than fifteen pounds.

After the chaos of landing the fish, peace would return, the low-pitch drone of the engine once again wrapping me in its secure embrace. It was during these moments of calm that I'd look over at my father, busied behind the wheel of the boat, and feel some profound wash of connection to him, reminding me that at my core I just wanted to be with him.

I left my father lying in bed and walked down the long hallway to my room. I sat on my bed, staring ahead at nothing at all. The late afternoon light filtering through the Venetian blinds eventually gave way to blackness. The jackhammers that seemed always to be at work in the courtyard below my window, re-making a space no one visited, eventually went quiet.

I got up from my bed and walked back down the hallway to check on my father. As I approached his room, I heard a sound vaguely familiar but so out of context I didn't immediately understand what it was: my father retching in the bathroom, then the inevitable surge plunging into the toilet.

I didn't know whether to offer help or leave him alone. I stood in the hallway, paralyzed for what seemed like several minutes, then turned back.

There was nothing I could do to help him.

Even as my father continued to waste away, even as I had to cover him in pillows to protect him from our thirty-pound Wheaton terrier Rosie who would jump up on the bed to kiss him, even as he gasped his last breaths with an oxygen tube shoved up his nose, he and I never spoke of the possibility of his dying. Only once did I hear him mention his feelings about his illness. It was after the cancer had taken a firm hold and he'd become extremely frail, his clothes hanging off him like they belonged to some fairy tale giant. My father was sitting at the kitchen table with my mother who was arguing with him about something, probably his constant working. Yet this time my father, who my whole life had calmly withstood my mother's verbal slings and arrows about his workaholic ways, finally snapped. He stood up from the table, barely able to muster the strength to push back the chair in a pathetic attempt to add dramatic flair and said in a voice that was weak but laced with venom, "Well, you may not have to worry about that much longer."

He shuffled out of the kitchen, leaving my mother and me in stunned silence. It was the cruelest thing I ever heard him say. It was also the only time I heard him acknowledge he might die, the only hint he ever gave of his own desperation. He always said his strategy was like the one he employed defending corporations from hostile takeovers: extend the fight until something else positive happens. I was never convinced, but I believed he was certain he'd beat it. Until that moment.

I'd like to say that I went over to my mother and gave her a hug, that I assured her, "Pops doesn't really think you'll be happier when he dies." But I didn't. I retreated to my room, put on my headphones, and cued up "Dark Star" by the Grateful Dead.

"Dark Star" is an intricate maze of a song—clocking in at over twenty minutes—with countless sonic cul-de-sacs where you can hunker down and hide, blind alleys of distortion and fuzz and faraway choral keys and piercing trills and mind-bending reverb and joyfully pulsating bass riffs and soul-quenching quietude and metallic, grinding guitar stabs, all ferociously pursuing some sacred core of mindful presence, with Jerry Garcia's blazing guitar notes draped over simple drum brushes, the absence of a popping snare drum leaving the music groundless, spiraling away to oblivion.

Why in that moment was I drawn to "Dark Star"? I think it was probably related to my being an anxious flyer. The slightest turbulence leaves me clutching the armrests as I wait for the oxygen masks to drop, convinced I'm about to die. And when things get really bad, when the pilot asks the flight attendants to please suspend beverage service and take their seats, I put on my headphones and take refuge in "Dark Star." I can shut everything down while listening to that song and luxuriate in a peaceful calm, even amidst the unnatural gyrations of an airplane in seeming freefall and panicked fantasies of my imminent death.

Witnessing my father surrender to the reality of his actual imminent death unconsciously catapulted me towards "Dark Star." I felt like this time I was in fact falling through the sky. Nothing made sense. What the fuck's a dark star anyway? Aren't stars the brightest objects in the known universe? I lay down on my bed, closed my eyes, and drank in the omniscience of Jerry's sweet, soulful voice, "Reason tatters, the forces tear loose from the axis."

2

PRESENCE OF AN ABSENCE

One of the best things about visiting my dad in his skyscraper office on Park Avenue was riding in the high-speed elevator. It was like being an astronaut in a rocket ship, the way that thing took off, my ears popping all the way to the forty-eighth floor.

When the ride was over, I'd stumble out of the elevator, feeling a little woozy from it, and also like I'd arrived on a different planet, one made of dark wood and glass doors, inhabited by men in dark suits and brightly colored ties, all of them wearing glasses, their noses deep in shuffling papers as they marched down long hallways zombie-like. It was so quiet in there, the only sound being the electronic *beep-beep* of telephone lines ringing at the receptionist's desk. I'd feel my stomach get all tight, look down at my white sneakers that weren't that white anymore, and wonder if I should maybe take off. But the receptionist would always spy me standing there all still.

"Hello, sweetie, can I help you?"

"Um, I'm here to see my dad," I'd whisper, not wanting to break the quiet of the place.

"Who's your father, sweetie?"

That question always confused me some—it'd take me a second or two to figure out how to answer it. "Um, Mister Fogelson," I'd finally say, the words sounding strange and somehow wrong.

"Okay, I'll let Ruth know."

Ruth was my dad's long-time secretary. She'd take me through the maze of the forty-eighth floor to my dad's corner office. "Matthew, darling, look at you, you've gotten so big," she'd say to me. "You want to make a quick pit stop in the kitchen?"

The answer to that question was always yes. The kitchen area of my dad's office was like something out of *Charlie and the Chocolate Factory.* It had anything a kid could want. Refrigerators filled with sodas, cabinets filled with M&Ms and other candy. All free for the taking. No permission or money needed. *Wow,* I thought, *I can't wait to get a job!* There were Welch's grape sodas in the fridge, which were my favorite, but I'd grab a Schweppes ginger ale since ginger ale seemed more like what you were supposed to drink in an office. I'd also take a packet of peanut M&M's and a Twix bar to save for later.

Ruth would lead me through corridor after corridor, past the xerox room and law library, finally leaving me in front of my dad's office with those strange words, "Mr. Fogelson," engraved in silver on the closed door. Ruth would knock and open the door all in the same motion, not waiting for permission to enter—like I did when I knocked on his study door at home. My dad would be talking on the phone, his back to the door, staring out the glass wall behind his desk.

"I can wait out here until he's off the phone," I'd tell Ruth.

"Don't be silly, darling. Your father wouldn't want you standing in the hallway. Anyway, it could be a while, so you might as well get comfortable."

When he noticed the door open, my dad would turn around, smile, and wave me in. I'd take a seat on his large leather couch and listen to him on the phone. He'd be saying nonsense words, words like "equity financing," "fiduciary," "illiquidity," "proxy," "undercapitalization," and "poison pill." It was all pretty boring, except the poison pill bit—that sounded sort of cool, like maybe my dad was involved in some type of shadowy Dungeons & Dragons situation. When I got bored enough, I'd stand up and walk over to one of the two glass walls, put my face up against it and stare down at the street below. The people looked like ants from so high up and the yellow taxis looked like the matchbox cars my mom would buy me at the stationery store on Madison and 76th when I was really small.

When I got bored with staring down at the street, I'd sit back down on the couch, rip open the packet of peanut M&Ms and check out the magazines my dad kept on his coffee table. A couple had pictures of him on the cover, with headlines saying something about M&A transactions—whatever those were—and my dad being the future leader of the legal profession. *That's pretty cool*, I thought. Not as cool as being on the cover of *Sports Illustrated*, but still, pretty cool.

Eventually my dad would finish his call and turn to me.

"I'm not so sure about eating candy right before lunch," he'd say. "But since you've got them open already, how about some for your old man?" I'd hand over a few and he'd give me a wink.

"So where do you want to go for lunch?"

My answer was always the same: "How about Brew Burger?" I liked Brew Burger because they had red vinyl-covered stools up at the counter that swung all the way around like tops. My dad would let me take a spin or two before telling me to knock it off and look at the menu. Not that I needed to look at the menu. I always ordered the same thing: a cheeseburger and vanilla milkshake. The cheese came out all liquid-y, like it wasn't even cheese. I loved that. Eventually my dad stopped taking me to Brew Burger. He said his doctor told him eating burgers and milkshakes wasn't good for him. Something about cholesterol. So we'd go to Oscar's, a restaurant in this fancy hotel, the Waldorf-Astoria it was called, which I didn't like nearly as much. It had white tablecloths, no fancy spinning stools, and the menu was written in a foreign language—*escargots, tartare, confit.* Plus, a lot of my dad's law partners seemed to go there for lunch. He was always introducing me to people at Oscar's, which required me to make eye contact with them. I hated that.

"Brew Burger it is, then," my dad would say. "Let's get out of here." But then his phone would always seem to ring at least once more and he'd race to answer it, even if we'd made it into the hallway. Or one of his law partners would stop in just as we were leaving and ask him a question and then sit down for ten minutes, the two of them exchanging more nonsense words. I didn't really mind, though, since I figured it gave me permission to go ahead and eat my Twix bar.

When we finally made it over to that high-speed elevator, I'd jump up just as it began descending, the floor falling out beneath me like the Freefall ride at the Great Adventure amusement park in New Jersey. My dad would shoot me a stern look if somebody else was in the elevator, but he never told me I had to stop doing it.

Meeting my dad at his office for lunch was the best. He seemed happy and relaxed at his office, always smiling and in a good mood. When he was home, my mom was always yelling at him, taking out her frustration at his working all the time and leaving her alone with Rob and me. Even when he wasn't home, she'd be yelling at him—over the phone. "Tell them to give the work to Bob Kramer!" she'd scream when my dad said he couldn't make it home for dinner. "He sits around all day doing nothing!" Mr. Kramer was one of my dad's law partners—my dad introduced me to him a few times at the office.

He always seemed plenty busy to me, but maybe my mom knew different. She seemed real sure about it, anyway.

So yeah, my dad worked lots, which was kind of a bummer, but that's because he was an important lawyer and important lawyers work a ton. My mom said that when Rob was born, she and my dad hired a baby nurse who told my mom she didn't believe my dad was staying so late at the office every night, that he was probably visiting a friend after work. "Go ahead and call his office," the nurse told my mom once at one in the morning. My mom did and of course my dad picked up on the first ring. "Well, I'll be," said the nurse. But I wasn't surprised to hear it. His work was super critical—not that I knew what it was exactly.

I worried a lot that my dad would get sick of my mom always yelling at him and just take off. Some of my friends' dads had done that. "Can't you just let him be?" I'd ask my mom. "It's not like he wants to work until midnight every night." But I'd also try to get my dad to spend more time with us since that seemed like the other way to solve the problem. I often did this thing where instead of giving my dad birthday cards, I'd write him poems. When I was ten years old, I wrote him one for his thirty-eighth birthday which included this verse:

Jim: let me give it to you straight
You can't keep working so late
Your wife and children get annoyed
And when Phylis gets mad it's terribly bad

Pretty good, I'd have to say. Although I now see that "annoyed" doesn't rhyme with anything. Not sure what I was thinking there.

My poem two years later for his fortieth birthday, which I called

"Advice for Old Age," was much better—everything rhymes in this one:

In your profession
You've always been the best
But now that you're forty
Try to get some more rest

Don't work from the rising to the setting of the sun
For now that you're forty, there are other things to do that are fun
Spend more time with your wife and sons
Let's go to some Yankees games, how about in the tons?

So here's wishing you
A happy birthday
And maybe you'll consider
Some of the things that I say

I really nailed it with that one! Going to Yankees games "in the tons"? Hilarious! We didn't end up going to that many games, though, maybe once a year or something.

When I was at sleepaway camp for the summer, I'd write to my parents each week—the counselors forced us to, which sucked. I mean, who wants to spend their time out of school writing letters? Anyhow, my letters home when I was ten all ended the same way, with a note to my dad, like this one, "Pops: I hope work is going okay and you take it easy now and then. Sometimes you work too hard (almost always). Oh, and please send the latest *Sports Illustrated*."

One day after school when I was eleven years old, I heard this song "Cat's in the Cradle" on the radio. It was by some guy named Harry

Chapin and I liked it so much I went over to Crazy Eddie on Third Avenue and bought the 45. It came in a gold paper sleeve which was pretty cool. The song is about a father and son who don't spend much time together because the father's too busy for the son when the son is a kid and then the son's too busy for the old man when he becomes an adult. The son wants to be just like his father when he grows up and that's basically what happens, which is sad because they don't see each other so much but also kind of cool since he got to be like his dad. It's a great song, although the part about the son blowing off his dad when he grows up didn't make much sense to me—I was pretty sure I'd want to see my dad lots when I grew up, want him to play with my kids and stuff. Whatever. It's still a great song.

I played "Cat's in the Cradle" a lot. Sometimes if my dad was around, I'd play it a little extra loud, hoping he'd hear it and like in that old Pied Piper story, magically come outside and follow me to Central Park to throw the football. But it never worked. Usually he'd just tell me to turn it down.

One weekend when Rob and I were really little, it was snowing like crazy and my dad said he'd take us sledding in the park later that day. But he never came out of his study where he worked on the weekends. It really screwed Rob and me when he'd spend all weekend in there because that's where the TV was, so we couldn't watch football or anything. Anyway, my mom went in after lunch to make sure he was still planning to take us sledding. When we saw her open the door to the study, Rob and I squeezed in after her. My dad was still in his red flannel robe because he started working right after he woke up. There were papers all over the floor. He said he couldn't take us sledding after all, that something had come up at the office.

Oh man, my mom started yelling at him, which was a little strange because usually she didn't yell at him right in front of us—we could usually hear her, but at least we weren't right there. Well this time, she just let it rip. "This is insane, Jimmy! What could possibly be more important than taking the boys sledding? This is their childhood and you're missing it! It's like they don't even have a father."

"Calm down, Phylis. You think I don't want to take the boys sledding?"

Score one for my dad—that's what I was always telling my mom. It's not like he didn't want to be with us. I mean, what dad would rather work than take his sons sledding or go to a Yankees game or throw the football around? No dad I could imagine. Why couldn't she get that? I wanted to tell her all that again but figured I should keep my mouth shut.

"I'm starting to wonder if you do, actually," my mom said in a quiet voice, her eyes moving away from my dad to the window and the falling snow.

"Well that's ridiculous," my dad replied. "Of course I do. Our biggest client just became the target of a hostile takeover and we have to come up with a counterstrategy immediately. That's the problem and it's not one I can solve in time to take the boys sledding."

A hostile takeover? That sounded pretty cool.

"It's always something," my mom said, shaking her head, "and it never ends. Never."

My stomach started to feel a little funny and I looked over at Rob. He was sitting on the floor looking through my dad's work papers, which was pretty stupid because I'm sure they were filled with lots of those nonsense words so there was no way he could've understood any of it.

"Boys," my mom said, turning to us. "Go get bundled up. I'll take you to the park."

Rob looked up from my dad's papers. "I don't want to go sledding," he said, looking at my mom. "I want to stay home."

I was surprised he said it, but on the other hand could kind of understand why he did. Although I still wanted to go sledding, I was pretty mad at my mom for yelling at my dad. I hated when she did that. I guess Rob did too. So I gave my mom a mean look and said, "Me too."

"Come on you guys," my dad said, "I'm really sorry, but Mom will take you. It'll be fun."

"No it won't," Rob said, going back to pretending to read my dad's papers. My dad looked at me and I looked down. I was about to say that I didn't think it'd be fun either, which wasn't true, when my mom turned around and walked out of the study. I could hear her footsteps down the hall and then my parents' bedroom door slamming. I wasn't sure if she was just mad at my dad or also at Rob and me for refusing to go with her. I knew she was trying to save the day, to make things better for us. She did that a lot. Like when she'd offer to hit tennis balls with me after my dad had bailed. But sometimes a son just wants to be with his dad. Honestly, there was nothing she could do to make it better. Nothing.

My mom was always taking me places when my dad wasn't around. One rainy summer day when I was eight years old and Rob was off at sleepaway camp, my mom and I were out on Long Island and she asked me if I wanted to go roller-skating in Riverhead, which was a few towns over from our place in Westhampton. I'd never roller-skated before but it sounded fun so I said sure, why not.

The rink was in a large concrete building that looked like an airplane hangar. As we approached the entrance, I could hear the pulse of "Macho Man" echoing through the walls. I myself was no macho man but a fat kid, self-consciously so with huge *pulkes* as my mother called my legs (*pulke* being Yiddish for chicken drumsticks). And honestly, the Village People carrying on about bodies—wanting to touch bodies and feel bodies and please bodies and tease bodies—made me more than a little anxious. I didn't want to hear about bodies at all, particularly about adoring bodies and exploring bodies. But I figured the song would be over soon, so I soldiered on.

Inside it was pitch black except for the flash of multi-colored laser beams and strobe lights that swirled around the walls and bounced off the ceiling. Notwithstanding "Macho Man," I was pretty excited, but also nervous as we got fitted for skates and hobbled our way toward the rink.

It turns out I wasn't a very good roller skater. No matter how hard I tried, my ankles just wouldn't stay straight. They'd turn so far inward they almost scraped the floor. I clung desperately to the side wall, like a rock climber hanging on for dear life, thinking this whole thing is more terrifying than fun.

"Try pushing instead of stepping," my mom suggested. She'd been a good skater back in the day. "Here, like this." She took my hand and pushed off with her skates, gliding around the rink with me in tow. "Now you try," she said after we'd made two trips around the rink. She let go of my hand. I inhaled deeply and gently pushed one foot back behind me and somehow didn't fall flat on my face. In fact, I was moving in a forward direction! I tried the other foot. Same deal! I was doing this!

"There you go!" my mom squealed, a huge smile plastered on her face. "That's my boy!" I wouldn't quite say I was having fun, but at least I was no longer terrified. A rush of air whipped through my hair, so I must've been moving pretty good.

My mom continued skating gracefully a few yards ahead of me.

She wore a red sweater that stood out in the dim light of the rink. Every few seconds she'd glance back over her shoulder to make sure I was still upright and to encourage me to catch up to her.

The rink was packed, and older kids rocketed around at warp speed while parents led younger kids by the hand. The teenage kids were definitely having more fun than me. I began to wonder if the constant breeze now rushing through my hair was less from my own forward progress and more from all the big kids whizzing by. I was hanging by a thread balance-wise and feeling a little anxious about the whole scene. Barry Manilow's "Copacabana" blasted out through the rink's sound system which didn't help my anxiety since it's about a horrific, bloody shooting by some unidentified gunman.

As my mom glanced back to check on me again, a huge guy, tall and fat, stopped in front of her to help his daughter adjust her skates. Wham! My mom barreled into him and fell on her back. In the process, she took the guy's legs out from under him and that mountain of a man collapsed on top of her. I could hear my mom's agonized scream above the thundering music.

The next thing I know, I'm visiting my mom in the hospital. She was "in traction" to address a "slipped disk." I had no clue what that meant but it sounded bad. She lay on her back in the hospital bed, each leg elevated at forty-five degrees, suspended in a harness of sorts. There were ropes and pulleys and weights attached to the harness, with everything running back to a set of poles above the headboard, like she was connected to some medieval torture device. She stayed laid up in that position for weeks.

After she was released from the hospital, the doctors put her on bedrest. She must've needed a lot of rest because she didn't get out of bed for like two years. On drives out to Westhampton, my mom would lie flat in the back seat with her head in my lap, her legs bent under a pile of pillows. Rob would ride shotgun. Every bump in the road caused her to seize up in pain.

"Jimmy, what are you doing!" she'd yell at my dad.

"What do you want me to do?" my dad would ask, "flatten out the road?"

Fair point, I thought. In moments like these, when it felt like the runaway train was about to go hurtling off the rails, I became like Batman getting a call from Commissioner Gordon: time to swoop in and save the day.

"Relax, Mom, he's just driving normally," I'd tell her. "The road has bumps in it, there's nothing to be done about it." I did that kind of thing a lot—tried to get my mom to take a chill pill. As the peacemaker, I figured the best way to restore the peace was to engage with the person who was disturbing the peace, which was my mother. She was always the one yelling.

For those two years, my mom was basically an invalid, either in bed or on the floor going through some weird stretching program. She hardly ever even took a walk outside. But all the bed rest and stretching didn't help any. At least that's what my mom says. She says she got better only after reading a book called *Healing Back Pain: The Mind–Body Connection*. I flipped through the book once. My mom had underlined entire pages and written all sorts of notes in the margins. The thing was pretty beat up, all dog-eared. I read the back cover but didn't really understand it. It said the body is really good at healing itself and if it's been a while after your injury and you're still having chronic back pain, it's probably because there's something mental going on, that you've likely got something called Tension Myositis Syndrome, or TMS. It said that TMS is caused by repressed anger and that once you recognize the emotional roots of your TMS and break the connection between your emotional and physical pain, voilà, you're healed! It sounded like hocus-pocus to me, but my mom swore by it. And after reading it, she did sort of rise from bed like Lazarus from the dead, walking around like the prior two years hadn't happened, even getting back on the tennis court.

My mom was always around, but Westhampton was where I'd get to see my dad. Most weekends, spring through fall, we'd head out there. Our house was on a small bay, just across from Dune Road, with the Atlantic Ocean beyond. When it wasn't too windy, if you went out to the end of our dock and closed your eyes, you could hear the waves breaking on the faraway beach. There'd be a gentle crash and then complete quiet before the next wave rolled in.

When I was real young, we had a small boat, a Cruiser, for zipping around the bay. Sometimes my dad would beach the boat on a barrier island near Moriches Inlet and we'd waddle ashore for a picnic lunch. Other times we'd head in the opposite direction, east towards Shinnecock Inlet, and get steamers out on the back deck of Nick's Restaurant, an old wooden structure on stilts above a small marina, next to the huge rock jetties that formed the inlet. Nick's deck always looked so wobbly up on those stilts, like at any minute it could tumble into the water.

Besides boating, the other family activity in Westhampton was going to the beach. My dad would take a hard right down the sand and go what felt like a mile past the last sunbather before setting up his chair, the rest of us following behind, me wondering why we had to be so far away from everybody else. My dad would plant the umbrella, bathe his nose in zinc oxide, and begin poring over the work papers he'd brought along, disappearing into all those nonsense words. But I didn't mind—at least he was there. I mean, you couldn't always count on him being there.

Once when I was ten or so, we were on the way to the airport for a Christmas trip, riding in one of those fancy Lincoln Town Cars my dad's law firm hired for its top lawyers, when the car phone rang. The car had an actual phone in it! I thought that was totally cool, although not so much this time. My dad hung up the phone and quietly told the driver to turn around, to go back to our apartment first and then head downtown to drop him at his office. Some big corporate deal of his was blowing up. The vacation was canceled.

"Jesus Christ, Jimmy!" my mom roared, slamming both arms down on the seat. "It's Christmas. Nobody else in the entire world is working, but you have to work?" I thought about reminding my mom that we were Jewish and didn't celebrate Christmas, so what was the big deal, but I could see her point. It seemed like my dad should've been able to get out of this one. And honestly, I was pretty pissed about it. The Christmas trip was the highlight of my year. We'd hang at the beach and could go scuba diving and play tennis. And at the restaurant at night they had hermit crab races where they'd paint the crabs' shells a different color and you could bet on them. Man, those crabs moved slow on their tiny legs and sometimes they'd just stop in the middle, like they didn't know they were in a race, and we'd all go nuts yelling at them, trying to get them to move. It was hilarious. And you could win as much as $5 on each race. So yeah, I was pissed. Not so much at my dad—I knew it wasn't his fault—but at whoever or whatever was making him work so much.

"There's nothing I can do about it," my dad said softly.

"Is Bob Kramer spending the holidays at the office?" my mom asked all angry like she knew the answer was no.

"He's not on this deal so I don't know."

"Well I do, and the answer is no way is he working over the holidays. He's probably already on the beach or in Aspen with his family.

But no, you're too important. The world will collapse if you aren't around for a week."

"The world won't collapse but our lifestyle will."

"Yeah, this is a great lifestyle. Just great."

"I'm really sorry, boys," my dad said, ignoring my mom. "I'll make it up to you, I promise."

"It's okay, Pops," Rob said looking out the window as the car turned off the freeway. I was going to tell him the same thing but couldn't—I was too pissed. Part of me hoped my mom would say the three of us could still go, but I guess she figured Rob and I wouldn't want to without my dad and she probably would've been right. It would've been super weird without him.

When we got home, I sprinted down the long hall to my room, slammed the door, lay face down on my bed, and cried for a good long while. Eventually, my mom came in and rubbed my back.

"I'm really sorry," she said. "I know how disappointed you are, how much it hurts. I wish I could make it better—more than anything I wish that."

I turned my head to look at her. "I know," I said.

My mom wiped a tear from my face with her finger. "I love you so, so much," she said. "You're my beautiful boy."

That was nice to hear, I suppose, but it didn't really help much.

I guess because it was such a rare thing, I tried to hang out with my dad whenever I could. That's why I'd go fishing with him even though it meant I'd have to get up at like 5:30 in the morning, which wasn't fun. It was so dark and cold, and my bed was so warm. No way would Rob get out of bed at 5:30 a.m. to go fishing. Or my mom. That's funny even to think about! But I would. Every time.

Speaking of not so much fun, sometimes I'd even go with my dad to the track at the Westhampton High School where he liked to jog. I couldn't understand the point of jogging—it seemed really boring, not to mention tiring. My dad said it felt good to "break a sweat," that it "cleared the mind," but that didn't make any sense to me. Why would you want to get all sweaty? And how would running in circles for miles clear your head? If anything, it seemed like it'd make you dizzy.

Even though the whole jogging thing was kind of weird, I'd try to do it myself, try to keep up with my dad decked out in his grey Adidas windbreaker and short shorts, the kind that Bruce Jenner wore. I'd usually make it just once or twice around the quarter-mile track before conking out, then go sit alone in the bleachers, waiting on my dad. Sometimes in the fall, the high school football team—the Hurricanes—would be practicing on a nearby field and I'd wander over there, the barking of the coaches, crunching of shoulder pads, and shrill of the whistle creating a wall of sound that distracted me from my boredom. But usually I'd just sit in the bleachers watching my dad run in long circles, lap after lap for no reason I could understand. And I'd wonder how long it would be before we could go home.

3

THE UNASKED QUESTIONS

One day in the second week of my senior year of college—a gloriously sunny Tuesday afternoon—I was indoors in a huge lecture hall listening to a geology teacher drone about the properties of igneous rocks. When the class mercilessly ended, I came out of the concrete building into the bright sunshine of early afternoon and started to cross the road towards the student union to get my mail when I heard somebody yelling my nickname, "Fogie!"

I turned to see my roommate, Chris, wearing a muscle tee and shades and standing beside his red Mitsubishi Montero jeep. He waved me over.

"Your brother called," he said quietly as he took off his sunglasses, his expression somber. "He asked me to find you. He said for you to call home as soon as possible. Your dad's taken a turn for the worse."

The world fell silent.

I looked up and saw the tops of the huge loblolly pine trees in front of the science building. I could see the treetops swaying but I couldn't hear the wind, couldn't hear the branches rustling. I saw students continue to pour out of the building, but I couldn't hear the crunch of the gravel path under their feet, couldn't hear their voices, their laughter.

"Rob asked me to book you on a flight to New York tonight," Chris said. "It leaves at seven."

That I heard.

He fired up the engine and I was jolted out of my trance by a repellant blast of Mott The Hoople's "All The Young Dudes." I've never been much of a Mott fan; on those rare occasions I'm moved to conjure sonic images of dreary 1970s England, I usually opt for Procol Harum. Chris sensed the disconnect and fumbled around to turn the radio off. I wanted to say "Thanks" but was reduced to an aphonic stupor.

We rode in silence, hurtling past strip malls that housed the hyphenated college staples of Chick-fil-A and Steak-N-Egg. The silence began to feel weighty, so I rolled down my window even though Chris had the A/C blasting. The sound of wind, of air whipping through the car, helped drown out the clatter in my head.

We passed a Walgreens and I noticed the florescent light of the W had gone out, renaming the store "algreens," which in my head became "Al Green's." That's funny, I thought, the rebranding bringing to mind Al's mesmerizing version of Sam Cooke's "A Change is Gonna Come." Oh yes it will.

When we got to our apartment, I took the phone into my room, closed the door, and called home. Our longtime housekeeper, Pat, answered. She told me my mother and Rob were still at the hospital. That they should be home any minute and that my mother would call me back.

"What happened?" I asked. "He seemed fine a week ago."

"I don't know, baby." There was nothing more to say, so we hung up and I waited.

As I sat on my bed bracing for my mother's call, I desperately wanted to put on my headphones and cue up "Sweet Jane," subconsciously hoping it might serve as a magical portal back to high school, to a time before I understood my father would soon be dead. But I couldn't risk not hearing the phone ring, so I just sat there frozen in silence, rocking back and forth on the end of my bed.

Of course I knew this was coming—I just didn't expect it to come so soon. I guess the mind plays tricks when you're trying to keep your shit together. In retrospect, anyone could see my father was fading fast. In pictures of him the final months, he's gaunt, skeletal, the skin on his face pulled tight, his eye sockets protruding, his arms brittle. But I didn't see it then. Maybe because as a family we conspicuously avoided any talk of the obvious, never risked breaching the emotional walls we'd all constructed around ourselves and each other, keeping the fear and horror at bay.

It seemed impossible that I might never see my father again. That he'd just disappear. He'd been scheduled to go in for another chemo treatment that morning. I'd planned to call my mother after class to see how it went and then fly up on Friday for the weekend to see him.

The phone rang. I took a deep breath and answered it.

"Matthew, sweetheart, Daddy's dying." My mother was crying, her voice was cracking. "Come home tonight. We asked Chris to book you a flight."

"He's still alive?" I asked, hopefully. "Can I speak to him?"

"No, sweetheart, I'm sorry." She reported that my father could barely breathe, that he was "air hungry" and had been given heavy sedatives to induce a dream state.

"Bring a dark suit," she added numbly.

A dark suit. God damn. A dark suit.

I hung up the phone and staggered into the bathroom, turned on the shower so Chris couldn't hear me sobbing, then held my head over the sink and pelted my face with water for several minutes, shaking and convulsing. When I finally composed myself, I came out into the living room. Chris stood there looking ashen.

"What's the story?" he asked hesitantly. He had a pained expression on his face. Chris and I had been close friends since third grade. He knew my father well.

"The story is the story's over."

Sitting in the plane on my way home that night, I felt my father die. I could pinpoint the moment. I had a window seat and was staring out at a beautiful sunset, one of the prettiest I'd ever seen. The red and orange hues were mesmerizing, like someone had brushed bands of fluorescent paint across the sky. And then I saw a star begin to flicker, the first of the night. As I looked out at that star twinkling in the vast sky, I felt my stomach tighten in a wave of nausea. And I knew he was dead.

When I got to the apartment my mother opened the door and hugged me. "He's gone," she said.

"I know," I told her. Rob came over and joined our hug, the three of us huddled together, overcome by the truth finally laid bare.

After the funeral, my mother, Rob, and I returned to the apartment to sit shiva. There was such a dazzling array of flowers and so much food spread all over the place it could've been a wedding reception. And so many people streaming into the apartment, like commuters into the subway at rush hour. If my father hadn't just been buried, it might've been a fun party.

Scanning the spectacle of the room, I wondered how my father knew all these people, most of whom I'd never laid eyes on. Some Wall Street banker I'd never met told me he'd worked with "everyone in the business" and that my father had taught him the most about how to be a good person. It was nice to hear that, but it didn't make me feel a whole lot better about things. It just made me think that if you rise to the top of your profession there's likely to be a large pool of people to attend your funeral. Which I guess should be, what—comforting?

I went into the kitchen to get some water and found my Aunt Wendy, my mother's younger sister by six years, squirreled away there, seeking refuge from my parents' friends. Dressed for a funeral, she was barely recognizable. Aunt Wendy always wore brightly colored sun dresses, no matter the season, along with hoop earrings, matching jingly bracelets—so many of them you could hear her coming a mile away—and clog sandals that still left her only about five-foot-four. But today she was wearing a black pant suit with a white blouse, black flats, and no earrings or bracelets, and her long dirty-blond hair that usually tumbled over her exposed shoulders and down her back—wild and frizzy like it'd never seen a brush—was tamed in some kind of bun.

Aunt Wendy lived in Carmel, New York, fifty miles north of the city, and she dropped by maybe once a year, twice at best, usually when my grandparents were in town from Florida. We never once drove to see her in Carmel. I remember her visiting us one time out in Westhampton when I was really little. She showed up in a forest green Volkswagen Bug. It was the coolest car I'd ever seen. I rummaged around the inside of that thing, exploring the interior as it sat parked in our driveway, crawling from seat to seat trying not to crunch the cassette tapes that had been flung all around like confetti at a Yankees World Series parade. The inside of that tiny car was a space where I felt big.

Aunt Wendy was shaking her head. "My poor boy," she said, tears welling up in her eyes as she leaned in to give me a bear hug. As I squirmed in her grip, I breathed in her distinctive scent; it was like the deep woods, a mustiness produced by either an over-application of some off-brand perfume or an under-application of soap. "You know, I don't believe in God or heaven or anything like that, but I think your dad is finally free. He was always working so hard and was so serious. I think he's at peace now."

I felt myself beginning to roll my eyes, a reflex imprinted from a lifetime of watching my parents do the same in their interactions with Wendy. But I checked it, suddenly confused. Had she just said my father being dead was a good thing? I think she had. I knew Aunt Wendy's comment was well-meaning, but it irritated me. How could my father being dead be a good thing?

"Yeah," I replied flatly.

"I think you are one of the bravest people I know," she continued, still clutching me tightly. "There is, however, a place in the mind where it's very easy to deceive ourselves or block out thoughts or feelings we have deep within our souls." She released the bear hug and looked at me hard. "Please don't be afraid to feel what you feel, however uncomfortable. Ride the waves of fear and pain. Many times we have to do that before we can truly accept things and then we finally free ourselves, a little at a time, until the pain and fear aren't so great."

I couldn't check the eye-rolling this time, although I put my hand to my forehead so she wouldn't see it. I had no idea what she was talking about. I just wanted to get out of there. She was freaking me out.

"Um, yeah, will do," I said as I headed for the door. She called me back.

"Your mother tells me you're going to apply to law school," she said as she sat back down.

"Yeah, that's the plan," I replied, giving in and joining her at the table. "I'm interested in environmental policy, and everyone I met last summer during my internship at the Natural Resources Defense Council was either a scientist or a lawyer. I missed the science boat ages ago, so law it is."

Aunt Wendy didn't seem persuaded by my explanation. She frowned and took hold of my hands from across the table, sandwiching them between hers.

"If I could give you just one piece of advice," she said, staring at me with the seriousness of a chemistry professor discussing nuclear fusion, "it'd be this: Follow your heart. Don't just do what's expected of you. You must be true to yourself. That's all that matters in life. Everything else is noise."

"Don't worry, I actually want to go to law school," I said sharply.

"If you really want to go to law school, I think that's great," she plunged on. "I just feel like you're capable of doing anything you want in life. And not just in the professions. You're so creative—a great writer—and I feel deeply your passion for music. You're so smart and you get along with people. That's a rare combination."

Unable to process the deeply felt emotional content of Aunt Wendy's message, antithetical as it was to how members of my family communicated with each other, I gave her a cursory "thanks" and retreated to my room. I sat down on my bed, took a deep breath, and closed my eyes.

Some time passed, maybe a minute, maybe ten, who knows? When I opened my eyes, they came to rest on my old Gibson electric guitar, a bit scratched and not so shiny as it once was, but still beautifully regal in its complete blackness. I remembered meeting my father down at Sam Ash on Forty-Eighth Street when he bought it for me, remembered my cringing when he jokingly asked the hipster clerk if they had any guitars for sale. It didn't seem like such a lame joke to me now. It seemed pretty funny, actually.

I got up, plugged the guitar into my amp, and sat back down on my bed. I watched my fingers shape out a chord and, almost involuntarily, start to play "Sweet Jane." As I strummed those four sublime chords over and over and over, deep within my psyche I felt something break loose and I disappeared into the song. "Sweet Jane" was New York, the New York I presently inhabited—it was cold, it was wind, it was hard earth, it was a hole six feet in the ground, it was me shoveling dirt into that hole, it was the dirt I shoveled into that hole hitting the casket with a sound both thunderous and hollow like someone throwing themselves on a grenade, it was worms slowly devouring what was in that hole, it was my mother sobbing, it was my brother stone-faced, it was my grandparents burying their son, it was a rabbi exclaiming that God is merciful and just, and at the end of it all it was me, alone.

I couldn't stop playing those four chords. I must've sat there for an hour, like a metronome, back and forth, back and forth. Those four chords kept me afloat, kept me from falling in that hole myself. I played those four chords every way I could think of: I played them thrashing, I played them plodding; I played them deafening, I played them hushed; I played them with distortion, I played them raw; I played them with rage, I played them with submission; I played them with the conviction of Lou Reed's bellow in the song's final verse that life's just to die; and ultimately I played them because I didn't know what else to do.

The truth is, I didn't know my father. Not in any fundamental way. And maybe I've always had a sense of that, felt that distance, even as a kid. Bruce Springsteen writes in his achingly revealing memoir—a book that from the day it was published I've parsed with the searching rigor of a Talmudic scholar, turning to it for parenting and life advice nearly as often as I turn to his music for emotional sustenance—that his music, particularly his *Darkness on the Edge of Town* album, was an effort to try to know his parents, to go deep into their lives, to understand the social forces that held them in check. Maybe that's why I was drawn to Springsteen's music from early on; maybe I could sense in his music a searching quality that expressed an unrequited desire for closeness with his father, that ached to understand the dynamic of their relationship. Maybe I was searching for something similar.

In the movie version of Norman Maclean's novel *A River Runs Through It*, the older brother says of his younger brother who has just died, "I guess all I knew about Paul was that he was a good fisherman." His father replies, "You knew more than that. You knew he was beautiful."

So, okay, there's that. I knew my father was beautiful. I knew it in broad strokes, in his essence. I knew his integrity; I witnessed it on our way home from vacations abroad when he'd painstakingly fill out the customs forms, going through each receipt from the clothing boutiques my mother visited and ignoring her when she said, probably accurately, "Jimmy, please, nobody writes down the real value on those forms." I knew his character; I was the beneficiary of it in his quiet counsel to tell the truth about my involvement in a beer-drinking scandal while on a high school trip. I knew his singular laugh, the beautiful progression of it, the way it started with his entire body convulsing so intensely that he once fell out of his seat into the aisle at the theater, then devolved into a coughing fit that came in triplicate guttural hacks and concluded with the wiping of the eyes and the blowing of the nose into the white hankie he always had close by.

What was missing were the critical details of his life, the things that made him who he was. What was he into as a kid? Who was his best friend? What sports did he play? Who did he have a crush on? What were his passions? What music did he listen to? And even more fundamentally than all that, what was he *like*? Was he the life of the party or was he quietly shy? A gregarious kid with lots of friends or a loner? Did he have a mischievous side or always play it straight? Did he ever let himself go, maybe even try pot, or was he too tightly wound? I didn't know any of that—never asked. And he never said.

In his memoir, Springsteen writes about accompanying his dad to Long Beach, California, to visit the *Queen Mary*, the ocean liner his father shipped out on for World War II. He confesses that although his father's experience on that ship was likely one of the most meaningful of his life, Bruce had no time for hearing about any of it; he just wanted to get out of there. "I'd pay anything now to be able to walk that ship with my father again," Bruce painfully laments with the benefit of hindsight. "I would treasure every step, want to know every detail, hear every word and memory he'd share, but back then I was still too young . . . to recognize my dad as a man."

Bruce was twenty-two when he visited the *Queen Mary* with his father. My father died when I was twenty-one. Perhaps at some point I'd have gotten around to asking him about his life, or maybe he'd have eventually volunteered some crucial snippets—maybe there's some pre-ordained point along the continuum of the father-son relationship where such conversations are permissible. Maybe he and I just didn't have enough time.

4

TALK ABOUT THE PASSION

My parents weren't all that into music. My dad would sometimes play classical music while he worked in his study, but it was background noise that helped him ignore stuff—me asking him to go to a Yankees game next weekend or play *Space Invaders*, Rob asking him for help with his homework or to throw the football, my mom asking him to come home early from work next Thursday so they could go out to dinner with the Cowens—and instead, concentrate on his work as a high-powered corporate lawyer, the type who'd sometimes show up at our house in Westhampton in a helicopter. That was so cool, although if Rob and I were playing football on the front lawn when the chopper arrived, it was a bit of a bummer having a gigantic mass of whirling steel sitting on our fifty-yard line. One time my dad arrived in Westhampton on a seaplane that landed in the bay behind our house and floated over to our dock. That was cool but not nearly as cool as the helicopter. With the sea plane, I couldn't feel the skin of my face peeling back.

No, the sounds that filled our apartment when I was in middle school were those of yellow cabs honking their way down Fifth

Avenue, of kids across the street in Central Park squealing on the swings, and of my mom yelling into the phone at my dad, almost always about his missing dinner yet again.

My parents did have a few decent records in their small collection—mostly albums by Simon & Garfunkel and The Beatles. Those albums were like stone tools you'd see in a museum that provide clues about how earlier civilizations lived. Was it possible my dad's well-tamed hair, like Paul Simon's on the cover of *The Concert in Central Park*, had once completely hidden his ears and flowed down his neck like the Fab Four's hair on the cover of *Let It Be*? In his pre-kids life, did my dad maybe ditch the Gillette Atra razor and green Skin Bracer aftershave and grow a thick black beard like Paul? Not likely. *Let It Be* was probably my mom's, although that didn't seem right either.

Why don't they still listen to this stuff, I wondered. I figured maybe there was something about having kids that was incompatible with listening to music, or maybe it was just something you outgrew, like comic books, although that didn't make a whole lot of sense. I couldn't imagine not blasting tunes when I grew up—even if I had kids.

The one place I did hear music was in the car on the way to and from Westhampton. If it wasn't a Sunday during football season, when obviously we'd be listening to the Jets game, my parents would play music, but it was stuff you'd never see on MTV, stuff like Barry Manilow and Shirley Bassey. Their favorite album was *Barry Manilow Live*, the one with the album title glowing in blue and yellow neon above a live concert photo of Manilow, who stands on a stage spread-eagled, back arched, head thrown back like he's just been shot, microphone gripped in his left hand, mouth wide open, soaking up the love of the crowd.

Although it was only like an hour and a half drive to Westhampton, the trip seemed endless, like sitting through a Yom Kippur service, mostly because my dad, who was criminally tone deaf, would try to sing along to Barry Manilow's soaring vocals. But also because Rob was always getting car sick.

"Um, can I get some air, my window's locked?" Rob would woozily ask, way too weakly for the task, straining to make himself heard over the swelling chorus of "Mandy." Beads of sweat would form on his upper lip. The blood would rush from his face, as if he were Jamie Lee Curtis in *Halloween* rounding a blind corner into a knife-wielding Michael Myers.

"Hey, Pops, Rob's gonna puke!" I'd lean forward and yell into my dad's ear.

That would cue my mom: "Jimmy, Jesus, put his window down! And pull over!" My dad would fumble with the child lock while veering across four bustling lanes of the Long Island Expressway, ignoring honking horns and obscene gestures to make the next exit. Rarely was he quick enough. Rob, who'd stick his head out into the traffic like some overeager, shotgun-riding dog, would, at the moment of truth, pull his head back into the car and then, for some reason I never got, turn my way and let it rip. This happened frequently, once to Manilow ironically belting out the chorus of "Looks Like We Made It."

I initially figured Rob's stomach issues were caused by my dad's tragic inability to carry a tune. But looking back, I blame Barry Manilow. I mean, I liked his music okay, but at the same time there was something a little cheesy about it that could turn someone's stomach. But more than the music, it was the dude's fashion sense that just didn't sit right. I'd stare at the cover of that *Barry*

Manilow Live cassette, him wearing some type of blousy shirt with broad pentagonal-shaped vertical "stripes" of blue, yellow, and white down the torso setting off solid blue arms, the whole shebang covered in sparkles. He's got on blue bell-bottoms that are also covered in sparkles, but there's an even brighter shimmering going on along the sides of the pant legs. Rhinestones, maybe? The whole setup gave me the heebies but I couldn't look away, wondering what kind of person would want to draw so much attention to himself, to stand out in the crowd like that. You're supposed to keep your head down and play it cool, right? Nobody I knew dressed like Barry Manilow.

Except my Aunt Wendy.

My parents once took Rob and me to see the Broadway show *Joseph and the Amazing Technicolor Dreamcoat*, and that's how Aunt Wendy dressed, like a girl version of Joseph. It was crazy. She was always decked out in flower-print sundresses of every color imaginable, real bright colors, too, not earth tones. There weren't any sparkles or rhinestones like with Manilow, but still, you couldn't miss her.

"Next time you come in, let's freshen up your wardrobe," my mom would say as she walked Wendy to the elevator after her visits to the city. "There're so many great boutiques on Madison Avenue you'd absolutely love. It'll be my treat." Aunt Wendy always responded with some version of, "Sure, Phyl, that sounds great," but as far as I know, it never happened. Aunt Wendy's outfits never seemed to change, anyway.

Only once did I hear Aunt Wendy say something back to my mom about the shopping thing, telling her they should look for matching leopard-skin pillbox hats, whatever those were. "Bob would love that," she added. My mom sighed and then did this thing with her eyes where it looked like they were going to disappear in the back of her head. She did that a lot with Aunt Wendy. My dad did, too.

Aunt Wendy was always referring to this Bob guy. I had no idea who he was since as far as I knew, Aunt Wendy wasn't married or in a relationship. One time when my mom was saying she didn't understand why the Palestinians were "carrying on so" in the West Bank during the First Intifada, Aunt Wendy replied, "Well, Phyl, as Bob famously said, 'When you ain't got nothing, you've got nothing to lose.'" My mom did the thing with her eyes. Another time Aunt Wendy suggested my mom not worry so much about getting invited to the Gersteins' Yom Kippur break fast, one of the social events of the year on the Upper East Side, telling her, "You know, Phyl, what looks large from a distance close up ain't never that big. That's what Bob says, and I've found it to be so true."

My mom, unmoved, flipped the thing around on Aunt Wendy. "Well sometimes what looks small from a distance is actually pretty huge close up, like a mountain. What's Bob say about that?"

"I think he'd say you're missing the point."

Who this Bob character was and why he'd love it if my mom and aunt went shopping for matching leopard-skin pillbox hats was a riddle I needed solved.

"Who's Bob?" I blurted.

"I'm guessing as usual your aunt is referring to Bob Dylan, the singer, although I'm not following the reference this time," my mom explained.

"Phyl, you've never heard 'Leopard-skin Pillbox Hat'? Oh, it's a hoot. You should check it out. And a word to the wise—you shouldn't refer to Bob as a singer. That's really ignorant. That's like referring to Einstein as a scientist or Neil Armstrong as an aeronautical engineer." Aunt Wendy turned to me. "Bob Dylan isn't just a singer, Matt. He's a visionary, a modern-day prophet, someone who sees America for what it is, with all its shortcomings, and isn't afraid to shout it out loud. His lyrics are really more like poems, beautiful poems that demand accountability from our political leaders and the capitalist system."

"Please, Wendy, can you spare Matthew the communist propaganda?" my mom pleaded. "He's only twelve years old, for crying out loud."

It's true I was having a hard time following the conversation but was glad finally to know who "Bob" was. Although it did seem a little strange that Aunt Wendy would talk about him like he was a good friend of hers.

So yeah, Aunt Wendy was a bit of an odd bird, what with the flashy outfits, the constant references to her pal Bob, and the political rants. But on the plus side, it was cool how she was so passionate about music. I'd never met an adult like that, or, really, an adult who was super jazzed about anything.

As far as Bob himself went, he sounded like kind of an interesting dude, but all that political stuff was a little grown-up for me. Plus, my mom clearly wasn't impressed with him, seemed to think he was a bit of a jackass, in fact. And I wasn't into poetry anyway. So when Aunt Wendy said I should check out his records, starting with *The Freewheelin' Bob Dylan*, I said I would but didn't mean it.

Sort of like how she said she'd go shopping with my mom the next time she came into the city.

I may not have taken Aunt Wendy's musical advice, but I sure as shit always took Murphy's. Murphy was my best friend in middle school and somehow knew all about the latest bands, bands I'd never even heard of—maybe because I read *Sports Illustrated* and he read this rock magazine called *Creem*. Seemed like a strange name for a magazine about rock music, but whatever. Murphy even looked like a young rock star, with long jet-black hair, a prominently arched nose, and dark skin that made his teeth look super white.

Murphy lived in a brownstone on the Upper East Side, not too far from our apartment, and I'd hang out there a lot on weekends. His room was at the back of the brownstone, on the ground level, and opened to an interior courtyard through a sliding glass door. That may sound like the high point of his digs, but my favorite feature of Murphy's room was a long wall of exposed red brick. When we listened to music, I'd stare at that brick wall and see in it—as if it were a movie screen—the aliens Styx sang about in "Come Sail Away" calling to me from their starship.

The first band with even the slightest hint of edge that Murphy and I got into was Def Leppard. Their second album, *High 'n' Dry*, was our absolute obsession in middle school. Before *High 'n' Dry*, Murphy and I mostly listened to groups like Journey and Styx, bands that could on occasion rock but were way too fond of the sappy power ballad. *High 'n' Dry* was a different animal. It was pure rock 'n' roll—raw, ferocious, and loud. The record's very first distortion-filled guitar notes were a literal wake-up call, commanding me to get up, grab something heavy, and start smashing things. Murphy and I memorized every word. This wasn't Barry Manilow all sad, saying he can't smile without you, or Journey's Steve Perry coming to you with open arms. Not even close. This was lead singer Joe Elliott bragging about tipping back whiskey and wine—at the same time—with his girlfriend by his side and the lights about to go out because it's Saturday night and he's high. I wasn't quite sure what all that meant but when

Murphy and I jumped around his bed, jamming on air guitar and howling along with the lyrics, we felt dangerous, like we were a couple of hardcore bad boys kicking ass, breaking hearts, and taking names.

Then came Def Leppard's next album, *Pyromania*. It was huge, like multi-platinum huge, but Murphy and I weren't impressed. Something had shifted with the group. Maybe it was the fact they'd booted lead guitarist Pete Willis for drinking too much and replaced him with some guy named Phil Collen who I guess was a more upstanding citizen. We hunkered down in Murphy's room to absorb the new album, staring at that red brick wall, but where was the edge? And what's with these electronic drums? And this Phil Collen's guitar solos, weren't they a tad too polished? A little too crisp and radio-friendly? And the lyrics? The lyrics no longer made me consider calling the cops. Take for example the album's first single, "Photograph." It just didn't seem like Joe Elliott's carrying on and on about his crush on some pinup girl was worth anyone's time. Honestly, it sounded like Air Supply lyrics.

Although Murphy and I did our damnedest to give *Pyromania* a chance, its fate was sealed one day after school in Murphy's room when we saw the video for "Rock of Ages" on MTV for the first time. The song's spoken word introduction, uttered in some kind of German gibberish, was cringe-worthy enough, but the absurd video that follows, with its medieval Excalibur theme, band of hooded druids, and tight shots of the backside of Phil Collen's even tighter white pants, was more than I could stomach.

"Whaddya think?" I asked Murphy, all tentative even though I knew it sucked big time. I still needed to hear what Murphy had to say about it since he was the ultimate authority when it came to all things music.

Murphy took a swig from his Sprite can and with a pained look on his face said, "I've got no idea what that was but we definitely need to take that record to the wall."

It was a death sentence. When Murphy and I decided we no longer liked a record because it was too lame or whatever, we'd violently scrape it against Murphy's red brick wall, scratching the shit out of it so nobody could ever again experience its lameness—it was like community service.

That red brick wall got a workout. Most of Cheap Trick's body of work made it there eventually. But sometimes the wall wasn't available to us. One time when I was over at Murphy's weekend place in Center Moriches, which wasn't too far from our house in Westhampton, I was thumbing through his vinyl and came across the Bee Gees' *Saturday Night Fever.*

"What's the story with this?" I asked accusingly.

"Wow, I don't know. I don't update my stash out here that often, I guess."

"We can bring it back to the city," I helpfully suggested. "Scratch the shit out of it next week."

"No, man," Murphy replied. "We don't have time for that. This is an emergency. Wait here a second." Murphy took off with the record and I sat in his room staring out the window at a large tree swaying in the wind. It was raining pretty hard and the window was all spotty and streaky. Then I saw Murphy tapping at the window, no jacket on, getting soaked, motioning me to come outside, which I did after grabbing my rain jacket. He was standing in the dirt driveway holding a hammer and shovel.

"What the fuck?" I asked.

But Murphy didn't answer. He just pulled *Saturday Night Fever* from its sleeve, tossed it like a frisbee onto the driveway, kneeled down, and started pummeling the thing with the hammer. It shattered into a dozen pieces.

"Start digging," he ordered, looking toward the shovel laying on the ground nearby. "We need to bury this shit before my parents get back."

Damn, I thought, *Murphy is hard core*. I grabbed the shovel and started digging up Murphy's parents' dirt driveway while Murphy continued to hack away at the vinyl. Luckily, the digging was easy because the driveway was soaked. So was I, but this was fun!

I dug down maybe a foot, and Murphy dropped the vinyl shards in the hole. We then both had at the album cover, tearing it to pieces and throwing it in with the vinyl. I filled in the hole, and we took turns jumping on it until it was good and flat, like a regular old dirt driveway. We caught our breath, looked at each other and started cracking up.

"Should we say a prayer?" Murphy asked through what looked like tears of laughter but maybe it was just the rain.

But before we could pay our final respects to *Saturday Night Fever*, we heard his parents' car starting to turn into the driveway, so we gathered up our tools and sprinted back to the house.

Around the time of *Pyromania*'s fatal trip to the red brick wall, Murphy and I quit shopping for records at our neighborhood Crazy Eddie and ventured downtown to hit the record shops of Greenwich Village. On Saturday mornings, we'd hop the Number 6 train at 77th and Lexington downtown to Astor Place. Murphy and I spent most of our free time, and all our allowance money, record shopping in the Village. Our favorite stores were Venus Records on 8th and Second Coming Records just across Washington Square Park on Sullivan.

Walking into Second Coming Records was like entering a religious shrine, if religious shrines played music deafeningly loud through sound systems delivering so much bass you could feel your bones vibrating in your body. Something very mystical was going on in there, something I always felt was beyond my complete understanding. The employees were like high priests: they wore special clothes (ripped jeans, leather, and lots and lots of jewelry), knew way more than everybody else (about music, anyway), and helped us commoners perform sacred rituals (of identification, inspection, and selection).

There were odd objects on display at Second Coming—vinyl of all shapes, sizes, and colors hung from the walls. The most bizarre was a 45 of the single "Africa" by the sort-of-rock band, Toto. It was shaped like the continent, with a map of Africa superimposed on the vinyl, the spindle hole obliterating most of central Gabon. I didn't buy it. Even though I liked the song, I could never admit that to the clerk since Toto was just barely cooler than Air Supply. But I did fork over hard cash for a single made of this crazy bright red vinyl by R.E.M., a band Murphy had clued me into a few years earlier. Murphy had scored their first EP, *Chronic Town*, after reading about them somewhere, probably in that weird *Creem* magazine. "You have to come over and check these guys out," he told me during lunch one day.

So when school got out, and after grabbing a plain slice at Mimi's Pizza on 84th and Lexington—it was a Wednesday and we always went to Mimi's on Wednesdays to celebrate hump day—we headed over to Murphy's house.

"The whole thing is great, but you have to hear 'Carnival of Sorts,'" Murphy said as we raced down the stairs to his room. In one athletic motion, he dumped his backpack on the floor and grabbed the record, which was sitting quietly on top of his Pioneer tuner, like it was wondering where he'd been all day. Murphy pulled the vinyl from its sleeve and dropped the needle on the last track of Side One.

The song started with some funky, swirling accordion sound, which I guess is where the "Carnival" title came from, before it kicked into high gear with the guitars and drums. The guitars sounded strange—there wasn't any hard-core distortion like with *High 'n' Dry* or the other bands we listened to like the Sex Pistols. R.E.M.'s guitars were all jangly or something. As far as the lyrics went, I couldn't make sense of them. It was like gibberish. I stared at Murphy's red brick wall, but even that didn't help make sense of them.

"What's the deal with the lead singer?" I yelled to Murphy over the second chorus. "Is he drunk?"

Murphy put his finger to his mouth, motioning me to shut the hell up. He sat on the edge of his bed, legs crossed, swaying back and forth like he was in an old-fashioned rocking chair, his eyes closed.

When the song was over, Murphy finally responded. "Forget about the lyrics, man. Who cares about that shit? Did you hear those drums? So crisp, man. And the guitars? Did you feel that tingling?"

"Yeah, it's a great tune," I said even though I didn't feel any tingling.

Anyway, by the time I scored that sweet red vinyl 45 at Second Coming, R.E.M. was Murphy's favorite band, hands down. We went at it a little over that R.E.M. single, which was a cover of the Velvet Underground's "Femme Fatale." By then, Rob had turned me on to VU, but Murphy wasn't that into them. So it was my VU thing against his R.E.M. thing.

"How about you buy it but I bring it home and check it out first?" Murphy had proposed. "Then you can have it for keeps." That sounded fair to me. Murphy was probably entitled to have the first listen, anyway, since he was the bigger music guy.

"Deal," I said and we shook hands on it.

I got the better end of it. Not only was the single pressed in that bright red vinyl, but you could see clear through the thing. Cooler still, it was bendable, and although it was the size of a regular 45 single, you played it at 33 RPMs. It was totally rare, a promotion given away with the June 1986 issue of *The Bob Magazine*. That's why Murphy and I kept heading back down to the Village—no way you'd find shit like that at Crazy Eddie.

Another time while combing through the bins of Second Coming on a gloomy Saturday, I scored a classic 1978 Springsteen bootleg—three glorious records recorded at the Winterland Theater in San Francisco during the *Darkness on the Edge of Town* tour. It was recorded from a radio broadcast and had perfect sound quality. I was so pumped to get home and listen to it that I blew off Murphy who was still shopping and beelined it to the closest subway station, hugging that precious Springsteen record the entire way to protect it from all those muggers I figured were jonesing for a perfect-quality Springsteen bootleg. When I finally got home, before I even took off my coat, I rushed to my room and gently placed the first record on my turntable as if it were made of gold instead of vinyl. After the initial thundering chords of "Badlands" boomed through my bedroom wall, Rob came busting into my room. "Holy shit! Where'd you get that?" he asked, incredulous. I still think of that bootleg as the best twenty dollars I ever spent.

Murphy, being more enlightened than I, mostly scored records by bands I'd never heard of, bands like Jesus and Mary Chain, Lords of the New Church, and the Cult. Despite their names, these bands didn't seem to me to be all that religious. Well, there was that B-side of one of the Jesus and Mary Chain's early singles called "Jesus Fuck." But other than that, not so much. Being Jewish, I wasn't bothered by the various forms of sacrilege, but I did worry a little about the fate of Murphy's soul.

By the time we began our pilgrimages to the Village, we'd come a long way musically from Def Leppard. But *High 'n' Dry* taught me something really, really important about life: certain songs just sound better LOUD! I'm not sure why that is. Maybe they generate extra brain chemicals at ear splitting volume or something. Who knows? But it's without a doubt the case, a scientific certainty, and *High 'n' Dry* was Exhibit A for me of that elemental law of nature. I needed to play that record loud—real loud.

In fact, I played that album so loud and so often in middle school that one day when I came home from school, my mom, instead of putting out milk and cookies, handed me a small, gift-wrapped box, complete with a purple bow on it. I was mightily confused since it wasn't my birthday and Hanukkah was still months away.

"What's this?" I asked, suspicious.

"Just a little something to help keep the peace," my mom responded all mysterious like.

Having no idea what she was getting at, but figuring it was unlikely my mom was trying to play some evil trick on me, I ripped the thing open.

Nestled in the box was a pair of gleaming black headphones, and not just any headphones; these were high-end Sony DR-M7s.

"This way you can listen to music and I can hear myself think," my mom explained. "A win-win. Just don't destroy your hearing, okay?"

"Okay," I shrugged, not sure yet what to make of the gift. It wasn't like I'd really wanted headphones; I was just fine cranking my stereo speakers to the max. But I headed to my room to give them a test run with *High 'n' Dry.*

Listening to *High 'n' Dry* through headphones was sort of like the first time I went scuba diving—I felt like I'd entered a different world, completely separate and physically apart from the one I'd just been in. As if I'd slipped underwater, the headphones wrapped me in a sonic cocoon that blocked out everything else, sealing off the outside world. I was physically inside the music, surfing its soundwaves; if somebody had cut the power to my stereo, I'd have wiped out, disintegrated into nothing, like the woman in that bible story who turned into a pillar of salt.

It was so freaking cool. When I listened to Def Leppard's "Bringin' on the Heartbreak" through my headphones, I could hear Joe Elliott whispering something just after the introductory guitar riff and before the first verse. I couldn't make out what he said but that just made it more mysterious, more hardcore. I heard drummer Rick Allen during the chorus alternating between hitting the snare on every beat and every other beat; it was like pulsating or something, and the next thing I knew I was bobbing my head all crazy-like. I heard the background vocals coming at me from every direction, like the final battle scene in *Star Wars* at the Loews Orpheum Theater on 86th Street, leaving my skin covered in goosebumps.

The headphones were cool not just for the stuff I could hear but for the stuff I couldn't. I couldn't hear my mom yelling at my brother to do his homework or for breaking curfew. I couldn't hear her yelling at my dad for having stayed late at the office again or for taking on another big case. I didn't hear any of that. I was underwater.

5

LISTENING FOR THE STILLNESS

The summer after my father died and I graduated from college, I spent three weeks backpacking and rafting in Gates of the Arctic National Park as part of a seven-person Outward Bound group. The park, well above the Arctic Circle in far northern Alaska, is a vast wilderness, over 13,000 square miles. No roads in or out. You either have to walk in or catch a ride on a float plane. I was starting law school at NYU in the fall and viewed the trip as a last hurrah before the academic grind set in.

The decision to light out for Alaska beforehand was downright bizarre. As the caricature of a sheltered city slicker, someone who considered Central Park a vast and unspoiled hinterland, I'd never done anything in the wilderness, not so much as a day hike. My family's vacations tended towards the beach resort end of the spectrum. Hell, I didn't even own hiking boots.

My college girlfriend Jodi and I had experimented with the car camping thing at a lake once, but that barely qualified as an outdoor experience, what with the cooler of beer we toted along, the bathrooms with hot showers nearby, and the country music blaring well past dark from the neighboring campsite which was itself just a spindly high schooler's shot-put throw away from our own.

Jodi and I had met our freshman year at Duke. My friend Jon asked if I wanted to go to a sorority formal with her, and although I sort of knew who she was, we hadn't hung out much. On top of which, there was an important Duke basketball game that night that I planned to watch with friends, so I shook Jon off. "No problem," he said. "I'll let her know."

Ten minutes later my phone rang. It was Jodi. "Jon tells me you'd be up for going to this formal on Saturday. It should be fun. Why don't you pick me up at seven?"

"Sure, sounds great," I mumbled as I cursed Jon in my head.

Turned out to be a good thing that Jon had screwed me. Jodi was fun and super smart. And hot. She was fit, had long dirty blond hair, a perfect smile, cute apple cheeks you could rest a dime on, and stunning hazel eyes. We started dating sophomore year and were still together when I hatched my crazy Alaska plan. For good reason, Jodi was a touch anxious about my lighting out for the Alaskan wilderness but ultimately encouraged me to listen to the mystical inner voice that was commanding me to go to the mountains—and to go big!

I'm not really sure where that voice came from, what fueled my desire, my primordial need to make a break for the vast untamed emptiness of Alaska. Springsteen told his biographer, Peter Ames Carlin, that after his father died he couldn't be inside. It rained for days on end after his father's death, but even so, he still needed to be outside. Maybe there's just something about losing your father that makes it feel like the world's caving in on you, that you're being hemmed in, buried along with him in a way that propels you to want to bust loose.

I do know I had a crazy suspicion I'd feel my father's presence out there, that I'd be able to commune with him some and maybe say a proper goodbye. Referring to the wilderness, Wayne Muller writes, "When we first glimpse emptiness, we taste the death in it. It feels like an abyss, a sheer drop into eternity, a dangerous negation of all that is alive, visible, safe, and good." Part of me wanted to stare into that abyss Muller describes, in the hope of glimpsing my father one last time.

Or maybe it would be a type of penance, to be in a place without any modern conveniences, a place where I'd feel small, insignificant, where my own mortality would be pounded ceaselessly into my head by the timelessness of soaring, majestic mountains and deep churning rivers, a place where I and my tale of woe could be dwarfed by the majesty of nature. Maybe I wanted to dangle from the side of a mountain, as Pearl Jam front man Eddie Vedder once described hiking with Chris Cornell, the lead singer of Soundgarden, a band with whom I'd soon form a deep, impassioned relationship. In Vedder's telling, they were hiking in "the middle of fucking nowhere . . . climbing up these crazy green mountains and then into this rock mountain. The rocks were like crumbling, it became kinda like light brown crumbling rocks and all of a sudden we were just both like two Spider-Man impersonators just hanging on the side of this thing not being able to move. Just stuck and about fifty feet above the freakin' valley floor." Maybe I too wanted to be high above a valley floor, courting my own death, staring it down as if to affirm I was still alive.

Or was it that I hoped to transform myself into the kind of person who walked comfortably in his own skin, self-sufficient, living in the moment—the person I had thought I was but who was now lost to me? Bob Dylan writes in his memoir that after suffering a serious hand injury, he felt as if "[t]here was a missing person inside of myself and I needed to find him." And so off he went into the wilderness, surrounded by moose and bear, listening for the call of the loon. "In nature there's a remedy for everything," Dylan writes, "and that's where I'd usually go hunting for it." Maybe I, too, needed to find myself again, having lost track of that person in the aftermath of my father's death.

My family was stunned that I wanted to go traipsing around Alaska for three weeks. My Grandma Toby summed up the collective reaction when she interrogated me, incredulous, "Matthew, why would you want to do that? It's so dangerous!" Only Aunt Wendy seemed to get it. Shortly before I left, she sent a journal for me to bring along. "Phyl told me you're headed to Alaska—I think that's sooo excellent," she wrote in an accompanying note. "I had a friend who went to the University of Alaska and she loved it up there, but you'll get to see so much more of the land. Oh Matt, I think it's so great you're going! I know this is a difficult time for you, but you should feel excited for the road ahead. I love you very much and think of you every day." It felt good that somebody in my family understood my strange yearnings, even if it was just my wayward aunt.

Our small group flew into Gates of the Arctic National Park on a float plane from the outpost of Bettles and landed on a sparkling lake situated in a long valley surrounded by huge, glaciated peaks. Having deposited us and our gear in the middle of a boundless and stunning nowhere, the float plane took off, leaving me feeling a bit on edge but also exhilarated for the uncertain adventure ahead.

Bill, the leader of our group, was in his mid-forties with wild brown hair, a Dalai Lama pendent around his neck, and a slight but strong frame that was well bronzed from spending most of his life outdoors. Bill had been an Outward Bound instructor for over twenty years, and he also led private groups through the Nepalese Himalayas and up Mount Kilimanjaro. Bill taught me how to read and orient a contour map, how to analyze the terrain to find the easiest passage, and what to look for when picking a campsite (a breeze to keep the mosquitoes down; an open, flat space fully visible to the bears; and, of course, access to water). Bill had spent most of his life traveling the world, trying to learn everything he could about the cultures he visited. I'd never met anyone so intellectually curious. He was equally fascinated by all types of life—plant, animal, and human.

The trip was a gauntlet physically. My pack alone weighed over sixty pounds. And the walking was relentless, entailing constant elevation changes, with some days our group hiking for nine hours, clothed in long sleeves and long pants—despite the heat—to protect us from the ubiquitous, maniacal mosquitoes.

But what made the hiking almost unbearable was the terrain itself, the actual composition of the ground. The surface of the land resembled a sponge, the top few inches of permafrost below the vegetation having melted in the July heat to create vast tussock fields. I wasn't sure whether to try to step on the large but unstable tufts of wild grass and risk turning an ankle, or maneuver painstakingly around them and sink into the boggy soil. It was like a giant field of moguls, except you couldn't just glide over them.

Back home, I always listened to music to keep my mind off the monotony when I'd jog or engage in other mindless tasks. But I hadn't brought any music with me to Alaska. It seemed like an extravagance given my already ridiculously heavy pack and it probably wasn't allowed anyway. But surprisingly I found I didn't need music in Alaska. More than that, I didn't *want* music there, in that setting. Not only did I not ache to hear "Thunder Road" even once over the three weeks, which was an odd turn since that craving typically surfaces every three days or so, it didn't even occur to me to hum the Allman Brothers' "Blue Sky" to myself as I trudged along beneath a sky that was as blue as skies come—like an Yves Klein painting. Instead, I listened for the breeze fluttering through the valley, for the gurgling of the creeks and the locomotive shrill of the rivers, for the screeching of eagles and the squish of the ground under my feet. Like an infant, I marveled at these sounds, all of which were new to me. I drank them in, feeling my mind expand as if to make room for their existence.

But most of all, I listened for the stillness, for the nothingness. It was as profound as any Dead jam, as any Duane Allman solo. And so much rarer. Even in Alaska it was rare. But I heard it unmistakably one night as we floated down the North Fork of the Koyukuk River at 1 a.m., hoping to spy wildlife in the half-light cast by the Alaskan midnight sun. We stopped paddling and circled in a small eddy, the only sound the trickle of water off our oars. And then that too ceased. I felt like Lucy slipping through that magical Narnian wardrobe into an entirely new world, a new dimension where nothing existed except the immediate present—there was no history, no future, no past; no thoughts, no worries, no fears; no sickness, no disease, no death. Just a presence, a physical state unmoored from all context. My eyes widened as I held my breath, not wanting to break the spell. And then a fish jumped, producing shards of sound that pierced the cocoon of silence. I exhaled as the ripples faded and the world grew silent once again.

One day after a grueling day hike to the summit of the highest peak in the Brooks Range, our group passed a small lake glistening in the late afternoon sunshine. I desperately wanted to dive headlong into that lake, both to cool off and to clean up a bit given it'd been five days since I'd last showered and I could feel the sweat and grime on me like a second skin. The other hikers, thinking I was insane to swim in a frigid glacial lake, just forged on, disappearing down the hill in the direction of our base camp which lay a half mile below. Alone in this pristine wilderness, the city boy who loved the Sex Pistols, crowded bars, and take-out Chinese, stripped down to his birthday suit, eased over to the lake's edge and breathed in the emptiness. The instant I waded into the water my feet went numb, which felt strangely liberating. I then plunged headfirst into the lake, knowing it was much too cold to inch my way in step-by-step. The shock took my breath away. My head immediately started pounding, like someone had taken a sledgehammer to it, and I could feel my heart racing from the deepest sensation of cold I'd ever experienced. I lasted only five or ten seconds in the water, worried I might have a heart attack.

So there I stood in the middle of the Arctic tundra, water dripping from my naked body, the sun slowly urging my blood to circulate again. With the expanse of the valley spreading out before me, the heart-stopping wildness and grandeur of the Brooks Range on full display as far as the eye could see, an endless tableau of mountains, moraines, lakes, and rivers stretching out to the distant horizon, the remnants of glaciers revealing themselves in the snow fields and huge u-shaped valleys carved out of the mountains, it hit me: I was completely alone. And not just that. Not only was I utterly removed from everything and everyone I knew, but I was thinking only about the next day, the next campsite, getting from Point A to Point B.

In "From a Buick 6," Bob Dylan quips, "I need a dump truck, baby, to unload my head." Music had always been my dump truck, but the Alaskan wilderness was like the Woodstock of mental sanitation.

In the entire first week, I hadn't even once thought about my father. I figured I'd be thinking about him all the time. I wanted him to see and experience what I was seeing, what I was going through, perhaps because this was who I thought I really was, a rugged outdoorsman, and I wanted him to see me that way so he'd actually know me. My father only knew me as a kid, when my top priority in life was getting into the Duke–Carolina basketball game. But now I was an adult, having graduated from college and on my way to law school, just as he'd done.

Or maybe this crazy trip to the middle of nowhere was something I imagined my father might've himself wanted to do if only he'd allowed himself the time; maybe I believed that so I could identify with him and claim a piece of him for myself, a piece nobody else ever knew about.

But my father never entered my mind that first week, perhaps because I did feel so alone in Alaska. Not only did the wide-open spaces foster a feeling of isolation, but it was so far from everything I'd known that I felt as if nobody from my life, from the "real world," could possibly be there with me. It wasn't until Day 15 that my father first entered my mind, albeit unconsciously. He appeared in a dream.

I dreamt I spoke to my father on the phone the day he died. In the dream, I knew he was going to die later that day, around 6 p.m., so I called his hospital room around 4 p.m. I called him from a golf resort, which was very strange because at that point in my life, I'd played golf no more than five times. Actually, saying I "played" golf would be a stretch. I mostly drank beer with my college friends while golf-cart drag racing down the fairways, the festivities occasionally interrupted by a slice so pronounced it defied the laws of physics. Maybe I associated golf with a type of careless frivolity, the ultimate counterfactual to my father lying in a hospital bed dying. Maybe I harbored some latent guilt about being MIA on his last day, felt that I should forever be holed up in a dark apartment, curled up on the couch in the fetal position.

In the dream, my father answered my call, his voice weak and cracking. He whispered, "I'm getting ready to leave this world. It's going to take a major adjustment, but I'll be with you all the time, everywhere."

This was not something he ever would've said. Not only did he rarely express a burning desire to be with me, he never admitted to anyone he was dying. He seemed to never accept the reality of it. My mother told me that the day he died, choking and sweating he asked the doctor when he planned to start the next round of chemotherapy. The doctor knew my father couldn't withstand any more treatments. "We'll do it tomorrow," he told my father, knowing full well my father wouldn't make it through the night.

I'll be with you all the time, everywhere. That had been my wish since childhood, but it was a wish that never came true. Was his dreamy declaration a too-late expression of regret, an acknowledgment that he did in fact want to be with me, if not *all the time, everywhere*, at least a lot more than he had been?

I woke up from the dream sweating even though it was snowing outside. The sound of falling snow was bizarre because it'd been near eighty degrees every day of the trip to that point. But I could hear the snowflakes flittering against our tent, could hear a tempestuous wind testing the tent's ground stakes. I peeked outside and saw the ground covered in a thin white blanket, the mountains hidden in the low, brooding clouds.

After my brief dip in that glacial lake, freed from the prison of those hiking boots, my beleaguered feet felt so good I couldn't bear the thought of putting them back on, so I slung them over my day pack and strolled the last half-mile back to camp barefoot, the bristling sharpness of the tundra, the grass, dirt, rocks, and pebbles massaging my soles as I ambled along.

I was on dinner duty that evening with Alex, a thirty-something divorced guy from North Carolina. Alex stood well over six feet tall with long blond hair that he typically kept under control via this ratty blue bandana tied around his forehead. He reminded me of someone, and after a few days I realized who it was—Gregg Allman, particularly after a week of not shaving.

My initial description of him in the journal Aunt Wendy had given me was decidedly unflattering: "Deadhead scumbag," which was a curious description since I was a huge Dead fan myself and had seen the band for probably the tenth time just a few weeks before heading to Alaska. But I didn't identify as a Deadhead. Deadheads were vagrants, rootless hippies, addled drug fiends. Everyone knew that. What with their tie-dye T-shirts (I owned several), trippy Volkswagen buses (my ride to school for many years was a red VW bus driven by the wife of my future high school science teacher, Ramblin' Bob Hipkens), unkempt facial hair (perfect description of me as I wrote that journal entry), and putrid scent of patchouli mixed with body odor (I would've killed for a vial of patchouli to counteract the odor emanating from my own unwashed body).

No, I was a professional, a straight-and-narrow type, a serious, no-nonsense individual like my father and much like another member of the Outward Bound troupe—Stephanie, a forty-five-year-old lawyer from New York. Interestingly, I described Stephanie as, "Extremely uptight and busy; basically an annoying person." I guess we sometimes don't like what we see in the mirror.

Looking back at those Alaska journal entries, it's clear I didn't think I fit in either the Deadhead or corporate camps. But maybe I just didn't want to admit that I fit in both. Acknowledging my Deadhead side in the wake of my father's death would've risked my feeling he was even further from me at a time when I desperately needed to keep him close. And yet there was something about giving myself over to the New York corporate world and following dutifully in his footsteps that felt stifling, even deadening. At the same time, splitting the baby by fully embracing elements of both sides didn't seem possible, didn't seem authentic. How could I claim to be a Deadhead if I'd be wearing a suit to work? And how could I claim to be honoring my father as an upstanding member of the professional class if I took a month off to follow the Dead around the country?

After I helped prepare a dinner of spinach fettucine with pesto sauce—which was delicious, not because of my culinary skills but because, as I'd learned, after a long day of hiking in the wilderness, everything tastes delicious—I wandered over to the bank of Ernie's Creek and sat up against a rock that overlooked the creek. The sun was still high in the sky, shining brightly at 9:15 p.m., and the Gates of the Arctic—Mounts Boreal and Frigid Crags—towered somewhat menacingly in the distance on opposite sides of the Koyukuk River, their glaciers shimmering in the warm light for miles in every direction. The mountains and valleys were vibrantly aglow, carpeted with myriad variations of lush green vegetation. Not a hint of metal or concrete here. Those materials were from another world, a world it was difficult to believe coexisted with this one. I wondered how I came to be in this place. How it was possible. And how I'd reenter "the real world," the concrete jungle of New York City. Would I violently careen like a spaceship re-entering earth's atmosphere? Or penetrate gracefully, like an Olympic high diver knifing through the water? Either way, the prospect of returning to New York broke my reverie. I could feel my neck and shoulders stiffen, could feel a chill start to take hold.

As if to re-center myself, I gazed up at the sky. Ever-morphing odd-shaped clouds—a guitar pick? A wayward pigeon? A Checker cab?—hovered in the distance, appearing frozen in place in the vastness of the high-country sky. For a moment I remembered a book I had when I was a kid, a cloud book full of pictures and tidy, scientific descriptions of all the different cloud types—cirrus, cumulonimbus, cumulus. Clearly, that book's author had never been to Alaska.

As I listened to the water rushing by in Ernie's Creek, I heard some inner voice posit, *Is the world really like this? Can it be this wrenchingly beautiful?* followed quickly by *Is this really me? Am I really this free?*

Although I returned involuntarily to those questions several times over the last ten days of the trip, most of which were spent rafting down the Koyukuk River back to Bettles—watching for the silver flashes of salmon in the crystal-clear water, camping on the river's gravel bars—I couldn't definitively resolve them. While I did believe the world could be unspeakably beautiful—welcome news after my father's death—and while I came to believe that my present incarnation out in the wilderness was the best possible version of myself, I wasn't convinced it was sustainable, that I was free to continue to be that person. Something about it felt fraudulent, as if I'd received a temporary pass to a fantastical world, one where I was playing the part of Cinderella at the ball, living on borrowed time, beyond my means and abilities, fated to be relegated back to the "real world" upon the clock striking midnight.

It turned out my reentry into "the real world" was more like an astronaut's into earth's atmosphere than an Olympic swimmer's into a pool. I met up with Jodi in Seattle to begin a three-week cross-country drive back to New York to start law school. Although Seattle is by any measure a beautiful city, with views of Lake Washington or Puget Sound from most vantage points, all I saw were traffic-snarled streets, crowds of people, and unbridled commerce, all things that felt foreign to me now. I felt deflated, on edge, and alone. A few days later,

Jodi and I stopped for lunch in a small, picturesque town perched on a bluff along the Northern California coast. I'd been weaned off sugar during the Alaska trip and after lunch found myself unloading on Jodi when she suggested we stop in some tourist-trap candy shop to buy a piece of fudge. Wild-eyed with irrational rage, I summarily informed her that her desire for fudge was reprehensible.

"Have you lost your mind?" she asked, staring in disbelief after I refused to stand with her in the huge line at the candy shop and instead stormed off to the car. She went ahead and bought the fudge anyway which made me even madder. We didn't speak for hours afterwards. Because of fudge. Maybe I *had* lost my mind. What was I trying to prove with that ridiculous outburst? That I recognized the existence of some superior realm, one that was pure and genuine, and that I was a creature of that realm, that I belonged there and not in this place of superficial and pretentious materialism? And if so, who was I trying to prove all that to? To Jodi? Or was I trying to prove it to myself? Was I trying to convince myself that I belonged in that realm because as much as I wanted to, I didn't really believe it? Clearly, I was in desperate need of that dump truck Dylan sang about.

I felt like I was my best self in Alaska, but I didn't know if I could ever find that person again. I felt the person I wanted to be slipping away, perhaps forever, and I was petrified. Petrified of becoming some nameless cog in the corporate wheel, someone toiling away just to become a face in an old photograph, gazed upon after his death by a wife or a child until they too died and the face was no longer recognizable to anyone.

Within a day or two of returning to New York, my nose started to run and my throat hurt. I figured my system wasn't used to Manhattan's filthy air, the same filthy air that in my mind had killed my father. While the runny nose and sore throat were upsetting, I was far more aggrieved a few days later when my nose stopped running and my throat stopped hurting and I realized my system had "readjusted." I was furious, telling myself I never wanted to "adjust" to living in New York again, that I wanted my experience in Alaska to shape my future. I didn't know what that meant exactly or how it would play out, just that I wanted to feel how I felt in Alaska: alive.

6

SHOULD I STAY OR SHOULD I GO?

For my bar mitzvah, Murphy gave me the first three records by the Clash and I immediately wore them *out*, cheering on the Clash's call to the working class to start a revolution. But then at some point it dawned on me that the Clash's new political order, if it actually came to pass, might kind of suck for me. Like, who'd cook dinner and do the laundry if Pat, our housekeeper, took off to join the revolution? And could the revolution somehow interfere with my weekends water-skiing and playing football on the beach? Seemed like it definitely could. It didn't really matter, though—I still loved the Clash even after I realized it was me they were coming for.

I told my parents that if Hitler were still alive and traveled to some world capital, he'd receive a full-on diplomatic welcome at the airport, complete with limousine, as lead singer Joe Strummer snarled in "(White Man) In Hammersmith Palais."

"That seems unlikely," my dad said without looking up from the business section of the *New York Times*. "He'd probably be tried as a war criminal like the others at Nuremburg. And executed."

"Hmmn, yeah, maybe so," I said, unable to think of a good

comeback to that since I had no idea what Nuremburg was. But I'd still defiantly spit out that lyric with scorn for the world's hypocrisies whenever the situation called for it.

In my mind, the Clash's declaration in "Death or Glory" that "He who fucks nuns will later join the church," was the most brilliant and insightful line ever written. I had no idea what exactly the metaphor was getting at. Or if it even *was* a metaphor. It didn't matter. It was punk!

Four days before my fourteenth birthday, I saw the Clash in concert. Well, kind of. It was 1984 and Mick Jones, who wrote and sang half their songs with Joe Strummer, had just been kicked out of the band by Strummer for prioritizing churning out Top Forty hits over inciting the workers' revolution. Some might make fun of me for claiming I'd actually seen *The* Clash. It'd be like seeing Paul, George, and Ringo but no John, then claiming I saw The Beatles.

But I didn't care that Mick Jones was no longer around. I was all about Joe Strummer. Mick Jones's songs were too pop for me. Strummer's were grittier, like his voice. He sounded like he had splinters in his throat. And because Mick Jones was gone, the Clash were downgraded to playing tiny venues like the gymnasium at Hofstra University in Hempstead, Long Island, where I saw them. Turned out they were way better without Mick Jones.

My friend John's mom drove Murphy, me, and a few of our other friends to the concert, sternly instructing us that we needed to be back at the car by eleven o'clock. "It's a long ride back to the city and I have a million things to do tomorrow," she said. We all nodded our agreement as we piled out of the station wagon and beelined it towards the gym's entrance.

We had showed up early, around eight o'clock for the nine o'clock show, to try to get as close to the stage as possible. A blue wooden NYC police barricade divided the gym into two sections with the good seats up front and a standing room section in back where my friends and I milled around waiting for the show to start. I sized up the crowd around the gym and noticed nobody looked anything remotely like me or my friends. Not one of us was sporting a Mohawk or hair dye. Far from it. My hair was its natural brown, cut short, with no particular styling to it except for a part to the right. I had no leather, no piercings. I was your basic square kid, blue jeans, a light blue Patagonia wind breaker over a brown V-neck sweater, a plain white T-shirt peeking out from the neckline.

It was body-to-body in the gym. Even though it was mid-April and chilly outside, once through the doors it was plenty hot. I briefly considered taking off my sweater but worried it might get too beat up if I tied it around my waist. Or worse, I might lose it. So I stood there sweating, as did everybody else—I guess leather isn't that breathable. There was no escape from the stench of B.O.

We stood around for like two hours waiting for the band to take the stage since there was no opening act. Then, just before ten o'clock, wham! A blunt object crashed into my thigh. Momentarily stunned, I looked down to see a section of the police barricade being passed hand over hand backwards through the crowd. What the hell was going on?

A quick scan of the crowd ahead of me told the whole story—fans immediately behind the barricade had secretly pulled apart then ditched the A-frame two-by-fours but then continued holding the blue crossbeam in place at waist level, giving the impression the barricade was still firmly in place while the supports were passed back through the crowd. Holy shit, these fans were hardcore! It was pure genius. But then a surge of anxiety passed through me. Was I about to get trampled like the fans at that Who concert in Cincinnati?

But before my anxiety could turn to panic, the lights went out, the hands that held up the barricade dropped it to the floor and the crowd surged forward. I was immediately separated from my friends, carried along like a surfer riding a wave. Somehow I stayed afloat and to my amazement ended up in the third freaking row! My friends were nowhere to be seen, but I figured that was their problem.

Something BIG was about to happen. Then, through the blanket of pitch black, a single column of white shone down on the stage, lighting up Joe Strummer. He stood defiantly on the band's drum kit, legs in a full lunge as if crossing a swollen river in one mighty step, arms pointing to the heavens. He sported a bright orange Mohawk and white three-piece suit. The dazzling combination of orange and white reminded me of the creamsicle I'd eaten earlier that day—but in a countercultural, regal way. His orange Mohawk was like a crown, the white three-piece suit his royal mantle.

Strummer's battered electric guitar hung limp before him, suspended by a black leather shoulder strap. I was close enough to read the sticker stuck above his guitar's pickups: "Ignore Alien Orders." I wasn't quite sure what that meant; I just understood it was dazzlingly hardcore. After allowing us a few seconds to take in his regal presence and pay tribute, which I did by spitting out a sound I'd never before heard come out of my mouth (it was like a cross between a chimpanzee's screeching holler and a hoot owl's mating call), he grabbed the neck of the guitar and jumped high off the drum kit. The orange Mohawk flew through the air, transforming into the feathers of some glorious and exotic punk rock bird.

Strummer's battered biker boots crash-landed on stage in perfect time to the first explosive chord of "London Calling." As Strummer madly pounded out the song's clipped chords, staccato style, like a musical assault and battery, it dawned on me how wrong Strummer's name was. He didn't strum his guitar; he pounded it like a boxer hitting a heavy bag. And yet "Strummer" was only a stage name. That he'd chosen such an ironic name only solidified his hardcore status.

I delighted in the thrashing of those guitar stabs. Unlike a literal stabbing, each insertion of this knife energized me, brought me life; it was like a modern-day bloodletting. I briefly looked around again for my friends who'd been swallowed up by the foul-smelling mohawked sea of humanity. Still no sign of them. A momentary pang of concern rose up but quickly passed; Joe Strummer stood directly in front of me, hammering out "London Calling." Nothing else mattered.

By the end of the second song I was drenched in sweat. I scanned the crowd around me, hoping to make eye contact with one of my crew . . . but still no sign of any of them, which was no big deal—I was sure as hell not giving up a third-row seat to go looking for them! But then through the fog of my punk delirium, I suddenly remembered that John's mom had commanded us all to be back at the car by eleven o'clock. Her request seemed reasonable enough at the time, but during the interval between the second and third songs, I checked my watch and saw it was already 10:30. *What*??? *No*! The trip back through the crowd and out to the distant parking lot could easily take thirty minutes! But leave after *two* songs? That would be idiotic. On the other hand, what if John's mom left without me? Were my friends obediently making their way out to the car at this very moment? Oh hell no. There was no way any of them were leaving a freaking Clash concert after just two songs. A week before, Ted had been kicked out of a bar mitzvah party for getting drunk on Jack and Cokes and writing "Keith Moon" in the "In Memoriam" dedication space of several of the synagogue's prayer books. Jacob, who would soon be suspended from school for running a fake ID distribution network, had recently befriended a Coors truck driver and now had a neon Coors sign in his bedroom which he used as a desk lamp. And Murphy had just started smoking cigarettes in the alley across from school. No way these guys were going to bail before the end. I figured I was safe to stay for the entire concert—encores included.

The last joyously defiant, fuzzed out guitar note sounded just past midnight. Because I was all the way at the front, I was one of the last to leave the gym, so by the time I weaved my way into the parking lot, it was past 12:30 a.m. The adrenaline was still coursing through my system; I was euphoric, on a non-pharmaceutical high. *Man, I can't wait to tell Rob about the show*, I thought as I scanned the parking lot for the wood-paneled station wagon. Rob, who was a big Clash fan himself, had seen them open for The Who at Shea Stadium a couple years earlier. Then I noticed there were hardly any cars in the parking lot, and my euphoria quickly melted away. My stomach began to churn. Had John's mom taken off? Sure I was a little late, but the concert had gone long. I stopped walking so I could focus on my search for the wagon. And then I saw it in the next sub-lot, sitting all alone in a sea of concrete and murky pools of industrial lighting. I sensed a real bad energy coming from the wagon, even from a distance. Just then, the driver side door opened with such force that it swung back again and pushed John's mom, who'd begun to leap out of her seat, back into the car. Even angrier now, she kicked open the door with her foot and hurled herself out of the wagon. She was an imposing figure under normal circumstances, tall with graying hair and a whiff of bitterness to her that I figured related somehow to her being divorced, but as she stepped towards me, coiled up like some furious animal, ready to strike, she was downright frightening.

"*Where* have you been!" she screamed at me, her feet in a wide stance like she was bracing for combat, her hands on her hips, her face so red in the parking lot light I thought she might pop like a balloon. "I was about to call the police. I thought you'd been trampled to death!"

My friends were in the car. Every one of them.

What the fuck? Nobody else stayed?

"Don't you have a watch?" she demanded. "We've been sitting here waiting for you for an hour and a half! What were you thinking? How selfish can you be?"

How is this possible? I'm the most responsible, rule-following, slapped ass of this whole bunch!

"I'm sorry," I stammered, "I thought that—"

"Thought what? That you can do whatever the hell you want no matter how it impacts other people? I should've left you here. Now get in the car!"

We drove back to Manhattan in stone silence. At some point Murphy whispered to me, "How was it?" Still too mortified to speak, I just nodded at him with raised eyebrows. He cracked a faint smile.

Man, were my parents pissed. Luckily, they were asleep when I got home, but by the time I woke up the next day, an overcast and gray Sunday morning, John's mom had already called them.

"What were you possibly thinking?" my mom thundered as I rubbed the sleep from my eyes and opened the refrigerator to grab the milk for my cereal. She slammed the refrigerator door closed. "Look at me, Matthew!" I knew I was in deep shit because she never called me Matthew.

"I thought everybody else was gonna stay," I replied weakly.

"Why would that have mattered? John's mom told you the rules. I don't care if everybody else ignored them. *You* shouldn't have. She was nice enough to drive you and your friends all the way out to God knows where Long Island and then sit around for hours waiting on everyone. And that's how you thank her? Jesus Christ, Matthew. I would've left you to hitch a ride back on the LIE."

"I get it, Mom. I screwed up. You can quit yelling."

"Don't tell me to quit yelling! I'll quit yelling when you stop acting like a spoiled brat!"

My dad drifted into the kitchen from his study, my mom's screaming having distracted him from his work.

"We're really disappointed in you," he said, piling on. "We'd expect that type of inconsiderate behavior from your brother, but not from you. You know better." Which was true. I did know better. My dad's disapproval battered me like some medieval stoning.

Before I could eat my cereal, my parents made me go back to my room and write John's mom a note apologizing for my delinquency. They also announced I was grounded for two weeks.

The following week, word spread like wildfire through the school hallways. "That is so cool, dude, what a punk move," gushed a kid named Max who earned his punk rock fame by breaking into the office of our gym teacher, stealing the teacher's prized silver-blue Adidas sweat suit, and then wearing it to gym class the next day, claiming it was his.

"Actually, it wasn't a punk move," I said in mild protest. "I thought everybody else was going to stay."

"Nah, man, you're the shit. Strummer'd be proud, dude."

Although I considered playing it cool, something about pretending I was a punk just didn't feel right. "Seriously, I didn't think I was screwing anybody. I actually feel like crap about it."

"Fuck that, man. You saw the Clash! Nobody got hurt."

"Yeah well now I'm grounded for two weeks."

"Just two weeks? That's awesome!"

Back home, Rob was also duly impressed. "Wow, nobody else stayed? Not even Murphy?"

"Nope, just me."

"Man, that's ballsy," he said. "Are your friends pissed?"

"Not really. They seemed sorry they didn't stay. But John's mom was not happy."

"Yeah, well that's to be expected. Collateral damage. I wouldn't sweat it."

I wasn't so sure. Maybe there was a passing wave of satisfaction at having earned my older brother's respect for my bad boy antics. But mostly I imagined being squeezed in that car for an hour and a half, waiting. I liked being a punk in my head, in my room, with my headphones on blasting the Clash. But in the real world, it kind of felt like crap.

As an adult, I've wondered how I'd react if my own kid pulled a stunt like that. Would I be pissed? Would I lecture him about the importance of following rules? Or would I only pretend to be pissed? Would part of me be happy he'd had the experience? I'm not certain about any of that. What I am certain about all these years later is this: I saw the *fucking* Clash!

7

I'LL HOLD THE PAIN

On the first day of law school I awoke to a cacophony of cabs laying on their horns three stories below on West Broadway, battling their way through the ever-present snarl of Greenwich Village traffic. A soft scattering of rays filtered through the window of my dorm room; had I forgotten to draw the Venetian blind the night before? Not that it mattered much. Sunlight in New York City is a rare commodity, and not one typically bestowed on lowly dorm residents. That's just life in the Big Apple. People in New York go about their lives in perpetual half shadow.

I glanced at the digital clock on my nightstand: 8:47 a.m. Shit! Criminal law started in thirteen minutes. It was the first time I'd ever forgotten to set an alarm. Of all days!

I threw on the same clothes I'd worn the night before to the Black Crowes concert at the Beacon Theater, still reeking of second-hand cigarette and pot smoke. A large yellow stain masked the face of the skeleton on the front of my tie-dyed Grateful Dead T-shirt where some slightly wasted half-wit spilled beer on me while executing an air guitar windmill.

I grabbed my criminal law casebook, ripped a banana from the rotten brown bunch on top of the refrigerator, threw some cold water on my face at the kitchen sink, and was out the door. Figuring the elevator would take forever to come at that hour, I bolted down the three flights of stairs and out the lobby door, plunging into a wall of stifling August humidity that nearly dropped me, like a drunkard sucker-punched in a barroom brawl. The overpowering stench of industrial antiseptic assaulted my nose, the sidewalk having just been hosed down by the building staff. I sprinted the four blocks down West Third, crossed Sullivan where Second Coming Records still sold bootleg albums, navigated around piles of garbage bags piled shoulder high, and finally arrived at the law school building. I took the main spiral staircase two steps at a time, passing a portrait of my father (a distinguished alum), and arrived in the classroom panting and sweating as Professor Crocker closed the door. I fell into my seat and wrestled the casebook from my backpack.

Professor Crocker, tall, bearded, and bespectacled, looked down at his class roster which contained some two hundred names. "Mr. Fogelson!" he thundered. He was about to make me the first person called on in our law school class. Un-fucking-believable!

"Mr. Fogelson, as you know, today we are discussing *People v. Spear.*"

That much I knew because I'd read the case before heading out to the Black Crowes concert. "Where did the case arise?" A softball question. I looked down at my case book which was opened to *People v. Spear.*

"King County, Washington," I replied, finding the court under the case caption.

"And what type of medical facilities would you suppose they have in King County, Washington?"

I had no idea, nor why he was asking—I didn't see the relevance to the case.

"Um, probably not the best," I responded, recalling the case involved a Native American man who lived on a reservation.

"And why is that?"

"Well, I don't know where King County is, but I assume it's pretty rural."

"Mr. Ferguson, please tell Mr. Fogelson what the largest city in King County is."

"Seattle," replied the student sitting next to me.

The class erupted in laughter. It was pretty funny, actually.

Of course, Mr. Ferguson was from Seattle, as was Professor Crocker. I'd been set up. I felt foolish and unprepared, not that I should have. What kid from New York City knows which fucking county Seattle's in?

Professor Crocker moved on, but that embarrassment stuck to me throughout law school.

It was in Professor Crocker's criminal law class that I received my first official law school grade. In those days, law school grades, which were based on just one exam taken at the end of the semester, were posted on bulletin boards outside the classrooms. Shortly after returning from Winter Break, I heard the rumor that criminal law grades were up and so I set off down West Third on that dank, drizzly January afternoon with a sense of dread.

The drizzle turned to a steady sleet as I made my way to school. An appropriate omen? The wind kicked up and I struggled to keep my umbrella from being blown inside out. When I got to school, I took a deep breath and trudged up the main spiral staircase to the criminal law classroom. There were maybe ten sheets of paper in a long horizontal line on the bulletin board, organized by student ID number. A couple of students were checking their grades and I waited for them to clear out. When I was finally alone, I found my ID number and ran my finger across the page to the right-hand column where the grades were listed.

It said A-. *What*? That didn't seem right. NYU's grading curve was notoriously harsh with only the top fifteen percent of the class receiving an A or A-. I ran my finger back across the page thinking I'd made a mistake, wishing I had a ruler. But there it was again: A-. "How about that, Pops?" I whispered under my breath, shaking my head slowly. I practically floated back down the staircase and out the front door feeling proud and a touch cocky, like I was rightfully at the top of the heap of all the incredibly smart people packed into that small law school building.

As I started to open my umbrella for the walk back to my dorm room, I hesitated. I could feel the wet sleet on my face, could feel the cold wind diving down the back of my neck like a wild animal attacking the soft underbelly of its prey, except that it felt strangely exhilarating to expose myself to the elements. I remembered a day in Alaska paddling down the Koyukuk River in a driving rainstorm, the rain pelting my face, the sky matte grey, remembered how invigorating it felt to be out in the squall.

I kept the umbrella closed and took a circuitous route back to my dorm room through Washington Square Park. Back in the days when Murphy and I crossed that park on our record shopping sprees, we were regularly offered a dazzling array of drugs, mostly pot, coke a few times, heroin once. But there were no drug dealers out in the sleet and wind that afternoon, Mother Nature having temporarily washed them away.

I had the park to myself and found myself wandering its meandering paths until I was good and soaked. Why? Why did I do that?

Why didn't I just go home? What was I looking for in that urban oasis? Was I flashing back to my childhood, courting the danger I perceived lurked there, maybe even courting death, searching for my father out in the storm, wanting to be with him, not to celebrate but to share in his pain?

What I do know is that in the twenty minutes it took to make it back to my dorm room, I'd managed to convince myself that the high grade was a total fluke, that I was a fucking idiot, that I'd never see another A-, let alone an A, for the rest of law school. It probably would've taken a shrink less than half of those twenty minutes to connect my self-esteem issues to my father's death. Just a few weeks after he died, I began studying for the law school entrance exam and was merciless to myself when I did poorly on the practice tests, convinced that not only was I an idiot but also a terrible person, someone who didn't deserve to get into law school. When Chris wasn't around, I'd storm around our apartment berating myself out loud—"What the *fuck* is your problem? What kind of moron are you? You think you're going to be some hot shot lawyer? That's fucking funny! You're a nobody!" When Chris was around, I'd retreat to my bedroom, pull at my hair, collapse on my bed in the fetal position, and cry as quietly as I could.

The tricky thing about self-loathing, I've since learned, is that it's not rational. If self-loathing were a person, it'd be a conspiracy theorist, someone unmoved by facts and incapable of being convinced by obvious realities. My scoring well enough on the law school boards to get into a top law school didn't undermine the self-loathing one iota. No, it laughed off that data point and continued to find other things to bludgeon me over, like, inexplicably, my A- in criminal law.

But during the walk back to my law school dorm, I didn't have a shrink to set me straight. So instead I wallowed in that self-loathing through the rest of law school, with help from a daily shot of grunge pathos via this new band from Seattle called Pearl Jam.

I was introduced to Pearl Jam by Mr. Ferguson—we became friends, despite Professor Crocker's awkward introduction. Mr. Ferguson, AKA Bob, felt bad about the setup and bought me a beer after class a few weeks later. As a lifelong Seattle native, Bob knew not only where King County was, but much more importantly, he knew about Pearl Jam and the burgeoning grunge scene in the Pacific Northwest.

"These guys are the real deal, Matt," he murmured reverently as we hunkered down and sipped our cheap tap brews in McSorley's, a fabled, sawdust-floor-covered dive offering only "light" and "dark" draft beer since before the Civil War.

Bob and I sat at the back of the pub where none of the sunlight streaming through the windows at the front of the place could reach us. "The real deal," he repeated, the darkness of the bar adding an air of gravitas to his pronouncement. Bob was a few years older than I was and wore John Lennon glasses, so I was inclined to take him seriously. Plus, he was an accomplished mountaineer. He'd scaled Mount Rainier and I figured mountain climbers must have good taste in music since they're generally self-contained loners with well-honed aesthetic sensibilities.

Pearl Jam, of course, fired some of the first shots of the grunge music revolution that swept the rock world in the early 1990s and with its raw and ferocious angst, laid to waste the synthesizers, slick over-production, and teased hair of the 1980s.

I can't count the times, while lying on my bed, headphones on, stereo cranked, that I lamented being born too late to be present at the inception of that magical epoch of rock 'n' roll, when the likes of Led Zeppelin, Jimi Hendrix, and Janis Joplin roamed the Fillmore

East. And although I've seen more than my share of legendary acts—the Grateful Dead, Springsteen, the Rolling Stones, The Who, the Allman Brothers, and a slew of other greats—none were in their prime. And what are the Allman Brothers without Duane? The Who without Keith Moon? The Stones without Mick Taylor? Pale shadows of what they once were (although those pale shadows could still kick ass). But my timing was perfect for grunge. And it exploded at the precise moment I needed it most. Shortly after my beer with Bob, I headed over to the Tower Records on Broadway to pick up Pearl Jam's debut album, *Ten*.

Like life's most profound moments, I recall the exact circumstances of my initiation into Pearl Jam. When I got back from Tower Records, I slipped *Ten* into my CD player while I folded laundry. I didn't put on my headphones for that initial listen; in an effort to preserve my hearing for as long as possible, I reserved headphones for deep, absolute immersions into a body of work, to explore sacred spaces, and at that point I didn't think Pearl Jam qualified. An hour later, my mind was changed.

Pearl Jam's music hit me like an eighteen-wheeler with busted brakes barreling down a mountain pass. The first track, "Once," captured the rage that had churned in me since my father's death. "I got a bomb in my temple that is gonna explode," proclaims lead singer Eddie Vedder over that trademark pulsating guitar riff that served as the foundation of most grunge. I too sometimes felt as if my head would explode, from a low-level but ever-present confusion that bordered on dizziness, a sense of displacement from my own head and body, and from a seething rage that had no outlet. "Once upon a time, I could control myself," Vedder howls in the song's chorus, a dark admission that he could no longer do so. Was that a pang of jealousy I felt at his abandon? Maybe so. I maintained my tenuous hold on self-control by jogging for miles and miles daily, having come to understand my father's attraction to the activity as a way to clear the mind, all the while telling myself to run faster, run farther, as if the exertion might bring some respite from the self-loathing, or enable me to outrun my grief. Often as I ran through the city's filthy streets, I wondered why my life continued but my father's didn't. I wondered whether I deserved to be the one still living, the very question Vedder asks in "Alive."

It seemed every line Vedder sang illuminated some unnamed shadow in my psyche. The shock of my father's death combined with my self-flagellation left me "spinning" at "how quick the sun can drop away," as Vedder croons in "Black." I reveled in the furious melancholy of that song, with the chorus structured around an E minor chord that sounded like the world after the apocalypse. Vedder's lamenting that his "bitter hands cradle broken glass" landed on me like a rogue wave hits a ship, motors failing, spun sideways and helpless.

I forgot about laundry, about the taxis honking their horns below, about law school, about everything. I put on my headphones and dove deep into "Black" again, then kept them on for the rest of the album. Some hidden nerve had been touched as one revelatory song followed the next. While every song packed an emotional punch, "Release," the last track on *Ten*, resonated with me like no other. The song is Vedder's gut-wrenching response to the death of his biological father. "Oh, dear dad, can you see me now?" Vedder asks, articulating the same question that ran through my head in a continuous loop in law school.

"I'll wait up in the dark for you to speak to me," Vedder admits in anguish. Check. Did that, too. But most of all, I heard myself in Vedder's defiant declaration: "I'll ride the wave where it takes me /

I'll hold the pain." Man, I loved that line. Clearly, I'd adopted some twisted ascetic notion that I should immerse myself fully in the pain of my father's death. Not that I walked around the city all dour, wallowing in the "unfairness" of life and adopting a self-pitying countenance. I didn't do that. It was more just a constant feeling of heaviness, of some invisible weight bearing down on me. Sometimes on the subway I'd catch sight of a stranger's face—a businessman suited up heading downtown to Wall Street, a teenage girl with an oversized backpack on her way to school, a cop on the beat—and think I could see in that face, in those eyes, the hint of some all-encompassing tragedy; I'd wonder what it was and if that person could sense the same thing in me, if maybe I was now a member of some secret sect, a mystically amorphous society of mourning. I couldn't seem to shake that heaviness—or more accurately, I didn't try to shake it. If I was out having a beer with friends and felt an uninhibited laugh coming on, I'd rein it in and settle for a smile or deep grin. It was a subtle thing—I'm not even sure I realized at the time that it was happening.

Mostly I communed with the pain through music, through Pearl Jam's music. It created a safe space for me to breathe the pain in deep, to feel it in every cell. And it was a space where nobody could see me, where I could lay down all my defenses and surrender to the pain. It felt liberating to be in that place. I could be my truest self there.

At the same time, though, the better part of me wanted to exorcise the pain, to be done with the suffering. Enter the final chorus of "Release" and Vedder's half-prayer, half-demand: "Release me!" howled over and over again, imploringly and yet with the threat of violence as clipped wah-wah guitar chords wage sonic battle against some invisible psychic restraint. "Release me! Release me!" I screamed along, headphones blasting at a deafening volume, hoping, praying that if screamed loud enough, a phrase from Vedder's lament might break loose the psychic logjam that'd been steadily growing in mass and density since my father's death a year earlier.

But it didn't happen. For some reason, I needed to keep holding the pain. Why was that? Did I think allowing myself even a fleeting moment of unbridled joy would constitute some grievous breach of loyalty owed to my father? I mean, what kind of son can strut around with even a fiber of good cheer in his heart after his young father is ripped from him by a disease so savage it aged the father fifteen years in fifteen months, rendered him utterly unrecognizable to the son, and at the end left the father gasping for air like the victim of a clandestine chemical weapons attack?

A few months after my father died, I was at our apartment uptown and passed by the small walk-in closet where he kept all his clothes—mostly suits, dress shirts, and ties. He must've had two dozen suits. Heavy wool suits for winter, light cotton suits for summer, pinstripes, solids, and check patterns, all in various shades of blue and grey. It didn't appear that my mother had touched anything in his closet, and for some reason I decided to peek in.

When I opened the door, I froze in my tracks, overpowered by a smell I immediately recognized but hadn't encountered in months: it was my father. I remembered it from all the times he'd check in on me after getting home from work. He'd make his way down the long hall, politely knock on my door, and then stand over me at my desk, his scent enveloping me as I looked up at him, enjoying a momentary break from my homework. He'd grab my shoulders and rub them hard—his strange form of intimacy. Every night the same drill.

My father's scent had left his study, it'd left his bed and his pillows, but it was still in that closet. I delicately eased myself inside as if entering some sacred shrine, closed the door behind me, and filled my lungs with his scent, hoping to keep it with me forever, wishing there were a way to preserve it the way a photograph captures an image. After a few minutes, I took one final deep breath and tiptoed out, pushing the door closed behind me with the full weight of my shoulder to make sure it was sealed tight.

That closet was the last physical vestige of my father, the last tangible reminder of his existence, and every time I returned home, I'd sequester myself in the pitch dark of that tiny room and breathe in that scent. But of course, it eventually faded and one day was gone, just like my father. Unlike his scent, though, I could hang onto the pain so I'd always feel my father with me, inside me. I didn't know how else to access that feeling. And so I held the pain. Held it tight.

8.

GIRLS AND GUITARS

I know it sounds sort of weird, but the only girl I knew before high school was my older cousin Emily. In my defense, my school was all boys until ninth grade. Plus Murphy and I swore off girls completely after we went to a middle school dance and stood around for two hours in a lame gym listening to Kajagoogoo and watching people make fools of themselves on the dance floor. Ugh. There was no way I was going to make an ass of myself by asking a girl to dance, even if I'd had the courage to do it, which I definitely didn't.

But there was no avoiding girls in high school. The weekend before the start of freshman year, the entire incoming freshman class of my now mixed-gender high school were forced to attend a camp retreat an hour outside the city. To be suddenly surrounded by girls was beyond bewildering. I hadn't the slightest idea how to behave in their presence. Was I actually supposed to talk to them? If so, how? About what? Do they like sports? Do they like music? And if you do figure out how to start a conversation, will they think you're hitting on them? *Are* you hitting on them? What's that even mean?

Forced by a group of annoyingly cheery counselors to mingle, we spent most of the retreat participating in cheesy group activities designed to create bonds between us freshmen. Some of the activities were downright terrifying—the three-legged race, for example. Having my leg strapped to some random girl's? Pretty damn scary. Those meddlesome counselors directed us to split off into two lines, with boys in one and girls in the other. Then they paired us all off, one boy with one girl, like we were in a wedding procession. *This is going to be a fucking disaster*, I thought.

"Matt, you're with Gretchen," one of the counselors announced without any fanfare, which seemed like a strange way to send someone off to the gallows. I had an urge to bolt, but there was no escape. Gretchen and I stepped out of our respective lines and met in the middle of the field. "Hey," I muttered while looking at the ground.

"Hey," I heard a voice say back. Was she looking at the ground too, or . . . at me? I didn't dare risk looking up to find out.

The counselor told us to stand next to each other so he could tie our legs together. We did as he said.

"C'mon, you have to get closer," he barked at me and this Gretchen chick. But it seemed to me we were plenty close already. Close enough for me to notice that Gretchen smelled like a field of wildflowers, like springtime itself. "Closer, this rope isn't that long," the counselor commanded, losing patience. I shuffled sideways maybe two inches, still looking at the ground. I guess the dude wasn't satisfied with our progress because the next thing I know, he's grabbing me by the shoulder and shoving me toward Gretchen until she and I collided.

There's this really old and totally awesome Springsteen bootleg from 1975 during which Bruce introduces "The E Street Shuffle" and tells the story of how he met Clarence Clemens, the E Street Band's saxophonist. It's a big buildup, lots of drama about a cold, windswept night and a random meeting in an alley. Bruce tells the crowd that

Clarence held out his hand for Bruce to shake. "And when we touched, there were sparks flying on E Street!" I don't know what Gretchen felt, but when our bodies touched, I felt sparks flying all around me. I was so startled I actually looked at Gretchen. Saw her flowing blond hair. Saw her long, bare, sultry legs, one of which was now tied tightly to mine, like we were prisoners on the shortest chain gang in history.

"Maybe we should practice a little," Gretchen said softly. She had beautiful green eyes.

"Probably so," I stammered.

"Let's start with the inside leg."

We started walking down the length of the field. We got the hang of it pretty quick and decided to speed up a little. No problems.

"I think we're a good match," Gretchen said, throwing me a quick smile.

I had no idea how to respond. Was that like one of those double entendre things? Or was I just imagining it?

My thoughts raced. If I agreed, and said, "Yes, I think we're a good match," would I be doubling down on the double entendre? Would Gretchen think I was acknowledging her hidden meaning and agreeing with it? How would I know if we were a good match in that way? On the other hand, suppose her comment was purely innocent, that there was no double entendre? Would she think *I* was hitting on *her*? Would I be? Because I couldn't sort all this out in the socially acceptable time allowed for conversational English, I said nothing. Instead, I snorted.

There were three other teams in our heat. As we gathered at the starting line, Gretchen turned to me. "Remember to start with the inside leg," she instructed. "That worked pretty well."

"Got it," I replied.

I stood there, leg tied to this beautiful stranger, poised, tense, waiting for my cue, for that starting pistol to fire . . . then *BANG!* Off it went. I leaped into action, leading with my inside leg just as I'd been told. So did Gretchen. But in my hyped-up zeal I guess I took a bigger stride than we'd practiced and with an explosiveness she wasn't expecting. This was the race, after all, not practice.

Gretchen went down immediately, like a Jenga tower. I then toppled nearly onto her, which created a whipsaw effect that rolled her over on top of me. We laid there in that dry hump position for what seemed like the whole afternoon, both of us too stunned to move, until Gretchen finally came to her senses and got up off me. The entire freshman class stood around us in hysterics. Even Murphy. Particularly Murphy.

We somehow managed to get up and finish the race, coming in a distant fourth. Which wasn't all bad news since it meant we didn't have to race again in the next round. I didn't hang much with Gretchen after that, or really for the rest of high school. Maybe we weren't such a good match after all.

Murphy and I hit on a pretty good strategy for dealing with all the girl-related crap. We'd show up at parties with a fifth of Gordon's Gin and sit in a closet trading swigs until we were loose enough to deal with all the craziness. I remember one time I asked Murphy if this chick, Molly, was coming to the party. Murphy seemed to like Molly—they were always smoking cigarettes together in the alley across from school. Not that he let on about it or anything.

"I have no idea," Murphy replied and took another swig.

"Well, I spoke to Nancy and she's coming so Molly'll probably show, too." Nancy and Molly were best friends.

"Whatever. Hey, I saw the funniest billboard out in Center Moriches last weekend. It was a plain white billboard and in black letters it said, 'Be Polite.' Like a public service announcement or something. But then somebody had spray-painted over the whole thing in huge block letters, 'Go fuck yourself!' So damn funny." He handed me the bottle.

"That is," I agreed, laughing, and took a pull of gin. A lot of our conversations were like that. I'd try to talk to Murphy about girls but he'd shut it down.

Murphy was a mellow drunk; after we came out of the closet (so to speak), he'd find a couch and pass out for the rest of the night. I was a more social drunk and drank just enough gin to allow me to play Quarters. Like most drinking games, Quarters didn't require much in the way of a setup. You just needed a glass, a table, a quarter, and a ton of beer. It also helped to have a bathroom nearby that didn't require a lot of effort to get to. The glass was filled halfway with beer and players took turns trying to bounce the quarter into the glass. If your quarter splashed in, you chose someone to drink the beer, and you kept your turn until you missed. If someone got on a hot streak and wanted to pick on another player, things could get ugly quickly.

One of the cool things about Quarters was it was a safe way to flirt with girls. By picking a girl to drink, I could signal I liked her without having to say so or, scarier, make any kind of physical move. On top of which, when drunk from playing Quarters, I convinced myself that, magically, I might get some action without having to do anything.

It almost sort of worked, one time, anyway.

Whenever my parents took off for Westhampton, as sure as thunder follows lightening, Rob would throw a party. At one of his parties during my freshman year, I was getting beat up at Quarters by Rob's friends—they thought it was hilarious to kick the little brother's ass—and I stumbled into the laundry room just off our kitchen to clear my head. I hopped up on the washing machine and was rubbing my temples when Julie, the most sought-after girl in my class—tan skin, athletic body, and husky voice that sounded kind of erotic—suddenly appeared in the door of the laundry room and scrambled up next to me.

I had a huge crush on Julie, as did every boy in my class. It was her image I held in my mind as I listened to "Born to Run" through my headphones late at night, dreaming of her strapping her hands across my engines. I don't remember what Julie said to me on the washing machine or what I said or if we even said anything. I do, however, remember her casually placing her hand on my knee, my bare knee—I was wearing dark green cargo shorts—and moving it around in a circular motion like she was buffing the hood of Greased Lightnin'.

I became disoriented, like some Loony Tunes cartoon character who got brained and suddenly sees stars and little birds whizzing around his head. I had no idea what to do. Should I put my hand on her knee? Around her shoulders? Should I do nothing, just play it cool? I had no clue. After a few tortured seconds of inaction, I finally hit upon a plan: I jumped off the washing machine, bolted down the hallway to my bedroom, locked the door behind me, put on my headphones, and cued up Springsteen's *Nebraska* album. Man, that record sounded good, those simple acoustic tunes with their faraway, hollow sound spinning tales about criminals and outlaws, the morally conflicted and the corrupt. It was like taking a cold shower, which was just what the doctor ordered. I mean, sure, part of me wished I hadn't been such a scaredy cat, wished I hadn't fled the laundry room like it was a crime scene and instead stuck around to see how the scene played out, but mostly I just didn't want to get involved, didn't want people at school talking about me hooking up with Julie. I didn't want to be the subject of hallway gossip. So yeah, I split. Although

I'm not sure what would've been so horrible about somebody talking to somebody else about me having scored with the hottest girl in the class. What was I so scared of?

Anyway, it was during this time of drinking for social survival that Murphy introduced me to a band from Minneapolis called the Replacements. We loved those guys, particularly how they were usually too drunk to make it all the way through their concerts.

The Replacements were a bit like the Sex Pistols in that they didn't seem to give a fuck about what people thought of them. But unlike the Sex Pistols' Johnny Rotten, the Replacements' front man, Paul Westerberg, was almost cerebral, I'd guess you'd call it. His lyrics made you think a little. I particularly loved the line about how he's sick of everything his money can buy. I mean, I had no issue with everything my money could buy, like kickass speakers, that awesome Winterland Springsteen bootleg, and all-white New Balance tennis sneakers, but the lyric hit me hard, made me think there was some greater purpose out there.

Living in New York, Murphy and I were lucky. Some kids never get to see their favorite bands play live. But Murphy and I caught the Replacements a few times at the Ritz, a small club in the East Village. The place had a wristband system to prevent underage kids like us from drinking, but it was no problem to find someone to buy us drinks. Murphy would scout the scene and find some dude, usually a long-haired guy in his twenties, alone and milling around the bar, he'd make contact with him, and then meet me back on the floor with our drinks—a gin and tonic for him, beer for me.

The first time we saw the Replacements the band was so wasted they could barely stand. Somehow they managed to crank out a few distortion-riddled chords and beats that when mixed together in my beer-soaked head sort of resembled the songs I knew, which was good enough for me and Murphy. Our respect for bands increased with the outrageousness of their behavior. The more they stuck it to The Man, the better. It didn't even matter that we were the ones getting screwed when they couldn't remember how the songs went. The music was loud, the beer was cold, and we were out past curfew, so all was good in the world.

Right around this same time, Murphy got me into an artist named Tommy Keene who'd just released this awesome record, *Songs From the Film*. I don't know what film Tommy was talking about—as far as I could tell, there wasn't any film to go along with the record. So that part was a little weird. But the music was really cool, a little louder than R.E.M. but still with that jangly kind of sound. It was even a little pop, much less hardcore than the Replacements, but such good stuff. Murphy taped it for me, put it on the other side of R.E.M.'s *Life's Rich Pageant*.

"Check out 'Kill Your Sons,'" Murphy instructed me. "It's a Lou Reed cover, about him getting electroshock therapy, but it rocks way better than Lou's version."

Even though I was a much bigger Lou Reed and Velvet Underground fan than Murphy, I'd never heard of the song and wondered how he had. But that was pretty typical Murphy—he knew everything about music. "Kill Your Sons" did indeed rock, with this amazing monster guitar solo at the end that seemed to go on forever.

After many, many nights spent boozing it up and listening to music, Murphy finally hit on the idea of playing music himself. Halfway through freshman year he talked his parents into buying him a drum set. Not just any drum set but a Pearl kit like the kind Jeff Porcaro of Toto played in the band's trashy *Grease* knockoff video for "Rosanna." Granted, Jeff Porcaro is no John Bonham and "Roseanna" isn't "When the Levee Breaks," but that's not the fault of the drum kit. That thing was Grade A. Right off the bat Murphy liked the physicality of playing the drums, the fact you could just hack away at the "skins," as he called them. It was a full-body workout for him and I suppose it helped calm his social stress some.

Soon enough Murphy formed a band with three other kids at our school. They called themselves The Amazings. I didn't understand why they'd want to call themselves that. Not only did it create serious pressure to be good, it seemed a little conceited. But I guess most rock stars are conceited—it's like a prerequisite. I have to say the name sort of worked because they'd often play in our school's chapel and blast out Sex Pistols tunes beneath a huge crucifix, singing about being Antichrists, and get away with it. That was pretty amazing.

Because Murphy took up the drums, it dawned on me that maybe I could learn how to play guitar. Several kids in my class played and if they could, why couldn't I? I borrowed a cheap Epiphone acoustic guitar from my school's music department and started to take lessons. Then, after a few months, my dad offered to buy me an electric guitar. We made a plan to meet after school at Sam Ash on Forty-Eighth to pick one out. Forty-Eighth between Sixth and Seventh, that one block, was like the mecca of musical instruments. Need a glockenspiel? No problem. A didgeridoo—cylindrical or conical? Pan flute—five or eight tubes?

Walking into Sam Ash I was immediately overwhelmed by the sheer number of guitars on display. They hung on the walls from floor to ceiling in every shape, size, and color. They all had a glow to them, shining and sparkling under the store's lights, like museum pieces. Did I dare touch them? Was that even allowed? Then from further back in the store I heard a blazing guitar riff explode, confirming that customers could indeed touch the guitars. The guitar riff, which I recognized as the opening to Led Zeppelin's "Rock and Roll," came courtesy of a thin, long-haired guy—probably in his late twenties—with a nose ring and goatee. He wore a leather jacket and sat on a stool with a guitar plugged into a Marshall amp. Was he somebody famous? Should I know him?

A clerk, a near twin of the guy churning out the Zeppelin riffs (minus the leather jacket), eased over and made eye contact with me. "You need any help?" he asked.

"No, I'm just looking," I said. For some reason, I was suddenly feeling all embarrassed and didn't want to let on I was there to buy a guitar.

"Okay, just let me know if you need anything."

I wandered around the store waiting for my dad to show. There were display cases packed with electronic guitar effects with strange names like fuzz, chorus, and delay. I recognized one as a wah-wah pedal—the kind Jimi Hendrix used at the beginning of "Voodoo Child"—but had no idea what any of the other devices were for. There was a room in the back with a drum kit and a guy banging away. I could see him through a glass window but couldn't hear him. I felt a strange closeness with this guy probably twice my age—he was playing air drums the same way I played air guitar: eyes squinted shut, shoulders hunched over, head gruesomely bobbing in a very unnatural manner, like it might fly off his body.

There were a few other customers in the store, none of whom looked like pathetically straight prep school me; I felt like I'd been dropped into Sam Ash from a Brooks Brothers catalogue. They were all some stripe of hipster, distinguished only by the type of facial hair and number of earrings and rings they sported. Nobody else wore a navy-blue blazer with a cross-themed school crest ironed on the breast pocket. Why hadn't I gone home and changed first?

Just then my dad came striding into the store having come straight from the office in his gray pin-striped suit, blue dress shirt with a red tie, and black patent leather shoes; he looked even more like an interloper than I did. I winced, then ducked into the very back of the store, hoping nobody would notice when he inevitably connected with me. But since he was paying, I eventually had to show myself.

"Wow, there's lots of guitars here," my dad said when he finally located me. "Should we ask for some help?"

"I guess," I replied weakly. But before I had to endure the indignity of my ultra-square dad asking a hipster clerk for help (there was no way I was going to ask), that same salesman who first approached me joined us in the back of the store. I guess he'd sussed out the situation and located the money source. What little cover I had was blown.

"My son is interested in an electric guitar," my dad told him. "You have any?" I stiffened at his lame joke.

"A couple," the clerk replied good-naturedly. He turned to me. "What type of guitar are you looking for?"

I froze. What type? I had no idea. The shame! Clearly, I was a fraud, a fact that any reply to the salesclerk would reveal in glaring detail.

"I'm not really sure," I admitted after a long pause.

"No problem," he said. "What type of music do you listen to? What music do you want to play?"

I sheepishly admitted I was a big Springsteen and Grateful Dead fan.

He nodded approvingly. "Cool, let me bring you a couple of things to try out." He then disappeared into the front of the store.

"This is really some place," my dad said. But I couldn't respond. I was focused on the last thing the clerk had said, the thing about "trying out" some of the guitars. How was I going to do that? I knew only a few basic chords. Led Zeppelin riffs were not in my repertoire, as everybody in the store was about to find out.

The clerk returned with two high-end electric guitars: a Gibson SG Special and a Fender Telecaster. He explained that Jerry Garcia often played a Gibson SG while the Telecaster was similar to the one Springsteen played. He brought me a stool, a Roland cube amp, and a cable. "See what you think," he said plugging in the Gibson and handing it to me.

I sat down on the stool and studied the guitar. It had an almost sinister appearance. Except for the brown fretboard it was solid black. The curved body resembled two women lying across from each other on opposite hips. The curves flowed gracefully toward the neck, ending in two smaller curves that reminded me of devil horns. The body was so shiny I could see my reflection in it.

I hoped the clerk would back off and let me "try it out" in private, but no dice—sensing a sale he stuck around. I played the three chords I knew—G, A, and D—in every possible progression, stopping periodically to admire the guitar, studying it like I knew what I was doing, like I was inspecting it for something.

"Check it out with the distortion," the clerk said, moving the cable on the amp from the "Normal" channel to "Overdrive." I played the same three chords but now they sounded like a volcano erupting. I could feel the energy surging through me like an electric shock.

"Wow," I said.

"Pretty cool, huh?" the clerk responded. "Here, let me show you what this thing can do." He took the guitar from me and began playing a ferocious solo, complete with Eddie Van Halen hammer-ons. While I knew he meant well, I was embarrassed he needed to play the guitar for me to show me what it could really sound like.

"Let's try out the Tele," he said switching out the Gibson for the

Fender and handing it to me. It did look like Springsteen's guitar from the cover of *Born to Run*, which made me feel like even more of a fraud. Who did I think I was playing Springsteen's guitar? Luckily, I didn't like it as much. It sounded a little tinnier than the Gibson, a little less muscular. Plus, I couldn't see my reflection in it. So I chose the Gibson.

My dad and I walked up to the counter to pay, and on the wall behind the register a bunch of photographs of famous rock stars holding court in Sam Ash caught my eye. Keith Richards was up there. Lou Reed was up there. Patti Smith. Joey Ramone. And some guitarists known only by their nicknames: The Edge, Little Steven.

Suddenly I heard the *cha-ching* of a cash register closing. "Enjoy it, Tips," my dad said to me as I tore my star-filled eyes away from the photos. My parents called me Tippy because I used to tip over in the crib; Tippy sometimes got shortened to Tips. Him calling me by that lame, baby nickname made me feel silly, but luckily nobody appeared to hear him.

I was pretty psyched walking out of Sam Ash with the Gibson SG nestled in its hard black case with deep-blue fuzzy felt lining. But as my dad hailed two cabs—one to take me uptown to our apartment, the other to take him back downtown to his office—that rush gave way to a terrifying realization: now that I owned a high-end professional guitar, I had to walk the walk. It just didn't seem possible that I could pull it off.

9

THE SOUND(GARDEN) AND THE FURY

I made it through that first bruising year of law school in large part because of my classmate Bob. We became good friends and his laid-back Seattle countenance kept me sane. Bob was the opposite of a vast majority of NYU law students, oblivious to the alpha compulsion to engage in intellectual puffery and just as interested in exploring the underbelly of the West Village as discussing constitutional theory. He always talked about hiking and climbing mountains, which was a welcome distraction from the grind of law school.

Despite Bob's calming influence, my debilitating intellectual insecurity persisted throughout my second year of law school, particularly since the A- in criminal law turned out to be harder to replicate in most of my other classes.

Jodi, who to her credit had overlooked my post-Alaska conflagration over fudge and hung in there with me, tried to buck me up. "You are literally the smartest person I know," she told me after I expressed frustration over a disappointing grade in administrative law. Given that Jodi, who was a law student herself at Georgetown, was the smartest person *I* knew—she was constitutionally incapable of getting anything other than an A in any of her law school classes—you'd think I would've credited her assessment some. Hah! No chance. My mental state was so damaged that even when Jodi's favorite professor at Georgetown came to NYU for a semester to teach a seminar on positive political theory—a seminar I took on Jodi's recommendation—and even after I got an A+ in the class based on a paper I wrote, which the professor said was one of the best pieces of student writing he'd read in his career, I still felt like an intellectual poser.

Enter the sweet, dark succor of Soundgarden. One of the preeminent grunge bands from Seattle, Soundgarden released their seminal record, *Superunknown*, in the spring of my second year of law school. Soundgarden's music was much more hardcore than Pearl Jam's, in large part due to lead singer Chris Cornell's nearly inhuman vocals which at the top of his almost four-octave range could send passing dogs into a frenzy. The searing raw emotion was astonishing.

The opening track on the record, "Let Me Drown," set the tone for the dark, worrisome journey to come. The song is punctuated by a primeval scream emanating from Cornell, the likes of which I'd never heard before. Sure, caterwauling is a given in rock music. Probably the most famous scream is Roger Daltrey's iconic outburst at the end of The Who classic, "Won't Get Fooled Again," but Daltrey's scream is one of defiance, of exhilaration. Cornell's scream in "Let Me Drown" is something entirely different: it's simultaneously a scream of desperation, surrender, and, above all, contemptuous, all-encompassing rage.

I too had a desperate fury bottled up in me but I couldn't figure out on who or what to unload it. Where exactly was I supposed to off-gas its steaming toxicity? Should I be angry at my father for abandoning me? That didn't seem fair—it's not like he wanted to get cancer and die. Should I be mad at God? It was hardly worth the effort since I didn't believe that old-timer even existed and anyway, venting in God's general direction didn't seem like best practices, just in case. Should I be mad at life's unfairness? That notion showed potential but how to operationalize it? How to take *life* to the woodshed, how to seek merciless, biblical vengeance on *life?* It's not so easy. Screaming, on the other hand, is easy. But I couldn't really do that either, confined as I was to my law school dorm room with a studious roommate I didn't want to piss off.

Plus, I wasn't a screamer. Which, come to think of it, could help explain why I was drawn to Soundgarden like a drunk to an open bar. As a kid, I'd developed a defense mechanism of suppressing my emotions, burying those pesky interlopers deep down in the murky depths of my psyche, to counter the disappointment of my father never being around. My mother, who *was* a screamer, took a decidedly different approach—she loudly and repeatedly laid into my father for never being around. As a kid I hated all the screaming—it scared me, which is another reason I never took to it. It's also why I always sided with my father—my mother was the one screaming and I wanted it to stop. I've since come to recognize how unfair that was to my mother, how all that wailing was my mother's effort—her very loving effort—to fight for Rob and me, to get my father to spend time with us, to just be with us, all together as a family. I now also recognize that, consciously or not, she was doing me a solid, that she was screaming *for* me, expressing all the repressed frustration and anger I felt but couldn't vocalize. But such mature reflections came too late—I had trained myself too well in the art of emotional reticence.

And so when my father died, I banished my disbelief, my fear, my outrage, my sadness—banished all of it—to that familiar, shadowy place. Locked it all away and tossed the key. That's all I knew to do. It's a horrible strategy, of course, for dealing with emotional traumas. Even Chris Cornell himself recognized as much, telling an interviewer about the darkness that perpetually dogged him, "My experience is you have to allow the expression to come and not be so eager to check it or critique it or be embarrassed by it or shut it down." Heck, Aunt Wendy had made the same point in the kitchen after my father's funeral. But I didn't have a clue what she was talking about at the time and didn't have the emotional tools to implement a strategy of unleashed expression anyway.

So I let Chris Cornell scream for me.

That helped for a little while, right up until I figured out there was in fact someone in the physical world at whom I could ever so quietly and surreptitiously unleash my rage: little old me. It was a master stroke, really. I mean, I was always there. What could be more convenient? Open 24/7/365, I was a freaking Waffle House! But without the friendly service and welcoming smile. I wore a scowl as I looked in the mirror and was greeted by the evil twin of *Saturday Night Live* self-help guru Stuart Smalley berating me over yet another B+ in this or that class and admonishing me not to join a study group because I'd be exposed as an intellectual fraud.

Where this self-anger came from was unclear to me. A flood of questions bombarded me kamikaze-style as I listened to Cornell's searing vocals, the music fileting open my tortured psyche. Was I somehow responsible for my father's death? Did I give up on him? Could he sense I never had any hope he'd beat the cancer, that I was only pretending to believe in him? Did I radiate unseemly karmic vibes that further compromised his immune system? And if our positions had been reversed, would he have ever—ever—given up on me?

Could I have been a better son to him, tried to really know him, expressed to his face instead of in a too-late eulogy that even with the shitty hand I'd been dealt, I still felt I was the luckiest boy in the world because I got to have him as my father, that I wouldn't trade places with anybody, even a boy whose father would one day hug him when he graduated from college, tell embarrassing stories about him at his wedding, and hold the boy's newborn son?

And what about the day he died? Couldn't I have been with him, by his side at his hospital bed? Couldn't I have held his hand? Couldn't I have kissed his cheek? Couldn't I have whispered goodbye? My mother was there. Rob was there. Even my rarely seen Uncle Arthur was there. Not me. Why not? Was I selfish? Did my father's death inconveniently conflict with my social life, with some epic fraternity party? Or was I a coward? Was I afraid to look into my father's vacant eyes?

Soundgarden gave clear voice to the inward anger, the self-loathing that pummeled me. In one song, Cornell commands, "Shame, shame, throw yourself away / Give me little bits of more than I can take," the follow-up command to "throw yourself away" given repeatedly over a stutter-step guitar riff, sounding like some poor, desperate soul being pushed off a ledge by the one person on earth they most loved and trusted. That tune was like lemonade on a sultry summer day, perfectly quenching my thirst for a shot of self-hatred.

When I managed to steal a brief respite from the constant churn of self-loathing and actually think critically about what had happened to my father, I wondered, like some dime store philosopher, what the purpose of life was. But probably unlike that guy, I concluded there wasn't much of one, that life was just a matter of waiting for bad shit to happen. I'd sometimes think about my mother's parents, my Grandpa Harry and Grandma Toby, who each lived to a ripe old age, happily married for some sixty-plus years until their bodies eventually wore out, leaving them in various states of discomfort, pain, and sadness. And that was the *best* one could hope for. They hit the freaking lottery.

If I'd had a mantra back then, it would've been "Expect the worst because it sure as shit is certain to happen." Soundgarden clearly shared my nihilistic outlook. One of their tunes is called "The Day I Tried to Live." Man, I loved everything about that song—starting with the title. Talk about dark. Not that the album's first track, "Let Me Drown," gives off a sunshine and rainbows vibe. But "The Day I Tried to Live"? To me it's even bleaker for the protagonist having foolishly believed it was worth trying to live in the first place. If the title of "The Day I Tried to Live" left any doubt about the depth of the menace Cornell perceived in the world—a perspective I'd internalized—his proclamation in the second verse surely resolved it: "The lives we make never seem to ever get us anywhere but dead."

This music transcended mere self-pitying; this was self-immolation, with Cornell starring as my surrogate Buddhist monk setting himself ablaze. On some deep foundational level it was exactly what I needed to hear. I too wanted to set myself on fire, at least symbolically. That was my unconscious strategy for releasing the anger. Burn the fucking house down! I told myself I'd never be a successful lawyer like my father because I wasn't smart enough, that I was an intellectual fraud, admitted to NYU based on pedigree, not merit. I told myself I wasn't worth my father sticking around for. The part of me that counseled mercy, that told me to take it easy on myself, had long since deserted the scene, knowing it had no chance of prevailing.

Aunt Wendy had tried to fortify me for this withering internal battle, one I never saw coming. Shortly after my father died, she wrote me a letter. "If you could step outside yourself and see you through my eyes, you'd see a beautiful humbleness and character and a wonderful warmth," she wrote. "If you get down on yourself, know your perspective isn't correct. You've had a traumatic loss and there's bound to be damage. Please have mercy on yourself." But I didn't internalize any of that at the time—I just rolled my eyes at Aunt Wendy's heavy-handed psychobabble.

Aunt Wendy, though, had correctly anticipated that a darkness would burrow its way deep inside me and fill the empty spaces left behind by my father's death. And she correctly suspected I'd commune with that darkness and conspire against the light, unable to hear its call at all.

Instead, I'd plumb the depths with Cornell and a tune called "Mailman."

The song opens with Cornell mischievously, almost seductively, asking,

"Hello, don't you know me? / I'm the dirt beneath your feet."

Yeah, I know you. You're the voice inside my head, always.

"I know I'm headed for the bottom."

I know it, too. I can feel it in my chest, in the tightness of my breath.

"I'm riding you all the way, yeah, I'm riding you all the way."

I want you to ride me all the way. All the way to the bottom.

"For all of the times when you made me disappear, this time I'm sure you'll know that I am here."

I know you're here. I'm glad you're here. I'll never make you disappear again.

I drifted through law school, often feeling desperately isolated. Sometimes it was the physical absence of my father that triggered my spirals. Sometimes it was the knowledge that no other person would ever understand my loss, that I was alone in my grieving and always would be. Sometimes it was the feeling that at any moment the world could consume me, that there was nothing to save me. And sometimes, oftentimes, it was all the above.

In such moments, and in some twisted way, Soundgarden's "Mailman" helped me feel less alone, as if someone understood me, had my back, even if their intentions were pure malevolence.

I listened to all these dark Soundgarden songs with the manic focus of a cliff diver leaping off some terrifying precipice. I'd squeeze the headphones tight onto my ears with both hands to completely seal out any competing reality. These silent primal scream sessions allowed me to access a dark place, a bruising place, a place nobody else could go, a place I caught fleeting glimpses of in my day-to-day life, forever lurking beyond my reach until I put on those headphones. I needed the music of Soundgarden and Pearl Jam like a plant needs sunlight, only in reverse. It was the darkness that sustained me, offering a surrogate soundtrack and human voice to my own eternally repressed pathos. Immersing myself in that music made life bearable, even exhilarating. I'd come to it empty, depleted, defeated, then, note by note, word by word, be revived. I couldn't explain it to anyone—my friends, my family—how it was I found perfected refuge in the dark howls of rage that grunge represented.

I couldn't explain it to Jodi either. I'd head down to Washington most weekends to visit her at Georgetown, needing to get the hell out of New York. I could no longer abide being in a place I'd come to associate with death and disease any more than was necessary. I'd also started noticing things about the city I hadn't before, seemingly innocent threads of the urban tapestry that now struck me as seismic affronts to civilization, like how you don't need sunglasses on a beautiful sunny day because of the ever-present shadows cast by the city's towering skyscrapers that bear down like prison towers, or how the garbage bags piled shoulder-high on the street create an outdoor Habitrail for rats, or how cab drivers treat pedestrians like pigeons, figuring they'll scatter at the last possible second before impact, and if not, serves the jaywalking assholes right.

I became so dependent on my grunge fix that I kept a second copy of *Superunknown* and a pair of high-end headphones at Jodi's house as a type of DC survival kit. At times when I felt the walls closing in and found no comfort in human interaction, I'd sequester myself in her living room by the stereo, crank the volume up to ten, then spend great stretches of time gazing half madly at the blurred image of Cornell's screaming visage on the CD cover, distorted to the point of no longer appearing human. Maybe I, too, wanted to disappear into abstraction.

Jodi could sense the pain I was in. One time I caught a glimpse of her in the mirror above the stereo, pausing on the staircase to gaze at me as I disappeared into the music, no doubt feeling helpless, wondering if she should say something or do something. She worried about me, interpreting my behavior as a cry for help. But she knew not to intrude into my private space, knew that I needed to commune with this primal scream called grunge, this deeply emotional outlet so intense it bordered on the physical.

"I wish I could make it better," she said to me when I reemerged exhausted. "Is there anything I can do to make it better?"

"I'm okay," I replied. "Although a hug wouldn't hurt," I added with a half-smile. Jodi frowned and held me tight.

As a kid, I had a lisp. When my mother told me I had to see a speech therapist I threw a tantrum. There was nothing wrong with me, I insisted. It was the same deal after my father died. I was committed to the idea that there was "nothing to see here," nothing for Jodi to be concerned with, and so I kept her at bay. I was just grieving, I kept telling myself, refusing to consider any alternative explanation, such as clinical depression.

Everyone grieves in their own way and this obsession with dark, nihilistic music was mine. It was almost like an addiction, leaving me high. I'd emerge from my listening sessions feeling alive, less empty and hollowed-out. And not as alone. But that's one of the things about depression: it can become like Linus' security blanket, something you wrap yourself in to make yourself feel better. Chris Cornell understood, once explaining, "If you're depressed long enough, it's almost a comfort, a state of mind that you've made peace with." So did Bruce, writing of depression that after a while you "welcome it in like an old friend." In absorbing the darkness of Soundgarden, in injecting it into my bloodstream, I felt that comfort, I welcomed in that old friend.

But like any addiction, it blinded me to the true depths of my growing despair. It was my smack—I couldn't survive without it, but it was slowly, incrementally ferrying me to a deeply fucked up psychological headspace.

While the music provided a vital emotional outlet that helped clear the fog, at the same time it trained a white-hot spotlight on my internal world, revealing what looked like the wreckage of some horrific, cataclysmic plane crash in there, with snarled metal spewed for miles across a desolate, horizonless landscape, jet fuel fires exploding all around, a blanket of asphyxiating black smoke blotting out the sun, deafening sirens blaring, tears falling in a heavy rain from a black sky, death's hooded henchmen calmly and malignly securing the perimeter of the entire scene, the black box that might explain how the fuck all this happened nowhere to be found.

When I listened to Soundgarden, it was like I'd taken some mind-expanding drug that laid bare this excruciatingly graphic and harrowing internal world. Part of me embraced the carnage I saw, while another part wanted to escape from it. But how?

I'd always thought of my connection to music as a judgment-free zone, a place of weightlessness where I'm comfortable in my own skin. Soundgarden upended all that. It passed judgment on me—and it was a harsh judgment. It confirmed my instincts that I was nothing, a nobody, a fraud. Their music tied a weight around my neck, made me wonder just who exactly I was.

In many ways, being a nihilist felt exhilarating; it felt true. After all, the world *is* totally fucked up, is it not? And honestly, what *is* the point of life? We're all just gonna die and in pretty short order, too. If we're lucky, a few people might actually give a shit that we died—or lived. That's where my head was back then, and the part of me that bought into all that quasi-nihilism rushed headlong toward Soundgarden like some hell-bent masochist hungry for the lash.

But Soundgarden's nihilism was by no means a perfect fit. I enjoyed drinking beer with my friends, my relationship with Jodi proved I was capable of loving and being loved (although admittedly, loving myself wasn't in the mix at that time), and truth be told, I did sometimes smile, if involuntarily. There was a tumultuous push and pull to the self-flagellation aspect of grunge music. On the one hand, it drew me in to wallow in the sordid depths of my battered psyche. Yet in doing so, it forced me to acknowledge and confront the existential noise in my head and, perhaps unknowingly, it prodded me to seek out the stillness, that all-encompassing emptiness I'd first experienced in Alaska.

I'd take early morning walks around the West Village when the streets were empty and revisit those same blocks Murphy and I'd haunted on our music-buying excursions back in middle school, perhaps trying to reconnect with the me untouched by death and confusion and grief. I'd jog down to Battery Park and plop down on a bench, gazing out at the Statue of Liberty standing motionless in New

York Harbor, watch the tugboats ply the filthy Hudson River. And when I really needed a respite, I'd hop the subway up to Penn Station, board the Long Island Railroad's Montauk line, and ride alone out to Westhampton. I'd go with a singular destination in mind, the one place I wanted to be, where I knew I'd be able to hear the stillness: the end of our dock.

When I'd arrive at the Westhampton train station, I'd catch a cab to our house. The cab would leave me in our driveway, where my father had erected a regulation height basketball hoop for Rob and me when we were barely old enough to dribble. But we'd eventually grown into that thing, which stood guard at our house for decades, pile-driven into the ground, unmoved by hurricanes, snowstorms, and errant shots from three.

I'd head straight for the dock, out at the end of a long boardwalk that ran parallel to a shallow slip where Rob and I sometimes set crab traps. We used to have an A-frame wooden swing out on the dock but it had blown into the bay during some long ago nor'easter and was probably now serving as a funked-out reef somewhere in the bay's depths. So I'd stand out there, turn my jacket collar up against the wind, and listen to the faraway waves breaking on the beach beyond Dune Road, the relentlessness of their crashing and receding, the way the waves, unmoved, went about their business, suggesting they were somehow indifferent to everything—indifferent to the rises and falls of our fates, to my father's death, to anyone's death, to anything at all.

And then in between the crashes, for a fleeting second or two I heard it, heard what I'd traveled two hours to hear: stillness, perfect, perfect stillness. I'd close my eyes to fully absorb the sublime emptiness of it. And I was once again a child, back on the boat with my father, out in the middle of the ocean, the engine silenced, the periodic lapping of the swells against the side of the boat the only demarcation of time and space. This is where I felt my father. Not in the city, not downtown at NYU, or uptown at our apartment, and definitely not at the cemetery where he was buried in the aptly named hamlet of Valhalla.

But on that dock.

The dock where he and I would set off in the pre-dawn blackness to go fishing. The dock to which we'd return in the dissipating heat of late summer afternoons, where my father would clean the bluefish on a wobbly, weather-beaten wooden bench, the seagulls circling overhead, awaiting their bloody spoils. The dock where my father would himself stand on summer nights and gaze across the bay, where in his last days he'd ask to be wheeled, perhaps so he too could listen to the stillness.

The primordial howl of Soundgarden had awakened me to the need for stillness and set me on a quest to find it. I figured I knew where to look: in beautiful, empty, untamed places like the Brooks Range in Alaska. Yet at the same time, I resisted fully embracing the outdoors, opting instead to keep it at arm's length. The summer after our first year of law school, Bob, recalling the glowing reports I'd given of my experience in Alaska, wrote me a letter encouraging me to join him for an ascent of Mount Shasta in California in late August. By all appearances it would've been the perfect getaway, but I never so much as considered joining him. Why? Fear of the danger? No, Bob had researched a non-technical route up the south side of the 14,000-foot mountain. But something deep inside me reflexively bucked at the idea, particularly since the dates conflicted with the annual job fair at NYU where corporate law firms from around the country conducted interviews for lucrative summer jobs the following year.

I told Bob about the conflict and he wrote back saying I should skip the job fair as he was planning to do. He signed off with a quote from *Zen in the Art of Climbing Mountains*: "Mountaineers decide to set out to climb a mountain, and from that moment, and at that time, everything else within their ordinary lives becomes secondary."

The quote was alluring and really hit home. It was almost a dare. I flashed back to Alaska and the high that trip had left me with, that feeling of singular purpose that made life suddenly seem so meaningful. It was summer break and I had the time. I deeply admired Bob for his conviction, his integrity, his passion. Some displaced inner part of me was drawn toward that way of being but an ancient, nagging voice in the back of my mind kept howling "No, that's not you, that's not what you're supposed to do." It was crucial that I land a summer job at some white-shoe corporate law firm which would lead to a permanent offer from said firm after I graduated in two years, thus marking the start of my ascent up the corporate ladder. The only mountains I felt I was permitted to climb, apparently, were professional ones.

The inner voice had spoken, the die was cast, but whose voice was it? Mine? Or was it some echo of my workaholic father, of my peers, of Upper East Side cultural inertia? Of course, now I recognize it as a muddled, soul-killing mélange of all those voices. But I didn't know that then. And so I let it keep talking.

10

TIME TO ADMIT DEFEAT

I brought that gleaming black guitar home from Sam Ash and set it up on a stand in the corner of my room. And I practiced—at least as much as I could, given all my schoolwork, team sports, and other extracurricular activities. Those, of course, took priority. I mean, I wasn't going to blow off my English reading to nail the guitar solo to "Jungleland," right? That'd be crazy.

But I did make some effort. I stuck with the lessons even though Hendrix, Springsteen, and every other rock star I knew of was self-taught. None of those guys took lessons when they were boys. Neither did any of the kids at school. And they were all better than me. One of them, a kid named Jason who played with Murphy in The Amazings, asked me one day in the hallway what songs I was learning in my lessons. It just so happened that the day before my teacher had written out the chords to U2's "New Year's Day" for me. Jason, who was a mega U2 fan and used nearly the same multitude of electronic effects deployed by U2's guitarist, The Edge, asked to see my notes about it. "That's not how they play it," he chuckled, handing me back the notes. "That's not even the right key." It was probably true—it didn't sound right to me either.

Despite Jason's dickishness, I stuck with it. I kept the distortion on my amp turned up full blast and mastered the entire Sex Pistols catalogue, which, to be fair, took only about a day since their tunes, in terms of complexity, are the cooking equivalent of whipping up a bowl of cereal. From there I worked through the Clash's repertoire (also pretty basic) and then moved on to the Grateful Dead who, unlike the Pistols and the Clash, typically used more than three chords in a song.

My buddy Eric, who played guitar, lent me a huge book of Dead sheet music and I asked my dad to xerox it for me at his law office. He said it was no problem, but I felt a little bad about it when I pictured him taking the book out of his leather briefcase high up in that Park Avenue skyscraper and handing it to the guy in the copy room. I mean the cover's got this freaky-looking skeleton wearing a crown of red roses! What must the copy room dude have thought? Did he offer to sell my dad acid at the next firm holiday party?

I'd started listening to the Dead maybe a year or so earlier. I was curious about them mainly because there was this kid at my sleepaway camp who had one of their skeleton concert T-shirts which I thought was cool. But I didn't really know anybody who was into the Dead—Murphy sure as hell wasn't; they were way too old and hippie for him—so I asked Rob which Dead album I should buy. Rob wasn't a Deadhead, but I figured he'd have some idea about them since he was older and wiser than me. Without even thinking about it he said *Europe '72*. I've no idea how he knew about the record; I guess it's just something older brothers know.

When I eventually got to Side Two and "Jack Straw," I was blown away by Jerry Garcia's lead-in riff. Those delicate little guitar notes fell on my ears like raindrops on the mountain lake at my sleepaway camp. The whole song is a bunch of similarly wispy riffs that sparkle and pop. There isn't really a traditional solo to speak of, mostly just those exquisite, airy riffs. I'd never heard anything like it. In that moment, headphones on, sitting on my bed, I felt my shoulders loosen, sensed my eyes closing, my head swaying back and forth.

When my dad brought the xerox of the Dead songbook home, I flipped immediately to "Jack Straw." Unfortunately, it had like sixteen different chords to it and although none of them were too crazy, I decided to focus first on "Scarlet Begonias" since I also loved that tune and it only had four chords—including the bridge. I got that one down pretty quick!

But the very first song I learned to play—by ear—was the Velvet Underground's "Sweet Jane." Man, I loved that song so, so much. I don't know why. All I know is when my friends and I wanted to get psyched up to go out and party, we'd cue up the original studio version from *Loaded,* grab a hat from my impressive collection (I had a bunch of safari hats, old-school golf caps even though I didn't play golf, mesh trucker hats, wide-brimmed sun hats, baseball caps, tennis visors, and triad pirate hats) and dance all crazy-like around my room. When I wanted to get lost in a muscular guitar jam, to block out the noise of my family, I'd put on Lou Reed's solo version from *Rock 'N' Roll Animal* and disappear into its wall of mind blowing distortion. And later in high school when I had girls over and hoped to get lucky without having to do anything (having eventually figured out how to talk to girls and still maintain eye contact), I'd put on the super mellow version from *Live '69*, the one the Cowboy Junkies would later bring mainstream.

One time at a school talent show in tenth grade, I performed "Sweet Jane" with my friend Mike who also played guitar. Some people are just natural performers and I'm not one of them. I could feel my knees shake as I stood onstage, catching a glimpse of my mom and

Rob in the small audience—my dad was MIA, stuck at the office—my hands sweating so much I could barely hold onto the guitar pick. But once we got through the initial progression and Mike started to sing, the soothing, basic chord pattern and melody helped me relax.

We finished with a theatrical flourish, both of us holding our right arms in the air like Pete Townshend about to administer a kick-ass windmill power chord. Our performance was met with dead silence, then quiet, polite applause coupled with blank looks. I'm not sure why the crowd appeared unmoved by our greatness. It could be we lost them in the song's final verse when we screamed at the top of our lungs that life's just to die. It's profound stuff, but maybe it was too much truth for them to handle.

As Mike and I hopped off stage, our science teacher, who played in an obscure band called the Central Park Chieftains and claimed to know Lou Reed, strode over toward us, smiling. I assumed he was going to congratulate us on our stunning performance. Instead, he informed us that one of the song's four chords that we'd played as a major chord was in fact a minor chord. "Just for future reference," he said with a smile. We took his critique in stride but I have to say, it was a little deflating.

For my sixteenth birthday, my dad, who apparently knew somebody with a connection to a recording studio in Midtown, got me an hour of studio time. I showed up there one rainy afternoon with Eric, my friend who'd loaned me the Grateful Dead songbook, and we laid down the Dead's "Sugar Magnolia" as the engineer tried out different sound effects on Eric's rich, stirring voice. The guy was patient with us and seemed to take us seriously, which is pretty funny since he was an old-timer—a grizzled type in baggy jeans and lots of grey hair all over the place, including in his bushy eyebrows and sticking out in strands from his ears—who must've worked with at least a few famous musicians. This was a studio in Midtown Manhattan after all! Who were we? A couple of prep school kids dripping rainwater in his studio.

But that engineer made us a multi-tracked professional-grade recording. At the end of the session he handed me a Sony UX-PRO 60-minute jewel case with "Matt Fogelson" printed on the spine with the words "Sugar Magnolia" printed on the sleeve under Side A. I had laid down the basic chord progression while Eric added the fills, riffs, and two blistering solos. I threw in a solo myself which isn't bad, even if the timing's a bit off. I had a big flourish planned for the finish that didn't quite crescendo when it should've, the underlying chord progression having ended a beat early, leaving my flourish hanging out there by itself. Oh well.

The grizzled engineer was right to take us seriously, though. At least he was right to take Eric seriously. Eric was a tall, charismatic kid, and, in my mind, a guitar prodigy. He had a beautiful Gibson Gold Top Les Paul Deluxe. That guitar was no joke; it was a striking instrument, and you needed real confidence to play it. If you didn't have the chops to do justice to that guitar, you'd just look flat-out silly with it hanging around your neck. Eric had the chops. His long, thin fingers flew effortlessly over the fretboard, like Stevie Ray Vaughn or Jimi Hendrix. But he didn't just play fast; he could play slow and mournful, like Jerry often did (think "Comes A Time" or "Row Jimmy"), lovingly holding a note like one might hold a baby. He also had an electric stage presence, charismatic and comfortable in his own skin, which was no small feat being that Eric was one of the only Black kids at our swanky prep school.

When we played together, it was clear to me I was, literally, the second fiddle. Which was fine by me. The music thing, it was like a hobby for me. I had no grand delusions of a sex, drugs, and rock 'n' roll lifestyle or even of hanging on the edges of the music scene. That was a universe apart from the professional world where I was headed. I was just psyched Eric stooped to jam with me.

Eric and I played a couple of talent shows, covering our repertoire of Grateful Dead tunes. At one of the shows held in the tiny basement theater at our school, my mom and Rob were again in the audience—my dad was stuck at the office, of course—and I gave Rob my Sony Walkman with a plug-in microphone to record the show. Unfortunately, I totally screwed up the bridge to "Scarlet Begonias." There's a very dramatic and stark chord change and I totally muffed it. My first move when I got home that night was to listen to the tape. Sure enough, there it was. I knew that chord progression cold; how could I have screwed it up so badly? I was pretty bummed out about it, but Eric didn't seem to care. And Rob didn't even notice. "You guys rocked!" he told me right after the show. "That was awesome!" But I didn't believe him. I felt like maybe I shouldn't have been up there playing with Eric at all.

When I wasn't drinking beer or listening to and playing music, I was bobbing and weaving away from girls I actually liked and wanted to hook up with, kind of like I did that time with Julie on the washing machine—although that was more of an all-out retreat than a bob and weave.

The summer after ninth grade, I convinced my parents to let me go to summer school in Hawaii along with a bunch of other high schoolers from the mainland. The cutest girl on the trip was named Mandi and although her name was a painful reminder of Barry Manilow and of Rob routinely blowing chunks all over me, she spelled it differently than Manilow's crush, with a final "i" instead of a "y." That was my out, how I managed to get past it—that and her long brown hair, golden skin, and deep brown eyes. Best of all, she was from Alabama and had a full-on Southern accent that was just heart-stopping. I'd never met anyone from the South and could listen to her talk forever. One afternoon she schooled me on some Southern dish called Brunswick Stew which sounded a little gross, at least until she rattled off the ingredients and pronounced "lima beans"; she held the first syllable ever so slightly with the rest slithering along like the snake in the Garden of Eden.

For some reason, Mandi had a key to a hotel room in downtown Waikiki. Occasionally, we'd break away from the dorms, score some wine coolers, and head down there to hang out. I'd bring a boom box, put it on the desk, and stand there playing her tapes of the Sex Pistols, Springsteen, and the Clash. Mandi would sit on the bed in her bikini top and tight cut-off jean shorts taking it all in. She didn't know much about music so I think she appreciated my exposing her to some of the greats, although now that I think about it, she never did say much about the songs.

Anyway, one time she asked if I wanted to come sit down on the bed, patting the spot right next to her.

"I kind of need to deal with the boom box," I told her.

"You could bring it over here," she replied, staring at me hard.

I hadn't thought of that. I had to admit it did make some sense—I could've easily dealt with the tapes from the bed—but I stood my ground. Although it seemed like Mandi was interested in me, and I was definitely interested in her, for some reason I pretended like I didn't know what was happening.

"That's okay," I said. "I'm about to flip the tape anyway."

That was the last time we hung out at the hotel.

It's too bad because I wanted to fool around with Mandi, like, *really* wanted to, but I was also scared to. I wasn't sure what to do after sitting down on the bed with her. And I guess I felt like I needed to know in advance what would happen. Which is pretty stupid, actually. I mean, what's the worst thing that would've happened if I'd just gone with the flow? I suppose it could've been a little embarrassing if things went south somehow. But on the plus side, man, it could've been awesome! Although if I'm being honest, I think part of the problem was that I was pretty self-conscious about my body. My *pulkes* were no longer as hefty as chicken drumsticks, but I still had a good deal of baby fat on me. I wasn't one of those boys who looked for any opportunity to waltz around with their shirt off. In fact, even at the beach that summer I'd leave mine on in ninety-degree heat, muttering something about not wanting to get sunburned. So my strong desire to mess around with Mandi lost to a slightly more powerful emotion—shame.

It was the same sad story the following summer when I went on a six-week "teen tour" trip to Australia and New Zealand. There was this really cool girl on the trip—Karen from Marin County, near San Francisco. She wore Birkenstocks, hoop earrings, and lots of tie-dye. She had wild hair, kind of like my Aunt Wendy's, except it was reddish-brown. And she was super funny, always teasing. She'd stay stuff just to try to get a rise out of me, crazy shit, like "You do know that Bruce Springsteen tries to act macho, don't you? It's all an act." She said it deadpan, as if it was some obvious thing that everybody but me knew. Clearly, she wasn't serious; she just knew it would irritate me. "Now Janis Joplin?" she continued, "She's got balls!"

Karen and I fooled around some at a nightclub in Melbourne when she followed me into the men's room and pushed me into a stall. We collapsed to the floor and Karen started kissing me hard. I was very drunk, having spent most of the night pounding Victoria Bitter beers and some type of Midori concoction with my friend Don and this local high school kid named Damien who, although he sported an orange Mohawk that strongly suggested he was a legit punk, listened to the Smiths and the Cure and groaned when I mentioned the Sex Pistols. But he did act like a punk when he scarfed down the decorative flowers at our table, stems and all. I was just drunk enough to follow his lead. Which is to say that my guard was way, way down when Karen made her move. I was glad to be defenseless, glad she took the initiative—in the moment, anyway. She unbuttoned my jeans and started touching me places I'd never been touched by anyone else. I wasn't sure what to do, so I did the same thing with her pants and touched her in places I'd never felt before. It was pretty crazy.

By morning, I felt gross about it, like I'd done something wrong, like I'd compromised myself or something. I desperately wanted to cue up *Nebraska*, like I'd done after my Julie whiff, but unfortunately I'd only brought *Born to Run* and *Darkness* on the trip. Those albums weren't what I needed. *Born to Run* was for when I was feeling fired up and thinking about adventure, and *Darkness* was for when I was feeling self-righteous about the failings of the American capitalist system—or when I just wanted to hear some kick-ass rock music. No, I needed *Nebraska* and its cast of criminals and outlaws. That's how I felt—like I needed to up and run from the cops who were surely on my tail.

Not that I decided to fend off Karen after that. I didn't. We kept fooling around. I just felt like shit about it. Like I was blindly giving in to my desires, my emotions, and not exercising self-control which I viewed as mission critical—although I had no clue what the mission was.

Things escalated in Sydney near the end of the trip after we all went out to dinner. It was a BYOB place so we brought our own, lots of it, barely finding our way back to the hostel. Karen and I ended up on the floor of the hostel bathroom and I made a mental note to someday fool around with a girl someplace other than a bathroom floor.

"Do you have protection?" she asked.

As fate would have it, I did have a single condom. I'd gotten it as a goodwill gesture from some drunkard at a bar in Airlie Beach just weeks before. The guy told me I wasn't holding my beer bottle correctly, that I needed to put my pinkie under the bottom of the bottle "in case you get jostled, mate, you won't spill any." I regripped the beer bottle as he'd instructed and thanked him enthusiastically—the advice seemed potentially invaluable moving forward. "No worries," he replied and for some reason handed me a condom. I'd been carrying it around in my wallet for four weeks, thinking I might need it someday, somewhere. But not here, not now.

"No," I sheepishly whispered to Karen, "I don't."

See, by this time I'd kind of decided I wasn't really attracted to Karen. "She's no Heather Locklear," I wrote in my journal. Which of course was true—Heather Locklear was the hottest woman on the planet, for crying out loud. But some small part of me felt like maybe that wasn't the whole story, that maybe I shut it down for some other reason I couldn't quite figure. I mean, Heather Locklear is a pretty high bar, is she not? Even Bruce in "Thunder Road" tells the girl he's leaving town with that she ain't a beauty but it's alright. It seemed a little strange that I'd have higher standards than Bruce Springsteen.

It was all so confusing that I actually started to question my sexuality. "It's so frustrating to try to be forward with you," Karen said to me one night. "All you ever seem to want to do is drink with Don." Karen was right that I gave top priority to hanging with Don, a long-haired hipster from Philly. Not only was he a blast to drink with, but he was also a mega classic rock fan who played the drums. We spent our first free afternoon jamming in a Cairns music store butchering Pink Floyd's "Comfortably Numb" and the Stones' "Tumbling Dice." Not surprisingly, I had lots of positive things to say about Don in my journal, going on about how he was "quite possibly the greatest guy I've ever met," and how the years it took me to build up my friendship with Murphy, "it took two days to build up with Don." "Jeez, I'm making us sound like gay lovers," I wrote by way of conclusion. "We weren't gay, but we were the best friends possible." Why would I include a comment like that if I wasn't wondering about it myself? And then there's this entry about our trip leaders: "It sounds gay, but I really miss Steve and Lyndsey. Fuck you, I'm not gay."

Reading those entries now makes me want to hit the time machine and have a little confab with that kid. *Wow, dude, relax. We get it, you're a red-blooded, pornography-curious, loins-ablaze-around-beautiful-girls, David Lee Roth-envying, virulently heterosexual teenage boy. You've made your point. Then just one simple question for you, stud: what the fuck? Why can't you ever pull the trigger? Even when girls are heaving themselves at you, twisting themselves in knots to spur you to action?*

Maybe it was because my mom really wanted a girl—I mean *really* wanted a girl—so much so that when I was super young, she'd sometimes tie my hair in a ponytail, tell me I was beautiful and carry on and on about how she'd give anything for my *gorgeous* eyelashes. Did that leave some nascent mark, causing me to question my masculinity in some subconscious way? Could it also explain why the only song I genuinely love by the Kinks is "Lola"?

We all find ways to blame our parents—for things we didn't try, lessons we didn't learn, opportunities we missed. So maybe it's their fault! How much did my parents even try to teach me about love, sex, dating? And what kind of example did they set? They were never really affectionate with each other so maybe that's why I couldn't be. Not that they ran away from each other like I sometimes did with girls, although I guess my workaholic dad did sort of use his office as a place to hide from my mom. But maybe it also had something to do with how my dad dealt with my mom when she'd yell at him. He'd just stand there and take it. I can't remember him ever really yelling back. More often than not, he met her emotion with a blank stare, with nothing. That emotional vacancy seemed to work for him; at least it got him through the skirmish at hand, so maybe I adopted it myself. Like the time he was going to take Rob and me to a Rangers playoff game but then bailed at the last minute because of work. When he said he was sorry, I told him not to worry about it, that it was okay. It wasn't okay—I was pissed! But I just bottled up those emotions and pretended they didn't exist. Maybe that's what I was doing with girls—meeting their emotion with stoicism and bottling up my own feelings.

A few weeks after getting home to New York a mix tape arrived from Karen. She'd decorated the cover with rainbows, flowers, and a large peace symbol and loaded it up with tunes by the Stones ("Let's Spend the Night Together"), the Velvet Underground ("I'm Sticking with You"), and the Grateful Dead ("They Love Each Other"). She wrote a note on the spine: "Matt, I have great taste in music. I hope you like this tape, and if not, just play it and think of me. I love you." First girl who ever told me she loved me. It was weird. When I read those three words from Karen, my stomach flipped and I felt almost like there was an electric current running through me, as if I'd touched one of those freaky metal globes that stands your hair on end.

I felt a little sad when I got Karen's tape, like maybe I'd blown an opportunity to put myself out there with a really cool girl—one who did in fact have great taste in music! But since she lived in California and I lived in New York, it wouldn't have amounted to anything. So it was probably for the best anyway.

At least that's what I told myself. But part of me wonders whether I was overthinking all that. Sure, Karen and I weren't going to get married or anything, but was that a reason not to open myself up to her, to just stifle my feelings? I mean, who knows? Maybe I would've grown by allowing myself a burst of uninhibited passion. What's that old, hippy tune, "Love the One You're With"?—maybe there's a kernel of wisdom in that thing.

After listening to Karen's tape, I cued up Joe Jackson's "Real Men," dropping the needle repeatedly on the next-to-last verse: "Time to admit what you call defeat / 'Cause there's women running past you now and you just drag your feet."

Defeat. Yeah, that's exactly what it felt like. The biggest defeat ever.

11

DON'T CLIMB AN APPLE TREE IN SEARCH OF ORANGES

After graduating from law school, I got a clerkship with a federal district court judge in Charlottesville, Virginia. I didn't have much of a social life that year since the only other person I knew in Charlottesville was my co-clerk and he kept to himself. When I wasn't working, I was mostly listening to WTJU, the University of Virginia's student-run radio station. Up to that point in my life, I'd survived on a steady diet of classic rock and the mainstream blues that spawned it, but my year in Charlottesville put lots of other dishes on the musical table. Friday nights on WTJU was the *Nothin' But The Blues* program from 9:00 p.m. to 11:00 p.m. followed by Professor BeBop from 11:00 p.m. to 1:00 a.m.

The Professor's playlist consisted exclusively of obscure old blues and soul tracks by the likes of Joe Beard and Willie Kent, musicians I'd never heard of. Some of the grooves he played rambled on forever. I'd drift off to sleep and wake up to the same groove. I taped a lot of those shows; still have the cassettes decades later. And it always blows my mind listening to them. The feeling of expansion they elicit—internal and external—of limitlessness, of there being so much more to learn and discover about music, art, life. Those grooves breed in me a sense of wonder and hope.

Sunday nights at 11:00 p.m. was *Walkin' The Blues*, acoustic blues from the '30s and '40s, musicians like Son House, Blind Willie McTell, and Big Joe Williams. It was my first time being exposed to old time blues and it opened the floodgates to Southern music in general. Soon enough the tight-assed law student from Manhattan started to get into bluegrass, attending the Graves Mountain Music Festival in the Blue Ridge Mountains. The fried bologna sandwiches were as memorable as the wild, slightly unhinged fiddle- and banjo-driven sounds echoing through the festival site. One thin slice of bologna fried on a griddle, slapped on Wonder bread, and coated with yellow mustard—nothing better.

My time in Charlottesville taught me that some music just sounds better in certain settings—like seeing an animal in its natural habitat instead of in a zoo. Bluegrass in the Blue Ridge Mountains is Exhibit A. Something about that twangy goodness reverberating across a small field in the shadow of the Blue Ridge, lawn chairs set out all catawampus, equal numbers of cowboy hats and straw hats, ice-cold lemonade helping to keep your core temperature down in the stifling heat and humidity after ingesting too much fried bologna. Since leaving Charlottesville, I've noticed the phenomenon elsewhere, that the Grateful Dead, for example, just sound better, more vital, on the Pacific Coast Highway than on the New Jersey Turnpike; the opposite of Springsteen, the characters in his songs coming to life as I imagined the Magic Rat driving his sleek machine over the Jersey state line in the lane next to me.

After my clerkship, I moved to Washington, DC, and worked at a large corporate law firm. Not the most fulfilling experience, lots of long hours and weekends reviewing documents in places like Peoria, Illinois. The excitement of travel wore off almost immediately. The first time I went to Peoria, I asked the hotel clerk where I could get dinner nearby. She recommended a place called Big Al's.

"The strip club down the street?"

"Yeah," she said, "they've got good burgers."

Although a burger sounded good, a strip club sounded less so. I opted for a turkey and cheese from the Subway shop a few blocks away.

After a year and a half, I quit the law firm and got a job as a trial attorney with the United States Department of Justice litigating environmental cases against corporate polluters. My mother's reaction to my job change was classic Upper East Side: "Why would you want to become a government bureaucrat?" she asked. She was trapped in a mindset in which lawyers worked exclusively at large corporate firms and made lots of money, like my father. That's all my mother knew. She may have thought the DOJ was no different than the DMV, but I knew better. And I knew my father would've as well. One of the only good things about my father not being around was I could attribute all sorts of thoughts to him. It came in handy whenever I needed to feel I was making the right decision about something. "Pops would definitely agree," I'd say to myself. And nobody could prove me wrong.

Before I started at DOJ, I went on a week-long Outward Bound backpacking trip in Arizona. I felt like I needed some emotional renewal; it'd been six years since my trip to Alaska and the head space I'd cleared from that experience was filling back in, like a garden being reclaimed by weeds. Mostly I felt nervous about the Justice Department gig. I wondered if I was up to the challenge and hoped a physically demanding week in the woods would help set me straight.

There were seven of us in the group, and we ranged in age from twenty to forty. My initial impression of these people wasn't great. At the orientation session on the first night, some of them asked anxious questions about the lack of showers and shitting in the woods. I was the only person not wearing brand new hiking boots. Although several opportunities presented themselves to mention casually that I had wilderness experience in the Alaskan backcountry, I kept my mouth shut. I didn't want to be dubbed an "expert." I didn't feel I was one, even among this lackluster crowd. When on the last night of the trip, the group voted me the most likely to move to the woods permanently, I laughed it off. To me, the honorific just showed how *not* outdoorsy this group was. Of course, another possibility was that they had it right; I just didn't want to believe it. Viewing myself as a true outdoorsman would've been disloyal to my father and pushed him away. That two things could be true at once—that I could've been someone who found genuine solace and meaning in nature while also being a lawyer—never occurred to me.

The highlight of the trip was a "solo"—an afternoon and night spent alone, separated from the rest of the group and confined to a small area, maybe twenty feet square, with just a sleeping bag, water, and a baggie of granola. Not sure how to pass the time in the sweltering heat, I sat under a shade tree with a view across a yawning valley to the distant mountains and took out my journal. I stared at the blank pages for a good while, and then out of nowhere found myself drafting a letter to my father. I'm not sure why I did it—it had been seven years since he'd died. I guess I felt close to him out there, felt his presence somehow.

I told him of all the times I needed him: the day I graduated from college, all the dark days of law school, and right now before starting my prestigious job at DOJ; I needed him to tell me, as he'd told Rob when

Rob made Law Review, that I was among the best because I *was* one of the best—I wondered if I was among the best only because he was.

I told him how his death had changed me, how I'd gained an appreciation for beautiful, empty spaces, filling them in my mind with him, fantasizing he could see what I see. I told him how stunning Alaska is, how he would've loved it, and how Outward Bound had special father/son courses—"Wouldn't it have been incredible if we'd done something like that?" I wrote.

And I told him that for all the changes over the past seven years, some things remained the same: the basketball hoop in Westhampton was still standing, the rust getting a little thicker each year; the ocean still crashed onto the beach across Dune Road, awe-inspiring in its vastness; and above all else, that I still loved him, cherished him, and needed him, that I missed him every day of my life. "I'll forever look for you in the beautiful empty spaces where heaven and earth meet," I told him. When I finished, I wiped my watery eyes with my dusty and mucous-soaked bandana, took several deep breaths, and signed the letter: "Love, Tips."

The last night of the trip, we held a group activity around the campfire called "gifts and appreciations." As the name suggests, we took turns telling each other what we appreciated about them and offering a "gift" by way of constructive criticism or positive advice. My gift to Don, a twenty-two-year-old who was about to move to New York to work on Wall Street, sounded like something Aunt Wendy had said to me. "Don," I said, "my gift to you is that you find it in yourself to check in periodically and make sure you're doing what *you* want." Shari, our leader, who was much more of a spiritual seeker type than I was, put it slightly differently: "Make sure you're not climbing an apple tree in search of oranges."

I could self-assuredly dispense my advice to Don because by quitting my job at the law firm to work at the Justice Department, I felt I was climbing up the right tree. It never occurred to me that maybe I shouldn't have been climbing trees at all, that maybe I should have been caving or skipping rocks.

After the trip, as I waited to board my plane back to Washington, I followed the sound of "Scarlet Begonias," one of my favorite Grateful Dead tunes, wafting from a storefront. Turned out the store sold products made exclusively from hemp. There were T-shirts and pants, milk and juices, jewelry, oils, and seeds. But my eye was drawn to a plain-looking briefcase. It was black with one large compartment and a simple shoulder strap. I wasn't in the market for a new briefcase, but something about trading in my leather briefcase for a hemp one spoke to me.

An information card hanging from the briefcase touted hemp's superiority to cotton, in part because no pesticides are required to cultivate it. The card noted that the original drafts of the Declaration of Independence were written on hemp paper. Nevertheless, "irrational and unjust laws prohibit cannabis hemp cultivation in the United States," the card inveighed. "Today, thousands of Americans are in prison because they had the courage to disobey these laws."

I brought the briefcase up to the counter.

"That's a great item," the clerk said. He was an older gentleman with just a few strands of white hair remaining. "It's real strong. Can hold lots of books. You mind if I ask what kind of work do you do?"

"I'm an attorney," I replied, proudly adding, "I work for the US Department of Justice."

"Really? That's fantastic."

"Thanks. Should I feel at all uneasy about bringing a hemp briefcase to work?" I asked half-jokingly.

"Well, I just sold one of these yesterday to an FBI agent so I think you're in the clear."

It took several years for that hemp briefcase to wear out. When it did, I switched over to a backpack. Never did return to my leather briefcase.

The Justice Department was a big improvement over the law firm, although there were some striking similarities. Instead of hanging out in Peoria, Illinois, I spent a good part of my first year at DOJ working in Warren, Ohio. Although the hotel clerk in Warren didn't recommend a strip club for dinner, she did suggest Red Lobster after asking if I liked seafood. "It's the best restaurant in town," she said.

I've got no problem with Red Lobster—their endless shrimp special is a revelation—but if I'm going to hit a chain restaurant, it's for sure gonna be Waffle House!

I was in Warren working on a case against a steel company that stored hazardous effluent in holding ponds that were not properly lined to prevent leaching into the groundwater. The company claimed the effluent didn't meet the regulatory definition of "hazardous." I spent weeks in depositions and trial prep. The trial lasted only four days, but they were long days. The judge started at 7:00 a.m. with one mid-morning break of fifteen minutes before lunch, which was itself only thirty minutes. Same drill in the afternoon—one fifteen-minute break until court recessed at 5:00 p.m. The first day I made the mistake of drinking water over the course of the morning. I didn't make that mistake again.

During that gauntlet I averaged roughly four hours of sleep each night (I was up late preparing for the next day's motions and cross-examinations), was perpetually dehydrated, and lost ten pounds in five days.

By this time, Jodi and I had moved in together. When I got back to

Washington after the trial, I told her, "Don't ever let me say I enjoyed this" even though my cross-examination of the defendant's statistics expert won the case for us, producing a Perry Mason–like moment when I handed the expert a calculator and asked him to perform one of his own calculations, the result of which proved the effluent was indeed hazardous.

"You should be very proud of how you represented the United States," our grizzled expert witness said to me in the hallway of the courthouse after the trial. He later told my boss I'd done a better job than any DOJ trial lawyer he'd worked with in his ten-plus years as an expert witness. But it didn't matter. I didn't feel any of the usual exhilaration other attorneys I worked with felt after a big trial. Sure, I was run-down and exhausted, but it was more than that. I felt defeated, like I wasn't cut out for the job, that I was an interloper or something. But I kept plodding down the road I was traveling, oblivious to the possibility of doing anything else.

Jodi, who was always more of an academic, head-in-the-clouds type, quit her job at a law firm and applied to sociology graduate programs. She was accepted to UC Berkeley, so we moved out to Oakland where I had to get used to pedestrians nonchalantly stepping out into the crosswalks of major streets as if they expected drivers to slam on the brakes to avoid flattening them. I continued to work at DOJ in its San Francisco field office, but eventually the DOJ gig became rote. I'd tired of litigating the same types of cases against the same types of polluters represented by the same defense counsel, so I took an in-house position at Pacific Gas and Electric Company, California's largest utility. I wanted to work in the renewable energy space and figured PG&E was the place to be since the company was in the process of converting large portions of its electric resources to renewables. And while I was assigned some renewables policy work, I quickly became somewhat of a rover, asked to handle the company's more pressing matters irrespective of subject area—be it a request to regulators for a rate hike or a change to an arcane rule or some other supposedly vital but utterly lifeless matter of corporate concern. I was a proverbial jack-of-all-trades who knew a little about a lot of different parts of the business, and my lack of in-depth knowledge about anything, while my colleagues were all steeped in expertise of one kind or another, made me feel perpetually inadequate. But for over a decade, I kept those feelings of inadequacy—of being a fraud—at bay, kept my head down, kept on keeping on, not once contemplating a career shift.

In his memoir, Springsteen writes, "Those whose love we wanted but could not get, we emulate. It is dangerous but it makes us feel closer, gives us an illusion of the intimacy we never had." He elaborated in a 2019 interview, explaining that when it came to his career, to making music, "I chose my father's voice because there was something sacred in it to me." In fact, Bruce adopted not just his father's voice, but his appearance as well—both the work clothes and the bulging muscles, hitting the gym every day to mimic his father's burly physique.

Maybe there was something like that going on with me. I mean, I'm sure my father loved me, but at the same time, some unconscious part of me may have felt rejected by him because I didn't get nearly as much of his time as I wanted. And maybe that translated into my not feeling loved by him. So perhaps to me there was something sacred about my father's path. Maybe the decision to become a lawyer—and to stay a lawyer—was an effort to keep my father close, by adopting as my own the critical component of who he was. With all due respect to Bruce, I didn't dress *like* my father—I literally wore his old suits to work, even though the tailor could never get them to fit right. When

I wore his suits, I looked like David Byrne in *Stop Making Sense*, but I didn't care.

Whatever the reason, I was hell-bent on following in my father's footsteps as a lawyer. There's an entry in my Alaska journal I keep going back to, about our leader, Bill, a guy who spent his life charging up mountains in successive incarnations of this or that wilderness: "I could never structure my life the way Bill has," I wrote. "You can't really live your life that way. Bill might be able to, but I could never live like that—at least I don't think I could."

Reading that entry decades later, it's the "I don't think I could" that resonates, activating some deep, seminal ache. For a few fleeting moments, as I wrote that journal entry, I had at least considered the possibility I could live in a way that felt free. But then I shut it down as just some crazy pipe dream. "I couldn't live like that—I don't think." *Why the fuck not? Why couldn't I live that way?* Bill was twenty-one when he became an Outward Bound instructor, just a year younger than I was during the trip. Why was I so beholden to the conventional? Why couldn't I break away from the mainstream grind?

Long before my father died, I was known as "Little Jimmy" in my family, my relatives always telling me how much I was like my father, not just in appearance but in temperament. It was a welcome appraisal—I loved being told that. I practically worshipped my father and modeled myself after him as best I could. In my eulogy for him I contended that my life's work was to "emulate my father, the most decent person I've ever known," believing that if I did "he'll never leave me completely." Maybe that's what I was doing, emulating him, so that in some ways I was less myself than my father's son.

Maybe the only way I could continue to feel my father's presence in the world was by becoming him.

12
MORE THAN A SPRINGSTEEN TICKET

The girl thing was a real mess. It didn't make any sense that I could never make a move. I still have no clue why I chose *Nebraska* over the hottest girl in my grade freshman year, but unlike Barry Manilow who I blamed for Rob always puking on me, I didn't blame Bruce for my poor decision-making that night. If anything, I felt even closer to him, as if we'd become partners in some shameful crime. He knew my secrets. And I knew those secrets were safe with him.

Yeah, I was way into Bruce. So much so that late one night in November of 1986, after the release of Springsteen's box set, *Live 1975–85,* I went down to 86th and Lexington and all quiet-like removed a huge poster of the album cover, maybe five feet tall by three feet wide, from the wood facade of a construction site. The glue hadn't totally dried yet which made it easy to pull loose. I hadn't anticipated that night's furiously howling wind, and I must have been a sight trying to walk nonchalantly home with this giant poster that I didn't dare fold, the bulk of it constantly slapping against me as the glue quickly hardened up all over my clothes.

But it was so worth a ruined pair of jeans. The cover's got Bruce in profile, mid-strut across a stage. A row of blindingly hot white floor lights casts a halo around him. The yellow fretboard of the guitar is in perfect alignment with his left leg, the bend of which forms a triangle with his right leg. It's an image of mastery, order, and control. I put that enormous image of Bruce up on the wall above my bed where it towered over my room like the giant crucifix in our school chapel.

Murphy was appalled by my obsession with Bruce. You could tell he was physically uncomfortable sitting in my room under that poster, sort of like me sitting in the school chapel under that crucifix.

"What do you see in that guy?" he asked me one day while throwing a tennis ball up against my bedroom wall, dangerously close to the poster.

It was a fair question. I mean, nobody I knew had lost their job or was struggling to get by. And I didn't consider my hometown to be a town full of losers I had to pull out of to win. But still, the lyrics kind of spoke to me.

"Well for one, I think his lyrics are pretty cool," I replied a little defensively.

"You focus too much on lyrics," Murphy said. "The music's the thing."

"Well sure, of course the music's important, but so are the lyrics. Take the Clash. Their lyrics are awesome."

"I guess, but the fire's in the music. You don't need the lyrics to feel the power of their shit."

"True, but I happen to think Bruce's music also kicks ass."

Murphy rolled his eyes. It didn't surprise me that Springsteen's music didn't speak to him. It was way too mainstream. Heck, Murphy had just turned me onto Malcolm McLaren's "Madam Butterfly," which is a crazy take on some opera with all this electronica stuff and spoken word dubs going on. It sounds insane but it was actually really cool. I bought the twelve-inch single of it down at Second

Coming. But it wasn't at all like Springsteen's music. Murphy and I just had to agree to disagree on The Boss.

As much as I loved Springsteen, I met my match Springsteen-fan-wise in high school when a new kid named Doug transferred in. Not only did Doug enthusiastically approve of my Springsteen poster, he took it even further, actually dressing like Bruce—well almost like him. While Bruce would stylishly break up the denim motif by wearing jeans of a slightly different shade than his jean vest, which he often wore *over* a black leather jacket for contrast, Doug was all-in on the monochromatic denim jeans and jacket. He also always carried a harmonica with him and during recesses would treat those of us hanging out in the hallway to the intros to "The River," "Thunder Road," and "The Promised Land."

Doug and I first crossed paths at that freshman retreat held before the start of the school year. His vintage *Born to Run* T-shirt caught my eye the first day in the cafeteria. I sat down next to him partly because I wanted to ask him where he got the shirt but also because he was by himself, far from all the girls. Doug told me *Born to Run* was not only his favorite Springsteen album, but his favorite album, period. I told him that *Darkness on the Edge of Town* was my favorite Springsteen record.

Doug had witnessed the three-legged race debacle that ended with Gretchen spread-eagled on top of me. "Pretty clutch move there, Fogie," he'd said when I sought him out afterwards. "That took some balls."

"Yeah, like I was trying to do that," I said, even though I knew he was joking. "What a nightmare."

I wanted to get as far away from girls as humanly possible. There was a lake in the middle of the park where the retreat was held, so I suggested we grab a canoe and paddle out to the middle. Once we were at a safe distance from all the girls, Doug and I swapped our concerns with *Born in the U.S.A.* which had just come out. It was too commercial, too pop, we told each other. Bruce's earlier records were *so* much better, although we did agree the title track was pretty cool. And maybe "Glory Days." And possibly "Downbound Train" if forced to pick another. But that was it. For sure. Other than, of course, "My Hometown," which was halfway decent.

"'No Surrender' is cool, too," Doug said. "The part about skipping school and learning more from records than some lame class. So true."

"Yeah, school pretty much sucks," I agreed, momentarily setting aside the fact I actually liked school. I'd found someone who was even more obsessed with Springsteen than I was. Doug was a needle in a haystack and I wasn't about to risk alienating the biggest connection to The Boss I knew.

Neither of us had seen Springsteen live yet. We both missed him on the *Born in the U.S.A.* tour which had come through New York a few weeks earlier; I was away at summer camp and Doug was out of town. We missed him again the following summer for the same reasons (why did Bruce come through New York only during the summer?). Springsteen, and the dream of seeing him in concert, saw Doug and me through much of high school—we spent a ton of time in each other's rooms talking Bruce and listening to his latest bootlegs.

One day senior year, Doug stopped me in the hallway between classes to let me know a benefit concert in honor of the late Harry Chapin at Carnegie Hall had just been announced and that Bruce was going to play. He'd probably play only one or two songs since there'd be a lot of other performers but Doug said he was going to see if his dad could wrangle a couple of tickets for us. Doug's dad was a big philanthropist in New York, had connections, and sure enough, came through. Doug came over before the concert and I cued up *Darkness on the Edge of Town* while we chugged a six pack in my room.

"What do you think he'll play?" I asked Doug as we pounded the last beers, the life-size image of Bruce gazing down approvingly at us from above my bed.

"Don't know. I assume a Harry Chapin tune. Hopefully not 'Cat's in the Cradle.' What a cheesy song," Doug muttered.

I was more than a little pissed by Doug's takedown of "Cat's in the Cradle" since I still loved that song, not that I wanted to get into it with him.

"Yeah, well, I'm sure Bruce's version would be amazing," I said.

Feeling sufficiently buzzed, we hopped a bus down Fifth Avenue to Carnegie Hall. Our seats were fantastic, in the lower level, left center, maybe fifteen rows back. People in the audience were dressed up. Lots of suits, ties, and dresses, plus an occasional tuxedo—which made sense since it was a benefit show. I wore a navy-blue blazer. My mom had insisted on it. "You're going to Carnegie Hall," she explained. "You need to look presentable." I didn't protest; it'd be easier to get served if I looked older. Doug, unaware of or uninterested in the high-class nature of our surroundings, sported his usual all-denim uniform.

As we settled in, marveling at the sophistication of the scene, Doug pointed to the woman sitting directly in front of us and whispered to me, his eyes nearly popping out of their sockets, "That's Julianne Phillips!" Julianne Phillips, of course, was Springsteen's wife at the time.

"You sure?" I asked. I could see only the back of a head that looked like it could belong to any woman in her late twenties or early thirties.

The hair was dirty blond, cut to the shoulders, sort of a perm going on. Black cable-knit sweater.

"Yes," he said with conviction. I'd learned to trust Doug's sixth sense when it came to all things Springsteen. This was a guy who'd buy obscure Gary U.S. Bonds albums just because Bruce sang backup on a few of the tracks.

"What should we do?" Doug asked.

"What do you mean what should we do?"

"We should do something, tell her how much we love Bruce."

"I doubt she really wants to hear that."

"Fair enough. Hey, let's write a note to Bruce and ask her to give it to him!"

"Are you serious?" I asked, but Doug was gone, returning a few minutes later with a cocktail napkin and a pen. He wrote feverishly, racing against the clock as it inched its way toward curtain time.

"Slow down," I said, "you're gonna tear the napkin."

Doug produced a love letter so cheesy that if he'd written it to a girl, she would've immediately cut off all contact with him. But still, I thought it was fantastic, soul-wrenching even, telling Bruce of our love of his music, how it helped Doug and me through hard times and made the good times better, how he inspired us to live lives of integrity and truth. I enthusiastically signed my name to it. At the bottom, Doug and I wrote our addresses and phone numbers just in case Bruce wanted to reach out.

All that was left was the task of giving the note to Julianne Phillips. I would've been too mortified to do it but Doug had no reservations.

"Ms. Phillips," he said to the back of the head. There was no response from the head. So Doug poked the woman on the shoulder. She turned around. "Ms. Phillips," Doug said, "I'm sorry to bother you but we're huge fans of your husband." She smiled a patient, slight smile. "We wrote him a note and were wondering if you'd mind giving it to him."

"I'd be happy to," she said, smiling for real this time. She put the napkin in her purse and turned back around.

Doug and I looked at each other in astonishment. We'd established a direct line with The Boss!

Bruce was one of the last performers of the night, and our anticipation kept building. I was sweating, both from excitement and nervousness—all the beers I'd downed prior to the show kept forcing me to hit the bathroom. I raced back each time worried I might miss even one second of Bruce's performance.

When he finally came out, walking slowly to the lone microphone at center stage, not wearing any denim, just a white dress shirt and black pants with black suspenders, harmonica rack around his neck, acoustic guitar melded to his torso by a strap around his shoulder, I could feel every muscle in my body tighten, as if commanding the focus of every cell in my body, every iota of my attention on beholding him, the master at work.

The audience started the obligatory chant of "BRUUUUUUUUUUCE!" but I was stone silent. Somewhere in the dream that followed, as Springsteen carried us along, I became aware of Julianne Phillips standing and gently applauding. A pang of jealousy rippled through me. *Man, she gets to eat breakfast, lunch, and dinner with him.*

Yes, Bruce performed only one song, but man, was it memorable. It was indeed a Harry Chapin tune; to Doug's relief it wasn't "Cat's in the Cradle," but "Remember When the Music." Ever the master performer, halfway through the song Bruce wove a humorous and moving story about what the song meant to him and commanded the assembled to honor its message to "do something" to better the world. He then sang the last two verses and concluded with four punctuating bars of shrill harmonica that fully confirmed that my belief in Bruce, my faith in him, my love of him, was, if anything, not all-encompassing enough.

After the show, Doug, equally fired up by what we'd just seen, confided in me that he possessed information that we had to act upon. He claimed that Springsteen had an apartment on Fifth Avenue, that said apartment was just a few blocks from the theater, and that we absolutely had to go over there immediately.

"Doesn't he live in Jersey?" I asked.

"Yeah, but he also has an apartment in the City. He'll stay here tonight," Doug declared like he was Springsteen's personal assistant. Even though it was a bitter cold December night and already 11:00 p.m. (not to mention a school night), the plan, which involved keeping vigil from a park bench across from the building, made perfect sense to me. Why would Bruce go all the way back to New Jersey so late at night?

"Maybe we should grab some beer," I suggested. "It could be a little while before he shows."

"Great idea," Doug replied.

I ducked into one of the three Korean grocers we passed over the course of our eight-block walk and grabbed a six-pack of Hamm's, the cheapest beer they had. Properly equipped with beer, we walked over to Fifth Avenue somewhere in the low sixties and found a bench across from the building in question, the world's two most unlikely private detectives.

We sat on that park bench for an hour, freezing, yet still drinking that cold, cold beer, assuring ourselves Bruce had probably grabbed dinner somewhere after the show and so wouldn't be expected to arrive home for a little while yet. There was nothing to be done except wait. I worried that holding a can of beer in my gloved hands would warm it up (the only thing more disgusting than a cold Hamm's is a warm one), so after each sip I gently placed the can underneath the bench, which had the added benefit of concealing my underage public drinking.

At some point, probably just as the beer ran out, I wondered: what would happen if Bruce *did* miraculously appear? Would we approach him and ask for an autograph? Maybe Doug would, but there's no way I would've had the courage to do it. Plus, we didn't have anything for him to sign. We didn't have a camera to take a picture, and even if we did, from our vantage point, all we would've captured on film was his back as he disappeared into the building. I vaguely entertained a fantasy that after we identified ourselves as the napkin letter writers Bruce would invite us up for a beer. But in a reversal of the usual order of things, the more I drank, the less likely it seemed my fantasy would play itself out.

This was a waste of time.

Around 12:30 a.m., I said as much to Doug. He seemed unsure at first. He took a swig of his beer, grimaced as he realized he was drinking warm Hamm's backwash, and reluctantly agreed. We gathered up our empties, tossed them in a garbage can, and split a cab uptown.

The Carnegie Hall show whetted our appetite for seeing Bruce again. It was just one song, after all. He was about to start a tour in support of his new album, *Tunnel of Love*, and Doug managed to score two tickets to a show at Madison Square Garden.

"That's amazing!" I said clapping Doug on the back when he told me in the hallway at school. "Which night is it?"

"Thursday, but Fogie, I'm taking Sue." His face was grim and flat, like a judge announcing a life sentence. I felt like the defendant on the receiving end of that sentence. I began to cycle through the five stages of grief, but only got as far as denial, depression, and anger. I never made it to bargaining or acceptance. Nope, I was stuck on anger.

Sue was a classmate of ours who Doug had been crushing on in vain since the freshman retreat nearly four years earlier. I had to admit she was cute, with golden hair and extremely large breasts. But Doug had no chance with her. Even with Springsteen tickets. This was ridiculous.

"You can't be serious!" I screamed. "How can you do this?"

"Calm down, Fogie, you're making a scene." Everyone in the hallway was staring at us. Doug ushered me around the corner behind the entrance to the chapel.

"I just want to take Sue," he explained. "No big deal."

"You're right, it's not a big deal. It's A HUGE FUCKING DEAL!"

"Look, I heard Bruce might be adding a couple more shows and if I get tickets, you and I will definitely go."

"Don't bother," I hissed at him. "You can take some other girl you have no shot at."

As the words left my mouth, I knew things were changed forever between Doug and me. I knew it from the roiling in my stomach and I could see it in his face. His eyes widened and his mouth opened slightly, letting out an inaudible gasp.

"Hey, remind me, wasn't that you at the Carnegie Hall show with one of my tickets?"

"The Carnegie Hall *show*? He played one song, Doug. If I'd known I had to choose between that so-called show and Madison Square Garden, I would've definitely picked the Garden." With that I stormed off.

"Fuck you, you ungrateful asshole!" Doug yelled after me.

I turned back to him. "Go fuck yourself!"

The nerve of him! I didn't speak to that jackass again for the rest of high school.

Did I overreact? I suppose it's possible. Truth be told, I did end up scoring my own tickets to the show. But that's not the point. The point is I didn't invite some girl in a Hail Mary attempt to get her to like me. In fact it never would've occurred to me to invite a girl—the thought literally wouldn't have passed through my brain. This was way too important for that bullshit. How could Doug not get that? How could he so nonchalantly stab me in the back? As much as I turned it around in my head afterwards, I couldn't make any sense of it. Screwing me out of a Springsteen ticket was just plain unforgiveable.

Although, if I'm being completely honest, there may have been a touch of jealousy in the mix there as well. I *so* wished I had the courage to put myself out there with girls. But I knew I didn't have it in me. And there goes Doug walking like a free man through this thrilling landscape of desire I could only gaze at through barred windows. Man was I furious at him—and at myself.

13

LIKE FATHER, LIKE SON?

As I continued to plod along in the legal profession, my father's absence still gnawed at me, still made little sense, at times seeming slightly surreal, as if it'd happened to a different version of me, to some poor fatherless clone.

After he was diagnosed, my father drafted a letter to Rob and me which he kept under wraps until he died. One of his law partners reverently handed it to us at the funeral. Once home, after the last shiva guest had departed, I retreated to my room, locked the door, and sat down at my desk to read it.

I studied the unopened envelope, unsure how even to physically handle this correspondence from the netherworld. Ultimately, I laid it flat on my desk, touching only the corners to turn the pages so as not to smudge the ink, as if it were the original copy of the United States Constitution or some other sacred text.

Typical of my father, he'd written the letter on a yellow legal pad. It went on for seven single-spaced pages, methodically walking Rob and me through the diagnosis, the shock of it (he had no symptoms and felt fine), the critical need always to face up to the truth, not to hide from it. Apparently viewing the letter as a last opportunity to discharge his fatherly duties, he wrote about the "bywords" through which he'd tried to live his life: the importance of being a person of substance, of having integrity, and of always treating people with respect even if you disagree with them.

He then urged Rob and me to treat our mother with unconditional love, frankly admitting, "I think she stayed with a difficult marital situation which was not what she'd bargained for because of her love and devotion for each of you." He wrote that he loved our mother deeply and made "the terrible mistake" of not telling her that every day. "Don't make that mistake when you meet your Phylis," he wrote. "Don't be afraid to express your emotions, even though you think it's not 'macho' to tell your Phylis every day that you love her. Life is so short and unpredictable."

He then concluded by saying he'd made the same mistake with Rob and me. "I love you Robert; I love you Matthew, and I regret not having said so to you more often. I can't imagine having been able to live such a full and rewarding life without the two of you. As they say, you made my day. Thanks."

I folded up the letter and put it in my desk drawer. Then I cried. Hard and long.

Over the years, I've gone back and reread that farewell letter many, many times. I've regarded it from different angles at different times in my life, my reaction to it shifting in the way a canyon wall reflects ever-changing details through the arc of the day in response to the bending sunlight.

While the ritual invariably elicits tears, sadness, and feeling sorry for myself, for my father, for the time we no longer have together, conflicting emotions have risen in the shadows of my psyche as I've gotten older. I often wonder about the choice he made to focus so blindly on his career, relegating his family—relegating me—to second-class status. What the fuck was that about? How could he have done that? How could any father do that to his son? Other times I get caught up in what was the biggest bait and switch imaginable: he gets to tell me he loves me, but I don't get to tell him? How exactly is that fair? Then there's Soundgarden-obsessed me, directing a hefty portion of rage at him, offering up my best Chris Cornell primal scream until my throat aches. He tells me *in a fucking letter* that he loves me? He admonishes me not to be afraid to express my emotions when he himself was?

I've tried to console myself, to fend off those negative emotions. After all, just because he couldn't walk the walk himself shouldn't have irrevocably disqualified him from encouraging Rob and me to do better—in fact, his inability to express his feelings, his love, likely made him even more desperate to ensure that we broke from his example. And at least he took the time and effort to write a heartfelt message for Rob and me, right? But hang on a second—he didn't bother to do that for my mother? Apparently not. When I showed my mother the letter, she moved right past the part about how much my father loved her. "He didn't write me a letter," she said, shaking her head. It was hard to tell if it was a statement or a question. My father declares that he loves my mother deeply, that he made "the terrible mistake" of not telling her that every day. So why didn't he tell her that himself? Why are Rob and I the ones who have to convey that information to our grief-stricken mother, that our father loved her deeply? Why are her children the ones who have to assure her of that? What a fucking emotional coward.

One morning shortly before Springsteen became a father, his dad drove five hundred miles to deliver a personal message, face-to-face: "I wasn't very good to you," he confessed to Bruce as the two of them nursed beers in Bruce's dining room.

"That was it," writes Bruce. "It was all I needed, all that was necessary. I was blessed on that day and given something by my father I thought I'd never live to see . . . a brief recognition of the truth."

My father never voiced any regrets about choosing his work over me, of choosing largely to absent himself from my life. There was no admission of wrongdoing, no recognition of the truth—of my truth, anyway. Maybe the letter was his attempt at a *mea culpa*, inadequate as it was. Or maybe, like Bruce's father, he would've come around to see the error of his ways in due time, when the full sweep of his life—of our intertwined lives—was more plain to him. Maybe time just ran out on him.

Of course I recognize the letter as a wrenchingly beautiful, genuinely heartfelt gesture, understanding that my father was doing the best he knew how. And I treasure it as such, keeping it tucked away in a protective sheathing away from all sunlight, like a museum piece. But it also highlights his emotional limitations, limitations that I struggle to understand.

My father loved me, I'm sure, and I loved him, but that love was never acknowledged in any observable way—at least until that letter. Prior to that it was all subtextual love. And while I'm grateful for the love he did offer in his own flawed manner, I struggle with the knowledge that it would've been so much more meaningful to connect with him in the physical world, not via those cool, distant words jotted on a legal pad.

Why was he like that, why so emotionally stoic with his sons?

Of course, we're all products of our vastly different upbringings, the specific circumstances of our lives creating their own indelible, psychic imprints. But some inner emotional circuitry of the father-son relationship has shades of the universal, seems somehow endemic to it. I suppose it's standard Feminism 101 fare that men are not given cultural permission to publicly show much in the way of emotions. Rage is okay, disgust is okay, pride is okay. But emotions further toward the loving end of the spectrum, toward empathy and caring, are socially verboten.

I certainly felt an emotional distance from my father, a lack of emotional presence, communication, and connectedness. I felt it my whole life but particularly at the end of his. He never once brought up the fact he might die, never once gave me a pep talk, telling me I'd be okay, that he loved me. In many ways, he just pretended it wasn't happening. Which is pretty fucked up if you think about it. Of course, I didn't bring it up either, never told him how I felt about the whole thing, how unimaginable his dying was to me, how I'd sometimes wake up in the middle of the night all groggy, wondering if it was real, if it was just a dream, only to be jolted from my wishful slumber by a terror so complete that come morning my sheets would be soaked through with sweat. But I was just a kid. It was on him to take the lead on such conversations. He never did and so I was the one left to carry forever the guilt for leaving everything unsaid. The love I felt for my father was a powerful thing, but as with my feelings about his approaching death, I could never bring myself to express it to him. And neither could he express verbally his love for me. It wasn't his way and because I was his son, it wasn't my way. It saddened me that we were so utterly incapable of breaking through the invisible wall separating us. But the inertia of family was too much to overcome—I couldn't change and he couldn't either.

It was comforting to learn that my father and I were in good company. Springsteen couldn't access his father sitting there at the kitchen table smoking and drinking every night in "monk-like silence," writing, "As a boy I figured it was just the way men were." Ditto for Chris Cornell whose father would pour himself a drink after work and just sit in his chair for hours without speaking, a template Cornell believed was "just handed down through generations—that Irish Catholic drunkard kind of way of suppressing all your emotions."

The father-son relationship, it seems, is often defined by the presence of an absence, by an ache somehow both inchoate and tangible, that gets handed down through the generations like some unwanted old-world tchotchke. It all leaves me wondering whether my father's emotional stuntedness got handed down to him by his father. And whether it's been handed down to me?

My father's dad, my Grandpa Dave, lived just short of forever, so I got to know him very well. There was a regal elegance about Grandpa Dave, perhaps attributable to his large size—he was over six feet tall and probably weighed close to two hundred pounds well into his eighties—wire rim glasses, and the shock of white hair he kept until the day he died. That and the fact I rarely saw him without a jacket and tie. Although he'd been retired as a lawyer for decades, he still carried himself as if at any moment he might be called into court.

While I understood he'd been a successful and hardworking lawyer, I always thought of Grandpa Dave as a fun-loving type with a freezer full of ice cream and a terrific sense of humor. Like the time at a surprise party for his sixtieth wedding anniversary when he offered extemporaneous remarks to a packed house on how he knew he was getting old (pushing eighty-seven at the time, he was), the gist being that not only did he require periodic injections to help with "the expulsion of urine," but the injections had had a most unfortunate side effect: they hampered his ability to maintain erections.

Then there were the times he'd audibly pass gas in synagogue—which happened with stunning frequency—side-eye me deadpan and whisper, "tight shoes."

While I thought of Grandpa Dave as easygoing and funny, at the same time he exuded formality. He maintained a file containing various documents related to me, including all our correspondence, most of which took place while I was away at camp each summer between the ages of eight and fourteen. Ever the fastidious attorney, he made photocopies of his letters and stapled them to the corresponding ones I sent back. Shortly before my tenth birthday, he sent me a letter typewritten on his personal letterhead, letting me know that he would be in Florida for my birthday but wanted to buy me a bike of my choice. "Once the decision has been made as to the model," he wrote, "let me know the price and I shall send you a check, or if you can arrange to borrow the money, temporarily, from your father, I shall reimburse him."

You really have to admire all those commas, each one exquisitely placed, and the use of the formal "shall" instead of "will" with the first-person singular. But even more revealing is his fulsome explanation of the underlying financial transaction. Like I would've cared about that? Just show me the bike, man! You adults figure out how the money thing works.

Grandpa Dave closed the letter by expressing how proud of me he was, writing "You are neat in your personal appearance and orderly at home, including the manner in which you fold paper money." I get that Grandpa Dave placed a premium on physical appearance, but how I fold paper money? What's that even mean?

What side of Grandpa Dave did my father see? Did he ever see the humorous, fun-loving side of his own father that I did? How did Grandpa Dave's formality express itself in my father's upbringing? What effect did it have on my father's ability to express love? I certainly don't recall any bear hugs between the two of them. From what I could tell, their relationship was based more on a mutual respect, a shared appreciation for their respective professional accomplishments, than a deep well of familial love. I sat bored stiff through countless conversations about my father's latest corporate deals, the business world, and politics.

I remember as a kid seeing an interview on MTV in which Jerry Garcia says something along the lines of how he's passionate about music, art, and literature, "basically all the things that make life worth living," is how he put it. I don't recall any conversations between my father and grandfather about those things.

I got a clue of what it must've been like for my father growing up in Grandpa Dave's household from a memoir Grandpa Dave wrote when he was eighty-seven years old. The document is forty-three single-spaced typewritten pages. Of those forty-three pages, less than half a page, a mere six sentences, is dedicated to my father:

"Jimmy was born in December 1942. Jimmy was accepted at Hunter College Elementary School and continued until he transferred to Horace Mann Grammar and High School—a private school.

"Jimmy attended the Wharton School at the University of Pennsylvania and the Law School of NYU where he graduated with honors and made Law Review. He was awarded a Pomeroy Scholarship. He took an evening course for a Master's Degree in Securities Law.

"Jimmy married Phylis Polakoff August 20, 1967; the wedding took place at the Hampshire House on Central Park South, New York."

That's it. My father's life reduced to a clipped, dry as dust summation, utterly devoid of emotion or affection. No adorable stories of my father as a kid, no reveling in his foibles, no mention of family vacations. An appendix describing the exact location and coordinates of Grandpa Dave's burial plot (to which he repaired at the age of ninety-four), receives as much ink as my father.

He likewise summarily dispenses with my Grandma Gertrude, his wife of sixty-plus years, whom he bombastically describes as a "Health Education Supervisor for the New York City Board of Education"—in less flowery terms, a gym teacher. He writes that they dated for two to three years before getting engaged—no discussion of how they met or where, let alone what drew him to her, why he fell in love with her. It's all so bare bones.

Were these opaque accountings veiling some hidden family secrets? Did he struggle with his connection to his family like my father did with me? I could believe it because knowing Gertrude as I did, I can say with something approaching scientific certainty that their family life was not drawn from the idyllic set of some whitewashed 1950s sitcom.

Nobody ever knew how old Grandma Gertrude was—she protected that information like it was the nuclear codes. Or as Grandpa Dave put it in his memoir, "Grandma's age has as yet not been finally determined; her family records are vague and a birth certificate is not readily available." But my guess is that she was at least as old as my grandfather, if not a year or two older.

To a young kid, Grandma Gertrude was positively scary. She was a tall, heavyset woman with elaborately coiffed hair dyed in a light blond color that required frequent visits to the beauty parlor to maintain. Her approach to cosmetics definitely came from the "more is more" school. She layered on makeup so thick she looked like an immense, terrifying porcelain doll. Drinking glasses would emerge from the bowels of my grandparents' dishwasher still rimmed with her garish red lipstick. To top it off, she bathed herself in some vile, astringent perfume that could halt a charging rhino at forty paces. Her cartoon-villain death grip was virtually impossible to extricate oneself from; those pudgy fingers and sharp nails of hers would dig into my flesh like an eagle's talons locking down on some unsuspecting salmon as she commanded me to get her a glass of water or a sweater or to do some other mundane task intended to make her more comfortable.

Her personality matched her appearance. Grandma Gertrude once told me when I was only eight years old that I couldn't have dessert because, as she delicately phrased it, "You're fat." I'm no psychologist, but I'm guessing that comment left a mark. It certainly didn't help with my burgeoning feelings of body shame. On another occasion involving food, I asked if I could have a last piece of meatloaf. No, she said, she wanted it for herself. I suggested we split it. She declined my offer, shoveling the entire piece onto her plate. She routinely took quarters from my ceramic Snoopy piggy bank when she came to visit, saying she needed the money for the bus, and didn't ever restock it. She never once wrote me a letter—Grandpa Dave exclusively wrote to me, always indicating at the end that Grandma Gertrude joined in whatever he was saying. I never could figure what Grandpa Dave saw in her. And his memoir gives no clues.

Although living with Grandpa Dave could certainly have presented its own difficulties, when I imagine my father growing up in a household with his mother, I'm filled with such profound sadness, it's near unbearable. But it does allow me to see my father more clearly, to understand better his emotional limitations. I mean it's hard to picture "game night" around the hearth or singalongs in the family car. By that measure, my father's letter to Rob and me was a veritable emotional breakthrough. He did the best he could.

I wonder if my father internalized his own father's unease with family and if maybe that's what drove him to become a workaholic, a lawyer whose commitment to his firm was "nothing less than astonishing in its completeness, much more so than it was fair to ask of any one man (or several men)," as one of his partners put it in a letter to my father two months before he died. Maybe my father was hiding from his family through his work.

Although he races past his family life like the Number 4 express train past 77th Street, Grandpa Dave ably conveys in his memoir how he pulled himself up by his bootstraps through hard work and unflinching dedication. The first few pages read like some archetypal Hollywood script depicting the Jewish immigrant experience. Parents emigrated from Russia in the late 1890s? Check. Processed through Ellis Island? Check. Settled in the greater New York City area? Check. The father makes ends meet as a peddler and then dies before the son hits double digits? Check. Son holds day job to support his family while pursuing an education at night? Check.

After providing this early background, Grandpa Dave spends nearly the entire balance of his memoir discussing in excruciating, highly technical detail his professional life as a lawyer in the entertainment industry. Reading Grandpa Dave's memoir, with its nearly singular focus on work and career (he doesn't even mention World War II), it doesn't surprise me that my father was himself obsessed with work and climbing the corporate ladder. He followed his father's example and spoke a language he knew his dad understood. Cliché for sure but sad nonetheless.

And ironic. When he was fifteen, my father typed a note to Grandpa Dave apologizing for some undisclosed transgression. "I am sorry about what happened yesterday," my father wrote. "I was wrong and you were right." He then makes a plea of his father: "But some of the things I said I meant. I hope that someday you will devote a little more time to the family than you do now. I hope in the days to come that the family will be together more often. With these words I am trying to give you a child's advice. I am sorry again."

It's downright eerie how his letter reads just like the birthday poems I wrote to my father when I was a young boy encouraging him not to work so hard, except his note is even more pointed, not veiled in an awkward attempt at humor. If I were in the market for a life coach, I'm not sure I'd hire Chris Cornell, but I was moved and impressed to hear him once tell an interviewer, "whatever bad cycles there were, the next generation's job or responsibility is to try their best to break those things." That's spot on—the goal of the father being to break the cycle for his son.

My father, it seems, repeated it.

And maybe it's not so hard to understand why. I've come to believe that sons feel an almost primal need to forge connections with their fathers. It's a need that probably goes back to the cave man and is as strong as the need for fire. And as I learned from life coach Chris Cornell, that need endures no matter how horrible the father is to the son, which makes me feel better about my father's inability to break the cycle with me. Chris had an atrocious relationship with his father, an alcoholic prone to violence, a man Chris so despised that he'd eventually take his mother's maiden name of Cornell. Yet when Chris, who hadn't seen his father in over ten years, was asked in an interview, "If he came to you and said, 'I'm an asshole, I fucked everything up, I want my son back,' that would melt your heart, right?" Chris immediately replied, "Of course—I would absolutely forgive him." He didn't pause for even half a second. If that doesn't make the case for the enduring need of a son to forge connection with his father, I don't know what does.

My father, I'm sure, was no different; he wanted to feel close to his father, to feel recognized, appreciated, and loved. If that meant sidelining his family and working every day as if it were April 14 and he a CPA, well, that's what had to be done. And so that's what he did, as naturally and uncritically as Chris answered that interviewer's question, his high-flying career as a mergers and acquisitions attorney a subconscious journey to close the most important deal of all.

Twenty-two years after I graduated from law school, I was at work when a news bulletin flashed on my phone: Chris Cornell had committed suicide. I closed my office door and sat slumped in my desk chair, staring at the draft legal brief on my computer screen that had seemed critically important just a minute before but now seemed utterly superfluous.

I couldn't focus the rest of the day and left work early. I listened to *Superunknown* on the subway ride home but the ride wasn't long enough to get through the whole album so I walked around my block a few times before going inside.

Listening to the record all the way through for the first time in several years put me right back in my law school room, in full spiral mode. I felt my chest tighten and my heart race as I thought about my father. And I realized what a gift that album had been to me. Not only did its darkness give perfect expression to my own, but decades later it still allowed me to access that darkness, to honor it, granting me entry to that deepest, truest part of myself, the part that will forever define who I am, the part where a son never got to experience his father as a person, and where a father never got to know his little boy.

On Cornell's final album, there's a song called "Before We Disappear," which he said was about "letting the people that you love know that you love them because we're all gonna die pretty soon." The song's chorus begins with a question that likely haunted Cornell his entire life: "How hard can it be / To share your love with me?" My guess is he was asking that question of his father, but it's a question his three children might now ask of him. Sadly, the answer is, it's very hard.

14

JUST TELL THE TRUTH

One evening during my sophomore year in high school, I was in my room blasting the new Replacements' album, *Tim*. I'd picked it up on a shopping spree with Murphy in the Village the day before and was trying to sound out on guitar the chords to my favorite track on the album, "Left of the Dial."

My mom appeared in my room like she'd been beamed in from the Starship Enterprise. She'd probably knocked, but I couldn't hear her over the roar of the stereo and guitar. I saw the red lipstick around her mouth moving but couldn't hear what she was saying. She looked angry. She threw herself at the stereo and turned it off, leaving my guitar chords floating in the air, naked.

"Jesus, it sounds like a war zone in here! The windows in my room are rattling!"

I apologized. Told her I'd try to keep it down in the future.

"Brian is on the phone for you," she said, referring to Murphy. "Dinner's ready, so please tell him you'll call him back."

I gave Murphy a quick three-word review of *Tim* ("Fucking awesome, man!") and joined my mom, my dad, and Rob for a rare weeknight family dinner around our kitchen table. It was a special occasion when my dad made it home for dinner and I was excited to see him. It felt like a holiday even though I had school the next day. We had a large dining room but never ate in there, except for formal events. It was painted a dark shade of red and there was this huge oil painting depicting some long-ago battle displayed on the long wall. There wasn't any window to provide natural light, so it was always dark in that dining room. It had a spooky vibe to it, like maybe ghosts had taken up residence in there, making use of the long mahogany table and leather high-backed chairs to conduct their supranatural business.

To me the round table in the kitchen was a much more relaxing option. A small window above the kitchen sink looked out to the back of another apartment building and provided a classic New York City view of metal fire escapes and the exhaust grids of air-conditioning window units. The kitchen was lit by two banks of fluorescent lights. One of the lights was flickering and emitting a quiet hiss as I walked in.

"Wow, that light is really annoying," I said to nobody in particular.

"I know," my mom replied. "I called down to Mr. O'Sullivan this morning." Mr. O'Sullivan was the building's super. He handled all the maintenance issues for the tenants, including tasks it seemed that any homeowner should've been able to knock out on their own in under five minutes.

"Can't we just go to the hardware store on the corner and get a new bulb?" I asked. "It doesn't seem like we need to bother Mr. O'Sullivan with changing a lightbulb."

"It's too late for that now, the store's closed," my mom replied. "And anyway, Mr. O'Sullivan probably has hundreds of these bulbs downstairs. Let me call down and see where he is. He said he'd try to come up once he dealt with something in the boiler room. Apparently the east wing of the building didn't have hot water this morning."

"Forget about it for now," my dad said. "I'm sure he's gone for the day, it's eight o'clock." My dad, just home from work, had taken off his suit jacket, unbuttoned the top button of his dress shirt, and loosened his tie. Those were his concessions to being home for the night. There was no Mr. Rogers-like wardrobe change into sweats and a soft flannel shirt. I'd routinely see him at his desk at ten o'clock at night still in his suit pants with a tie dangling around his neck.

"Someone will be down there," said my mom. "This flickering is ridiculous. How long could it possibly take to fix a hot water boiler?"

"I bet quite a while," Rob said, stating the obvious. But my mom was already heading for the house phone in the laundry room just off the kitchen that linked directly to the lobby. She passed by our housekeeper, Pat, who was fishing oven mitts out of a kitchen drawer.

Pat was a tall, thin black woman from Trinidad, in her late forties. She had a breezy calmness about her that I associated with the Caribbean. Maybe it was the accent. Nothing flustered her, the opposite of my mom who was quick to blow. Pat was coolheaded. She was good-natured, always trying to be helpful. She responded dutifully to whatever my mom asked of her.

"What's for dinner, Pat?" my dad asked as he unfolded his paper napkin out on his lap.

"Eggplant parmigiana, Mr. Fogelson," Pat said as she served it up from the baking dish, a blue and yellow apron setting off her all-white pants, T-shirt, and sneakers. For some reason, Pat dressed like a nurse.

"Ah, the specialty of the house, excellent!" My dad leaned back in his chair to accept a serving. I'm not sure why, but Pat liked to cook Italian food. Probably thought we couldn't handle the island spices.

My mom totally resented that we all liked Pat's cooking better than hers. But there was only so much enthusiasm you could generate with my mom's signature meal: shake 'n' bake pork chops.

"How was school today, Matt?" Pat asked as she served me some eggplant.

"It was okay, although I got some bad news. We're reading *To Kill a Mockingbird* in English class and my teacher told us today that we're going to do a mock trial of Tom Robinson. I got assigned to be Atticus Finch, Tom's defense lawyer, so it'll be a lot of work."

"Jeez, I should have Pat ask you every day how school was," my mom interjected from the laundry room where she waited for someone downstairs to pick up the house phone. "That's more than you've told me about school all semester."

She wasn't wrong about that. My mom was on a need-to-know basis.

Pat bought me my very first rock album: *Escape* by Journey. The one with "Don't Stop Believin'" on Side One, Track One. She'd asked what I wanted for my twelfth birthday and that was a no-brainer. My mom's mouth got all tight when Pat presented me with the record. I guess she could tell I was more into it than the fancy electric pencil sharpener she and my dad had gotten me. I didn't hug them like I did Pat. Just gave them a polite "thanks." I mean it was cool how the pencil sharpener's red light lit up when the pencil was fully sharpened—how did it know?—but it wasn't freaking Journey's *Escape*.

"Can't you wait five minutes?" my mom called after me as I ran into my room to throw *Escape* on the turntable. "I want to talk to you about your birthday dinner—I made a seven o'clock reservation at Elio's." But I was gone. Cranked "Don't Stop Believin'" way up. I, too, was a city boy wanting to take a midnight train going anywhere. That sounded awesome, like a real adventure. My mom stormed into my room as the chorus swelled and told me to turn it down. Which was not unusual. But this time she added, "For crying out loud!"

Pat served us all another helping of eggplant and then went to fold laundry in the laundry room. My dad told me he thought it was great I'd been assigned Atticus Finch. "It's really important to be able to get up and speak in front of a group of people," he said. "It'll be good practice." That may well have been true for him, but me—I would've preferred to stick tacks in my eyes than be the center of attention.

My mom hung up the house phone and returned to the kitchen. "Well, Mr. O'Sullivan took off but José said he'd come up first thing in the morning."

"Okay," my dad said. "In the meantime, let's turn off that bank of lights. It's like a disco in here." Pat came in and hit the light. We continued to eat, now in semi-darkness.

"Jimmy, the Costume Institute's fundraising gala is next Thursday," my mom said as she took a fork to her eggplant parmigiana. "I'd really like you to come this year." My mom worked in the communications department at the Metropolitan Museum of Art's Costume Institute, drafting press releases, helping fundraise, and planning events. Before that, she'd been a kindergarten teacher at P.S. 145 on West 105th but had quit that gig when Rob was born.

"Next Thursday? I need to be in Houston," my dad said. "I'm really sorry."

"What's in Houston?"

"A meeting."

"What kind of meeting?"

"A board meeting."

"For what?"

"I can't tell you. It has to do with a potential merger. I can't talk about it publicly."

"I'm not the public."

"According to the SEC you are."

"That's just ridiculous. Are the cops going to come crashing through the door? Is the apartment bugged?"

"Mom," I interjected, "why do you care about the details? What difference does it make? He needs to be in Houston."

"You want Pops to get busted for insider trading?" Rob asked, piling on. "Anyway, I can go with you. I saw the flyer on the mail table. Looks fun."

"Nice try, Rob. You just want to go because Christy Turlington is the guest of honor." Christy Turlington was a supermodel who happened to be Rob's age. "And it's a school night so no way."

Rob gave a sheepish shrug of the shoulders.

"But maybe Matt can come with me," my mom said, brightening a bit.

"Last time I checked it's a school night for him, too," Rob protested.

"It is, but he knows how to budget his time to get his homework done. You don't."

Rob raised his eyebrows, his tell that he was planning an aggressive counterattack. Ever the peacemaker, I prepared to jump into the breach.

"I don't really want to go to the gala, Mom," I said. Which also happened to be true. Adult social events were real low on my priority list. My parents once held a fundraiser in Westhampton for a congresswoman and toted me around introducing me to everyone. Lots of direct eye contact. It was a nightmare.

"Why don't you want to go? You'll get to meet Christy Turlington. She's gorgeous." That just made me want to go even less. Being introduced to a supermodel sounded terrifying.

"I think you should consider going with your mother," my dad piped up. "It's important to her."

I looked at my dad shoveling away the eggplant. He was throwing me under the bus to save himself. Then I looked at Rob to take his temperature on all this. He shrugged his shoulders, apparently realizing that hanging with a supermodel for thirty seconds probably wasn't worth sitting through three hours of gala with our mom.

"Fine," I said, "but you can't introduce me to Christy Turlington. That's the deal."

Just then the phone rang. Our apartment was equipped with an extra telephone line that rang when somebody called my dad's office at the law firm, like a real-life Bat Phone. It allowed him to be available to his partners and clients 24/7. My dad put his fork down mid-bite and went to his study to answer it.

"Jesus Christ, Jimmy, it's eight o'clock," my mom said to his back as he hurried out of the kitchen, giving no sign he'd heard her. Pat put my dad's plate in the oven on "keep warm," filled our water glasses, and returned to folding laundry just off the kitchen.

"Speaking of that, Mom, you think we can let Pat go home?" I asked. "We can clean up dinner ourselves."

"Good point," my mom replied. "Pat, leave the laundry. We can take it from here. We'll see you tomorrow."

Pat thanked my mom and headed out.

"You guys know Grandma Toby and Grandpa Harry are coming to stay with us for Passover next week, right?" my mom asked, referring to her parents who lived in Hallandale, Florida, a strip of beach between Miami and Fort Lauderdale filled with high-rise condos and shuffleboard courts.

"Sounds familiar," I said.

"When's the seder again?" Rob asked.

"Saturday, the fourteenth," my mom responded.

"That's a problem," Rob said. "Maltby's having a big party that night. Kind of a spring fling."

"As much as I wish I could rejigger the Jewish calendar to accommodate Maltby's Spring Fling, it's just not possible."

"Actually, the party will go late. I can swing by after the seder."

"That's not happening. Grandma and Grandpa will be here. Plus, you can't drink beer over Passover. Beer's like liquid bread."

Having been to some of Maltby's parties, I knew Maltby would have a lot more than beer on offer. If he wanted to, Rob could definitely keep Passover.

"Whatever," Rob said. "And why does it matter if Grandma and Grandpa are here? Am I not allowed to go out that entire week?"

"After what happened last year, yes, you should be grounded for the week."

"What happened last year" was vivid in my memory. Rob's girlfriend at the time was creeping her way to the hallway bathroom late at night but decided not to turn on the hallway light. Why? Well, because she was naked. Grandma Toby was staying with Grandpa Harry in the spare room just off the hallway. She headed to the very same bathroom at the very same time as the naked visitor and also opted not to put on the hallway light—not sure what her reason was. She was having a hard time getting her bearings in the pitch dark of the windowless hallway so she walked with her hands out in front of her, mummy-style, to feel for the wall and the doorknob to the bathroom. Her hands eventually did find something round, but it wasn't the doorknob. Dual shrieks woke the household.

"I already did my time for that," Rob argued.

"Fair enough. But there are to be no girls over here that week. Grandma almost ended up in the hospital."

My dad returned from the Bat Phone and after finding his plate in the oven, retook his seat at the table.

"Jimmy, can you impress on Robert that there are to be no girls here when my parents come for Passover," my mom said. Rob had already conceded the point so I wasn't sure why she was asking my dad to relitigate it. "And in fact I think maybe we need to be clear going forward that there are no girls allowed in the apartment, period," she added.

"That sounds right," my dad said with little conviction. Didn't even look up from his plate. My mom stared at him, eyes wide. She'd given him a softball, the perfect opening to have a conversation man-to-man, maybe sprinkle in some fear-laced warnings around STDs and unwanted pregnancies. But he didn't take the bait—my dad liked to leave the parenting to my mom.

"Hang on a second," Rob said through a mouthful of eggplant. "I thought you said no girls the week Grandma and Grandpa are here. That's fine. But now you're totally changing the rules. 'No girls ever' makes no sense. Matt has girls over here all the time."

"The girls Matt has over are just friends," my mom said. "That's different."

It was sadly true. What was going on in Rob's room looked nothing like what was happening in mine, which was nothing—just sitting around talking and listening to music. But it stung that my parents assumed I wouldn't be hooking up with girls. I mean, I could've been.

"This is ridiculous!" Rob thundered in response to my mom's no-girls-in-the-apartment edict. "I can't wait to get the hell out of here next year. It's like a fucking prison!" He got up from the table and stormed down the hallway to his room.

"With your grades you'll be lucky to get into college!" my mom yelled after him.

The slam of Rob's door reverberated through the apartment like an earthquake's aftershock. As if on cue, the Bat Phone rang again and my dad disappeared. My mom looked down at her plate and finished eating like nothing had happened.

I cleared our plates and my mom joined me at the sink, helping to put the dishes in the dishwasher. She left as my dad came back in, and I watched to see which way she'd turn, towards the front of the apartment to her bedroom, or down the hall to rejoin the battle with Rob, to make some final point that wouldn't be final at all but would open up a whole new front of the war. It was a toss-up; I'd seen her go both ways in the past. This time, she turned towards her bedroom.

"Sorry about that, Tips," my dad said. "I had to deal with something quickly. Sit with me while I finish dinner." He made no mention of Rob's storming out of the kitchen. It was just as well. "What was going on at school today? Anything interesting?"

"Not really. We got crushed again in basketball. Collegiate beat us by like thirty points. But Coach Maxim still never put in any subs. I got no time."

"That's too bad. Sorry I missed the game, although it sounds like it was a good one to miss." My dad gave me a thin smile. He never made it to any of my games. It didn't really bother me since I knew he had to work. That my dad missed all my games just proved how important he was, which made me even prouder of him.

"Yeah, it wasn't worth anybody's time," I told him. "I'm actually thinking of quitting the team. It's a big waste."

My dad leaned back in his chair, raised his eyebrows. "Really? I know you're frustrated, but I've never thought of you as a quitter."

"I have to get up at 5:30 in the morning for practice, wait for the crosstown bus in the pitch dark, it's freezing out, and then I never get any time in the games. What's the point?"

"I get that, but you have teammates, and you made a commitment to them. If nothing else, they need you to be able to run practice. That's not nothing. How much longer is the season?"

"Like a month. No way are we making the playoffs."

"It's your decision, but I think you should stick it out for your teammates. It's not that much longer and it's important to follow through with your commitments. And selfishly, I'm still hoping to make it to a game, play a little hooky from work." My dad reached across the table and gave me a light punch on the shoulder.

I always treated my dad's advice like he was some kind of prophet. Senior year of high school I got caught up in a drinking scandal that unfolded during a three-day Model UN conference in Boston. There was no evidence I'd been drinking and I hadn't officially been accused of anything. But because I was the leader of the Model UN Club, the principal set up a meeting for the two of us to talk about the trip. I suspected I'd be asked whether I'd gone out drinking with everyone else, which I certainly had. I needed my dad's advice on how to handle the meeting. I'd just applied to colleges and was concerned how the episode would affect the process.

Although there was a pay phone at school, I left to call my dad from a phone booth around the corner. I was so paranoid I tried several times to jam the phone booth door all the way closed, but it was warped and wouldn't seal. As I waited for my dad's secretary to put me through to him, I watched the black exhaust of the buses rumbling down Columbus Avenue spiral skyward and disappear.

"Did you have anything to drink?" my dad asked after I'd been patched through and had given him the backstory. I could picture him in his corner office high above Park Avenue. I imagined him closing his office door, taking off his glasses, rubbing the bridge of his nose, and doodling mindlessly on a yellow legal pad—drawing boxes on top of boxes, as he often did when he was on the phone.

"Yes," I replied.

"Just tell the truth and everything will work out," he said calmly without any trace of alarm or disappointment. "Just go in there and tell the truth," he repeated.

I hung up the phone. I hadn't considered that approach. But when he said it, somehow it made perfect sense. I no longer felt anxious. Just go in, tell the truth, and let the chips fall. I'd never been in trouble before, so it seemed unlikely they'd throw the book at me anyway. I went into the principal's office and told the truth (well, mostly the truth—I may have rounded down the exact number of beers I drank). Although I was suspended for two days, my father was right: it did work out fine in the end.

But I wasn't sure about his advice to stick it out with the basketball team. I wasn't convinced my teammates would notice my absence. "I'll think about it," I told him.

I did think about it and decided to soldier on for the rest of the season. I never did get any playing time, though. And my dad never did make it to a game.

15

IT'S ABOUT EVERYTHING

The night before the seder, Murphy and some other friends and I caught blues legend Johnny Winter at the Beacon Theater. Johnny was a sight to behold—a spectral, rail-thin albino with fine white hair down to his waist, sporting a black cowboy hat that was itself cause for worry; strapped to the face of it were the heads of two snakes, mouths open and fangs primed. As my eyes adjusted to Johnny's alluring menace, my ears were treated to a blistering rendition of "Sweet Papa John," with Johnny taking the volume down a notch at the chorus and carefully enunciating each word so the assembled wouldn't miss the import of his tidings—that a candy cane he kept on his person was not only rock hard, but it dripped a certain sweetness, not unlike honey, that would leave any girl who tasted it invariably wanting more. A devilish smile peeked out from under Johnny's hat that should've rightfully curdled the blood of any man with a daughter over the age of, say, eight. Even though I was a fairly literal-minded kid, even I grasped the candy cane metaphor.

Returning home after the show I made my way quietly down the long hallway to my room. I was about to flip on the light when I heard a strange noise coming from the other side of the shared wall with Rob's room. I froze, standing there in the darkness, my finger suspended in front of the light switch. It sounded like a woman's voice, making guttural noises and panting. How could that be? Hadn't Rob been sick that night and stayed home? A series of short high-pitched primal exclamations confirmed it: there was definitely a woman in Rob's room. My head started to spin, this time not from beer. If I lived to be a thousand years old I couldn't imagine ever having the audacity to do what Rob was doing—I mean, my parents were just down the hall! And on some level I guess I was jealous, too, envied his boldness. But I also felt a trace of anger at Rob's complete disregard of propriety. Something just seemed so wrong about it, so disrespectful to my parents, to our shared physical space.

I plugged in my headphones to drown out the provocative noises, then lay down on my bed and turned on the radio, tuned as always to WNEW, New York's main classic rock station, just in time to hear the iconic conclusion of "Stairway to Heaven" and Jimmy Page's ferociously mournful guitar solo. I cranked the volume to ten and disappeared into the wall of sound, the total immersion helping to soothe my frazzled nerves.

"Stairway to Heaven" segued directly into a song I'd never heard before, but I could tell from the first words that it was Bob Dylan. As his distinctive, raspy voice spat those initial words, "Early one mornin' the sun was shinin' / I was layin' in bed," I was instantly drawn into the storytelling feel of it, like I'd suddenly found myself in some intriguing adult fairy tale.

There was a slightly unsettling quality present in those opening lines and I couldn't wait to hear how the setup played out. The lyrics were a little hard to follow, although it seemed to be about a relationship gone bad. But the sweep of the narrative was the cool thing about it; I felt like I was being transported to some faraway place in a long-ago era, with the music spinning sonic webs around the words. An unmistakable sense of adventure, danger, romance, and yearning swirled through the chords and verses of the song, enveloping me completely; I was mesmerized.

I must've fallen asleep soon after because the next thing I knew it was morning. I sat up in bed, fully dressed, and heard blissful silence from Rob's room. I hit the shower and was slipping on a dress shirt for the seder later that afternoon when Rob came into my room wearing a robe open at the chest like he was Hugh Hefner, his hair all disheveled. "Dice Man, have I got a story for you," he said, his voice still gravelly from sleep and being sick.

"I think I know how it ends," I told him.

Turns out, he'd gone to the video store down the street to rent a movie just as the store was closing. He and the clerk started to chat and I guess she told him the movie he planned to rent wasn't that great, that there was a better way to pass a couple of hours. Rob was game and so smuggled her into the apartment. They took the service elevator which opened into the laundry room just off the kitchen near the back of the apartment where our rooms were located, completely bypassing the danger zone at the front of our apartment. Crafty. He smuggled her back out the same way.

Rob retreated to the shower and I made my way to the kitchen. Grandpa Harry and Grandma Toby had arrived the day before from Florida and Grandpa Harry sat at the kitchen table reading the *New York Times*. My mom and Grandma Toby were huddled around the cutting board, collaborating on a brisket for the seder, chopping carrots and peeling potatoes. I could tell from the light on the phone console that my dad was in his study talking on the Bat Phone.

"How's my boy?" Grandpa Harry said, putting down the newspaper and standing up to give me a hug. Grandpa Harry was short, with a strong, lean, athletic build, skin heavily wrinkled and golden from years of exposure to the South Florida sun, light green eyes, and a strand or two of blond hair. "How was your concert last night?"

"Good," I said, hoping he wouldn't ask any more about it. I was still a little rattled by Rob's recounting of his evening. Not to mention that Johnny Winter's howling about his candy cane melting in some poor girl's mouth was still kicking around in my head. All of which seemed wildly incompatible with having a conversation with my grandfather.

A few minutes later, here comes Rob, all showered up and acting like nothing had happened the night before. He sat next to me at the table, a shit-eating grin spread across his face. "Whatcha got there, Dice Man?" he asked, snatching my bagel and taking a bite.

"Let Matt eat his breakfast," my mom said to Rob. "You can toast your own bagel."

Rob moseyed over to the counter to get a bagel.

"So, how was Johnny Winter?" Rob asked.

"Good," I mumbled through a glass of milk.

"Did he play 'Sweet Papa John'? I love that song."

"He did."

"'Sweet Papa John'?" Grandpa Harry asked. "That sounds familiar. I think I've got the sheet music for that in one of my books for the organ. Is it an old standard?" Grandpa Harry was the only family member with even a shred of musical talent. He had an organ loaded with all sorts of preprogrammed schlocky music that could be magically accessed with the push of a button—waltzes, polkas, other outdated mainstream drek from the Old Country. He'd play over these rhythms, his ancient body stiffly swaying back and forth with the melody.

"No, it's definitely not in your song book," I said trying to snuff out the discussion.

"Are you sure? What are the words to it?"

I stopped chewing my bagel and looked at Rob. He leaned back in his chair, his eyebrows raised ever so slightly. The usual low-grade post-concert ringing in my ears seemed to be getting louder.

"It's about a guy who likes candy," Rob said deadpan.

"Huh, that doesn't sound like the song I'm thinking of," Grandpa Harry conceded.

I changed the subject. "Hey, Mom, is Aunt Wendy coming over for the seder?"

"Yes, she should be here any minute, assuming she remembers," my mom replied with a roll of her eyes.

"Great," I said and got up to head back to my room.

"Don't forget to put on a jacket and tie for the seder," my mom called after me.

"Really?" I asked looking back over my shoulder. "It's just Grandma and Grandpa and Aunt Wendy."

"Hey, what are we, chopped liver?" Grandpa Harry asked smiling.

"Still, I think it'd be nice for us all to dress up some," my mom said.

She turned to Grandma Toby. "Ma, I assume you have something other than that *shmata* to wear?" Grandma Toby was wearing the same drab tan house dress with pink and yellow flowers she never took off when Rob and I visited my grandparents in Florida.

"Don't worry, Phyl, I won't embarrass you," she replied curtly.

Just then the doorbell rang, which set Rosie off barking and sprinting for the front door. "That must be Wendy," my mom said from over at the sink where she was washing carrots. "Matt, can you please go answer the door? I'll be there in a minute."

I hurried to the front door since I knew Rosie's barking would annoy my dad, who was still on the phone.

"Hey, Aunt Wendy," I said as I shooed Rosie away from the door.

Aunt Wendy, dressed in a blindingly bright pink and purple sundress, her hair all over the place, wrapped me in a bear hug that tested the starch of my dress shirt. The smell of the deep woods engulfed us both.

Releasing me, Aunt Wendy handed me a brown paper shopping bag. "A few more Dylan records," she said. "You'll dig these better than the last bunch."

A while back I'd mentioned to Aunt Wendy having liked Dylan's video for "Sweetheart Like You" on MTV. It was one of the first Dylan songs that bypassed all my prejudices about namby-pamby folk music and let me see the other sides of Dylan's music. The lyric, "Steal a little and they throw you in jail / Steal a lot and they make you king," stirred up my disdain for the economic order, sounding like something Joe Strummer could've written.

I guess Aunt Wendy had taken my passing mention of "Sweetheart Like You" to mean she'd discovered a fellow convert in the family circle because she broke into a huge smile and hugged me tight. "Oh, Matt, that's so great!" she squealed like I'd just told her I'd gotten into Harvard. On her next visit she brought me three or four old Dylan albums, the covers beat up, the edges frayed. "These are some of the essentials, to get you started," she croaked, her voice gravelly as sandpaper from years of smoking. "They'll get you to 1965, just before he went electric."

I gave her beat-up Dylan records a listen. The poetry of it was a little heady for me and the music way too folksy. Dylan, in my view, just didn't really rock. I eventually returned the records to Aunt Wendy, telling her I thought they were okay. The lightness went out of her eyes and her shoulders slumped. She seemed really sad, like *she'd* let *me* down and not vice versa. It was weird.

But apparently, she hadn't given up on me. "These are from his early electric period," she said gesturing at the brown paper bag that I'd put down on the floor. "They really do rock. 'Like A Rolling Stone' is on one of these." I thanked her for the records and was actually excited to give them a listen, hoping the tune I'd heard the night before might be on one of them.

My mom appeared from the kitchen and looked her sister up and down. "Gee, Wendy, aren't you cold?" she asked, fixing her gaze on the colorful sundress. "I'll get you a sweater."

"Phyl, it's seventy degrees outside."

"Yes, but it's chilly in here with the air conditioning," my mom replied even though it was early April and the air conditioning in our apartment hadn't been turned on for six months. "I'll be right back," she said and disappeared in the direction of her closet. Aunt Wendy shook her head almost imperceptibly and smiled.

My mom quickly returned with the outer-most layer of a white cashmere sweater set for Aunt Wendy to wear over her dress. Playing the good sport, Aunt Wendy put on the sweater and walked off to use the bathroom.

"We're going to start the seder soon," my mom said to me, "so please go put on a tie and jacket and gather everyone in the dining room.

"Come on, Jimmy, let's get started," she called out to my dad. "It's the weekend; enough already." My dad looked up from the phone, raised his eyebrows in annoyance, and held up five fingers. My mom sighed and headed to her bedroom to change for the seder.

After fishing a blue and yellow striped tie and navy blazer out of my closet, I made the rounds of the apartment and corralled everyone into the dining room. My grandparents and Rob exchanged hugs with Aunt Wendy.

Just then my mom walked in wearing a cream-colored leather

jacket, black pants, and high heels. A small diamond triangle hung from a gold chain around her neck. She sat at one end of the table; the other end was vacant, waiting on my dad. The rest of us filled in with my grandparents on one side and Rob, Aunt Wendy, and me on the other.

"How's work going, Wend?" Grandpa Harry asked as he poured himself a glass of water from a pitcher in the middle of the table. Aunt Wendy worked at an insurance company tied to the healthcare industry. It wasn't clear to me what exactly she did there.

"It's fine," Aunt Wendy responded breezily with a flick of the wrist that caused the several metal bracelets she wore to sound like wind chimes. "It's still paying the bills." She looked towards Grandma Toby. "Gee, Ma, those are great earrings. Where'd you get them?"

"Oh, these?" Grandma Toby tugged on the single pearl studs embedded in her ear lobes. "Aren't they nice? They're not real, though. I got them at a yard sale." Grandma Toby loved yard sales.

"I don't know about that, Ma. If you got the earrings at a yard sale, you've no idea where they came from," Aunt Wendy pointed out. "They could be real."

"Wouldn't that be something?" Grandma Toby laughed and put a hand over her heart.

"You should have them appraised, Mom," my mom said, laughing. "They could be worth a fortune!" She reached over and replaced a strand of Grandma Toby's gray hair that had fallen in her face from the laughing. Grandma Toby pushed her hand away. My mom smiled weakly.

"Yeah, then maybe when Dice Man and I come to visit we could actually eat dinner when it's dark outside instead of in the middle of the afternoon at some early bird $4.99 special," Rob said, only half-joking.

"Oh come on, Rob, it's much healthier to eat dinner early, it helps with the digestion," Grandpa Harry countered with a laugh.

My dad eventually showed up dressed in a dark suit with white pinstripes, like a Yankees uniform with the colors reversed. After saying hello to Aunty Wendy from across the table, he asked everyone to join in the traditional candle-lighting prayer to begin the seder. Unsure of the proper melody, we each chanted it differently and had to restart several times before getting on the same page. We were what's known as High Holiday Jews, ones who attended synagogue only twice a year. "Better hope God isn't listening," Aunt Wendy said with her signature laugh, a cackle that emanated from her nose as if she'd sneezed. I smiled but nobody else seemed to think it was funny.

"It's crazy," Aunt Wendy said when we reached the point in the seder where Moses demands that Pharaoh let the Hebrews go. "How many thousands of years has it been since the Jews escaped from slavery and yet freedom is still illusory, even in America."

My mom took the bait. "You seem fully capable of living freely, Wend."

Aunt Wendy ignored her. "I'm talking about freedom for minorities. It's just like in 'Hurricane.'"

"'Hurricane'?" my mom asked. "What are you talking about?"

"It's a Bob Dylan song."

I took a deep breath. My parents rolled their eyes.

"It's about a black man set up by the police and convicted of murder," Aunt Wendy continued. "It's a true story. He's still sitting in prison even though everyone knows he's innocent."

"Not everyone must think he's innocent," interjected my dad. "You know, sometimes the answer isn't just blowin' in the wind. Life's complicated."

"See, Jimmy, you do know some Dylan!" Wendy said triumphantly.

"Jesus, Wendy, can't we just once make it through dinner without talking about Dylan?" my mom implored her. "It's really not the stuff of adult conversation."

I could feel my shoulders slump and my head drop. I mean, I sort of got what my mom was saying about Dylan not being appropriate dinner conversation since all we ever talked about at family gatherings were serious subjects like Middle East politics or the economy. But at the same time, my mom's dissing of Dylan felt a little offensive. Aunt Wendy clearly thought Dylan was important and I could get that too.

"Well, I think discussions about injustice in this country are always appropriate," Aunt Wendy responded, "particularly in front of the boys." She turned to face me. "Not only is 'Hurricane' an important statement against injustice, but it rocks. It's on one of the albums I brought you. Let me know what you think. See if it speaks to you."

"Please don't get Matthew started with that business," my mom pleaded in vain.

"I'll check it out," I said softly, not looking at Aunt Wendy but down at my plate.

We got through the rest of the seder without any more discussion of Bob Dylan. Afterwards, we all said our goodbyes to Aunt Wendy and I walked her to the door.

"Give those records a listen," she reiterated as she gave me a tight hug. "I really think you'll like them." Figuring I had an opening since my parents weren't around to roll their eyes, I decided to pick Aunt Wendy's brain about the tune I'd heard the night before.

"Actually Aunt Wendy, there's a Dylan song I want to ask you about," I said as she released me from her hug. "I heard it last night on the radio. All the verses ended with the same line, something about 'blue.' It was like a long story or fable or something, hard to follow all the lyrics. Kind of mellow, acoustic, but it soared and swirled and had a great harmonica solo at the end. It was clearly Dylan but the DJ never gave the name."

Aunt Wendy's eyes became glassy. I thought she might start to cry. Trying to compose herself, she sat down on one of the twin green upholstered chairs in the foyer and took a deep breath. Then, in a hushed voice, like she was letting me in on some great secret, she said, "Matt, darling, that's 'Tangled Up in Blue.'"

Truth be told, her reaction freaked me out some. It seemed a little dramatic and I felt an urge to roll my eyes. But her response was also kind of intriguing. I mean, I loved music too, but it had never made me cry. Except maybe "Cat's in the Cradle." I'd teared up once or twice listening to that one.

After an awkward few moments of her just sitting there and me just standing there, not sure what to do, I broke the silence.

"What's the song about, anyway?" I asked.

She sat silent for a while, staring down at the floor. I saw her brow furrow and her eyes narrow. Then she got up from the chair, opened the front door, and rang for the elevator, her gaze fixed like she was in a daze. I wasn't sure if she was pondering my question or if maybe she hadn't heard it. But then the whirr of the elevator cable quieted, the elevator door slid open, and she stepped in, turned around, and murmured something just as the elevator doors began to close, something that stuck in my gut for a while after. She whispered, "Everything."

16

THE VAGABOND RAPPING AT YOUR DOOR

I floated somewhat aimlessly through the rest of high school on a wave of repressed sexual desire, beer binges, and concerts (with a fair amount of studying thrown in), heading down to Philadelphia a few times to see some shows with Rob who was in college at Penn. One night, our fake IDs somehow got us past the bouncers and into a bar to see the Ramones; I think I can date the onset of my tinnitus to that show, but it was worth it. They packed so much energy into their ferocious two-minute songs, bound them so tight, I thought the place might spontaneously combust.

I also saw my first Bob Dylan concert in Philadelphia when he played there with the Grateful Dead. By then, Dylan's music had seeped deep into my pores, his mystical and stirring lyrics the gateway to a deep appreciation of all his different sounds. Dylan opened the show with "Tangled Up in Blue," the first few notes of which got me all fired up, but it was underwhelming. I understand nobody throws on a Dylan record to get lost in his vocal stylings but hearing him sing live was a seriously grating experience. On top of that, he'd reimagined "Tangled Up in Blue" as a rocker, which it isn't. It was all so disappointing. I made a mental note to share my concerns with Aunt Wendy but never did.

On a decidedly more awesome note, I caught Lou Reed at Radio City Music Hall, and his rendition of "Sweet Jane" was full of bounce and vigor. Several months later I saw Stevie Ray Vaughn perform at The Pier on the Hudson River. He took the stage playing "Couldn't Stand the Weather" and I looked around for a second guitarist, incredulous that Stevie Ray made all that beautiful sound by himself. And junior year I cut class to stand in line for several hours to see the Jerry Garcia Band perform at a small theater on Broadway. Probably the most subversive thing I've ever done in my life, other than maybe standing up John's mom at that Clash concert.

For his part, Murphy continued to play with The Amazings, his social life revolving exclusively around those guys. By the beginning of eleventh grade, we'd started to drift apart. He kept to himself and to his inner circle, which no longer included me. He'd begun smoking pot—a lot of pot—which I wasn't into. The drug scene scared me some, having drunk the Kool-Aid on offer in health education class about how pot caused birth defects. I'd occasionally run into Murphy at parties and he'd be totally wasted, completely out of his mind, his eyes red and expressionless, his speech reduced to a withdrawn whisper. He grew his jet-black hair long, past his shoulders, and dressed like R.E.M. guitarist Peter Buck, always sporting a black suit vest and bolo tie. To the (now) outside observer, he'd adopted a nihilistic attitude towards the world—the hell with everybody, everything is bullshit. There was this dark cloud that followed him everywhere and we could all see it. According to the editors of our senior yearbook, Murphy's theme song was Phil Collins' "I Don't Care Anymore," and his catch phrase was, "Everything sucks."

After we graduated high school, I never saw Murphy again.

While Rob and I may have been the first generation in our family to attend a concert (other than Aunt Wendy, of course), I also enjoy the notable distinction of being the first in my immediate family not to attend an Ivy League university. I'd been accepted to Penn, where my dad had gone and where Rob was now a sophomore, and my mom badly wanted me to go there. But I decided on Duke University—perhaps not the biggest rebellion a son has ever visited upon his parents, but still. Asserting my independence felt like a pivotal moment of autonomy to me.

The essay prompt for the Duke application was to write about the most significant innovation of the twentieth century. I argued it was pop music—loosely defined. I wrote that music's ability to bring different types of people together—a prerequisite for overcoming societal prejudices—was unmatched and cited a typical Grateful Dead concert as proof positive, a place where you'd find old-timers "in their fifties" along with infants in diapers, Wall Street yuppies and pan handlers, drug addicts and valedictorians, all coming together in perfect harmony. I contended that if Shakespeare came back to life to recite *Hamlet* in Central Park, the crowd would be uniform in comparison. I also touted music's ability to shine a spotlight on pressing social issues, giving a shout-out to Bob Dylan, Aunt Wendy style. I closed the essay by noting that music "is a release for people," citing myself as an example, writing that "I lock myself in my room for hours and do not stop playing guitar until I am physically exhausted"—a slight exaggeration, but hey, I was trying to get into college! "So while some might talk about the computer or the telephone," I concluded, "on serious inspection it becomes obvious that, socially and spiritually, pop music is the most important innovation of the twentieth century."

Reading that essay now, I realize how important music was to me then—not just that I enjoyed music, which I've well understood for a long time, but rather that it was a vital part of who I perceived myself to be. But I also sense in the essay an effort to ridicule that part of myself, to undermine it by placing it in the context of a tongue-in-cheek essay that insinuates the absurdity of the position taken. It all makes me want to hug that kid and tell him he's on the right track, that it's okay to take music seriously, to embrace that part of himself.

My mom was devastated by my decision to attend Duke. She'd gone to Cornell and wanted me to attend an Ivy League school as well.

"Are there even any Jews in North Carolina?" she asked exasperated.

For his part, my dad thought it was great I wanted to go to Duke, to chart my own path. So did Aunt Wendy. She wrote me a note congratulating me on my "self-determination" signing off with a Bob Dylan quote: "If I'd-a paid attention to what others were thinkin', the heart inside me would've died." I knew the lyric well; it was from one of my favorite Dylan tunes, "Up To Me," and Aunt Wendy's invocation of it resonated in my gut, so much so that I checked the Pavlovian eye-rolling that came on every time Aunt Wendy referenced Dylan.

Late in my freshman year, Aunt Wendy sent me a package. I hadn't heard from her since her letter congratulating me on my decision to attend Duke. I stood in line at the campus post office to retrieve it, wondering what she could possibly be sending me. Knowing Aunt Wendy, I figured it was probably pot brownies, but instead the clerk handed me a small, padded envelope.

Inside was a cassette tape of a rare cover of Dylan's "It's All Over Now Baby Blue" sung by Van Morrison. She included a note: "I heard Van's version in approximately 1964 before I even heard of Bob Dylan! When I went to college (1966) my roommate played 'Baby Blue,' this time sung by Bob himself. I thought it was a goof (laughed real hard!). But my roommate swore he was for REAL! Sooo, I listened up and started to appreciate the difference of his sound and what he had to say—a real mindblower for me, and in a sense Bob's been a great friend for the past thirty years."

Cassette in hand, I beelined straight back to my dorm room jazzed to hear the song, one of my favorites of Dylan's. By this time, I'd become increasingly captivated by Aunt Wendy, in part due to her robust support of my blowing off the Ivy League but also because I'd finally worked out the big family mystery that helped explain so much about the tension always present at family gatherings: Aunt Wendy lived with a married couple, and when I say lived, I mean, really lived—she'd been in the threesome relationship nearly her entire adult life.

Now I'm not saying the revelation was on par with, say, Pearl Jam's Eddie Vedder finding out at age fifteen that the person he thought was his father was actually his stepfather. But when I did finally connect the dots, certain things about my childhood started to come into focus, like why Aunt Wendy was rarely seen or heard from, why she always arrived alone, and why my parents were so dismissive of her when she was around.

I wouldn't say I now felt close to Aunt Wendy—just more open to her. I'd started to see her more as a person, as an individual, rather than as some undifferentiated background character in my own personal family drama. And even more than that, I started to see her not just as any person, but as one with whom I shared a deep passion for music, a passion not shared by my parents or by anyone else I knew from their generation. Part of me was curious about her, how she could be so different from my parents, and it struck me that I had no idea at all what her day-to-day life was like—we'd never gone to visit her even once.

As I walked past the main library towards my dorm, my mind filled with imagined images of Aunt Wendy's life. I pictured her at her house in upstate New York, a house I'd never seen, her green VW Beetle parked on the sidewalk. I imagined Aunt Wendy sitting barefoot and cross-legged in front of the stereo in one of her trademark colorful sun dresses. A window looking out to a back garden is open, siphoning off the smoke from the joint Aunt Wendy is toking on. She serenely places a pair of ratty old headphones with ripped ear pads spewing yellow stuffing over her wild brown hair, hits some buttons on the stereo, and closes her eyes.

This looks familiar to me; it's the same scene that played out in my own room hundreds of times growing up—minus the joint toking, of course. I recognized that state of immersion, of connection, of disappearance. It struck me that for all the things Aunt Wendy and I didn't have in common, for all our differences, we shared the ability to know enough to revere that space, to both lose ourselves and find ourselves in the solace of music.

The cassette! I picked up the pace back to my dorm room. When I got to my room, my roommate sat at his desk ostensibly studying, although the two empty beer cans next to his open textbook suggested some multi-tasking was taking place.

"Hey, Tom, you mind if I pop in a tape real quick?"

"Sure, bro, no problem," he replied without looking up from his book. "Grab a beer while you're at it. You know how I hate to drink alone," he added straight-faced.

I cracked a beer and slipped the tape into the stereo.

"Is that Van the Man covering Dylan?" Tom closed his book and fished another beer out of the mini fridge.

"Indeed it is. You've got a good ear."

"Wow, that's pretty wild. Where'd you find that?"

"My crazy flower-child aunt sent it to me," I said, immediately feeling bad about my characterization of her.

"That's solid. My aunt sends me newspaper articles about chess."

"You play chess?"

"Not since middle school."

As I listened to Van Morrison's version of "It's All Over Now, Baby Blue," I wondered what kind of instrument gave it its trippy vibe. It sounded like a cross between a xylophone and an electric piano. I wondered if Aunt Wendy knew. Then I heard Van sing one of those classic Dylan lyrics, the eerie mysticism of which I could never quite wrap my head around: "The vagabond who's rapping at your door / Is standing in the clothes that you once wore." Hearing the lyric this time around made me wonder if Aunt Wendy was the vagabond rapping at some inner door deep in my psyche, ferrying me some urgent message, and if so, what it might be. It also made me wonder if she and I were somehow cut from the same cloth, wearing the same proverbial clothes—and what it'd mean if we were. Was I the person I thought I was? Or was I pretending to be someone I wasn't?

Although at times I may have wondered who I really was, I was pretty sure of one thing—I wasn't an outlaw. That notion got tested one night freshman year when Jodi and I got pulled over at 2 a.m. in rural North Carolina. A bunch of us were returning to campus from the South of the Border roadside attraction on the North Carolina–South Carolina border when my friend Seth, who was driving the lead car of our small caravan, stopped by the side of the road to take a leak. While relieving himself, he noticed a large plastic pink flamingo lawn ornament in the front yard of a nearby house and apparently that flamingo made quite an impression on him because he went into the yard, grabbed the thing, and threw it in the trunk of his car.

"Did Seth just steal that flamingo or am I hallucinating?" I asked Jodi sitting next to me in the passenger seat.

"No, you're good," Jodi replied. "He definitely stole it."

"Huh, interesting," chimed in my friend Tim from the back seat.

Five minutes later, flashing red lights appeared behind my car. I pulled over.

"Shit," I said under my breath. The homeowner, despite the late hour, had obviously witnessed Seth's delinquency and called the cops. I was a little freaked out because although I didn't have a stolen plastic flamingo in my car, I did have a stolen plastic pelican—Tim had nabbed it from South of the Border two hours earlier. For some reason, South of the Border had a menagerie of fake, life-sized animals lining its grounds and Tim thought the pelican would be a nice memento of our excursion.

"This isn't good," said Tim as the officer lingered for a moment in his squad car, no doubt running my license plate through the system. "You think we should come clean about the pelican?"

"He's not looking for a pelican, he's looking for a flamingo," replied Jodi, exhibiting the precise analytical thinking that would serve her well in law school.

"I'm not sure the cop will be able to make that distinction at two in the morning," countered Tim.

"Have you ever seen a pelican?" Jodi asked, glancing at Tim over her shoulder. "They couldn't look less like flamingos. We may as well have a salmon in the trunk."

"I think we may be missing a larger point here," I interjected. "What if he asks why we have a large plastic pelican in the car? Seems like that might strike him as unusual."

"He's not going to ask about the pelican," Jodi said confidently. "He's looking for a flamingo."

I wasn't so sure about that but decided to just play it cool, like there was nothing weird about having a life-sized plastic pelican in my car, should the cop ask about it.

The license plate check completed, the officer came up to my window and shined his flashlight in my face, temporarily blinding me.

"You wouldn't happen to have a plastic flamingo in your trunk?" the officer asked as he moved his flashlight all around the inside of the car.

"No sir," I said, my voice quivering a little.

"You mind if I take a look?"

I told him to go ahead. I looked in the rearview mirror at Tim in the back seat. He met my gaze and our eyes locked in a "this could get ugly" kind of way. I glanced at Jodi in the passenger seat. She was calmly staring straight ahead. The officer moseyed on back to the trunk, popped it open, and moved his flashlight around the inside. He spent quite a while back there and I could hear him moving the pelican around some, no doubt trying to make sense of the thing. *We are so busted*, I thought.

The officer came back around to my door, shone his flashlight in my face, sighed, and said, "Well, there ain't no flamingo in there, son, so I 'spose you're free to go."

"Thank you, sir," I said catching a peripheral view of Jodi grinning.

Jodi and I, now full-fledged partners in crime, became partners in the real world and started dating at the beginning of our sophomore year. In our first days together, the logistics of being in a romantic relationship were as foreign to me as the seasonal droving of cattle from river valley to high mountain pasture. Could I make plans with my friends without first consulting Jodi? Apparently not, since "we" sometimes had plans I didn't know about. And was I allowed to go a day without at least talking to her on the phone? Again no, although what people were supposed to talk about when they'd just had a long conversation the day before eluded me. Were we supposed to hold hands as we crossed the Quad? Judging by the way Jodi violently slapped my mitt away, I gathered the answer to that one was also a definite no.

Jodi was and still is a strong-willed Midwesterner. She's from Cleveland, very sure of herself, and extremely sensitive to the plight of others, with a tendency to treat every injustice as cause for a federal lawsuit. While Jodi influenced me in certain humdrum ways, like helping me to become a feminist and overall critical thinker, I influenced her in more profound ways, like igniting in her a love of eggplant parmigiana, and, most importantly, helping to hone her musical tastes since her passion for music did not, shall we say, match her passion for justice. Hell, when she arrived at Duke, she'd never heard of the Grateful Dead! How's that even possible?

"Have you ever heard of William Shakespeare?" I asked, incredulous.

"Yes, asshole," she replied, apparently not fully crediting the point I was making.

I deeply admired Jodi's forcefulness, her take-charge attitude. She once cut off nearly all her long, dirty-blond hair and then dyed what was left burgundy red. I barely recognized her. Even though we'd been dating for a few years by then, she didn't tell me she was going to do it. Just showed up as a different person. As shocking as it was, I had to admit it was a huge improvement over her big Midwestern perm. She looked downright cosmopolitan.

I was also particularly grateful for Jodi's assertiveness when it came to sex since I had long ago locked myself in a jail cell of sexual ascetism.

One day shortly after we started dating, she announced she was going on the pill.

"You know we haven't had sex yet," I lamely said, a little confused.

"I know, but we're going to," she replied with the certainty of the sun rising in the east.

Her pronouncement was welcome. And prescient. We did have sex—a ton of sex as it turned out.

But I first had to overcome an initial squeamishness bordering on terror about the whole deal brought on by my one prior experience with actual intercourse. I was away at summer school after eleventh grade and had started hanging out with a girl I had nothing in common with—a daughter of a minister from somewhere deep in the Jersey suburbs whose favorite musical artist was Bach (and not Skid Row's Sebastian Bach, mind you). Yet for some reason I was attracted to this girl. Sure, it could've been her strikingly blond hair or perfectly proportioned body. Or her dazzling intellect—she read books by philosophers I'd never heard of and whose names I couldn't even pronounce. Kierkegaard? But I wonder if some small part of the attraction was her status as a minister's daughter, if that made me feel safe, as if things couldn't possibly go too far. If so, it was a miscalculation.

Towards the end of the summer we found ourselves in my dorm room in a compromising position with her naked on top of me—I was naked as well except for a condom—when my roommate busted in and threw on the light. Of course the obvious thing for him to have done in that unfortunate situation was to mutter some lame excuse of an apology, turn off the light, and quietly back out of the room, closing the door behind him. But instead, this guy lets out a riotous holler, as if he'd never seen anything funnier in his life, walks over to my bed, pulls the sheet off of us and slaps the girl on her bare ass. Whack! He then walks out without bothering to turn the light off. Was he drunk? Probably. Was he high? No question. But still, come on, dude. Show some human decency.

I must say, that incident was rather traumatizing. Looking back, I recognize it as a perfect storm. Uncomfortable about sex to begin with, thinking my desire was something to be ashamed of, something to be hidden away, and then here I am finally letting myself go and in waltzes this guy who exposes me in every possible way—yes, physically, but more importantly he exposes the sexual desire I desperately tried to keep secret, literally shining a light on it. And then he laughs at me, at what I'm doing, bringing down the shame truncheon on my naked state with stunningly brutal force. Not exactly how I pictured my first experience would go.

Of course, I had no fear of Chris acting so bizarrely should he ever walk in on Jodi and me, but that episode did make me feel even more self-conscious going forward. Happily, Jodi's take-charge attitude put me at ease and after we had sex a few times, I was no longer haunted by the sound of my erstwhile roommate's open hand making violent contact with smooth, bare skin. Mercifully, my other senses took over as I luxuriated in the sight, smell, taste, and feel of my body interlaced with Jodi's.

17

A DOG FOREVER CHASING ITS TAIL

Jodi and I dated for the rest of college and all through law school as well. She was with me every step as I navigated the nightmare of my father's cancer diagnosis and subsequent death, giving me a sense of being loved, of being deeply cared for.

Jodi spent the summer after our sophomore year in college abroad, taking economics classes in Amsterdam. While she was away, I put together a mix tape for her which I called "The Matt-in-Mourning Mix." I loaded that tape with all sorts of mushy love songs—Dylan's "You're Gonna Make Me Lonesome When You Go," Springsteen's "Drive All Night," U2's "The Sweetest Thing." I drafted handwritten liner notes explaining my reasoning for including each song—it went on for six single-spaced, legal-sized pages, nearly as long as my father's farewell letter to Rob and me. I waxed poetic about the Rolling Stones' "Moonlight Mile," telling Jodi that, as in the song, maybe she and I were just a moonlight mile down the road from each other, and how that didn't seem all that far at all. Jodi loved John Waite's "Missing You," so I included that one, writing that "my worst nightmare is having my headphones on one night and missing your call. Corny? I guess, but so is most of John Waite's music."

I also put on "Cat's in the Cradle." This was the summer after my father broke the news of his diagnosis and was starting to show the ill effects of the chemotherapy treatments. I told Jodi that I included the song for me, that I felt as if it encapsulated my relationship with my father. "I realize that my dad may not make it to retirement or meet my kids," I wrote, "and so I understand that I have to start making a bigger effort with him. And that's what the song is about: making time for people you care about. Because whether you live to be one hundred years old or not, time is slippery. I love my dad so much, Jodi. It's tough. When I look at him, I get frightened. He is very sick."

Jodi wrote back that as much as she missed me, she was glad I was home and able to spend time with my father, to talk with him. Of course, I never really did talk with him. Despite my understanding that I needed to start making a bigger effort with him, I didn't. I couldn't. As I put it in another letter to Jodi that summer, "I think it's that despite everything I've said and written to you, the *real* possibility of his dying hasn't hit me. It's just some hazy notion, far off somewhere." The whole thing was just too crazy to comprehend, to truly absorb. And then he died and even then, it was still too crazy to comprehend, to truly absorb.

One night during law school, eighteen months after my father died, I woke up with a start in the middle of the night. I'd had a nightmare that Jodi had been in a car accident. I suppressed the urge to call her at Georgetown, to make sure she was okay, and instead got out of bed, fumbled around for a pad and pen and found myself composing a poem to her at my kitchen table. According to a note I included at the top, it was 3:40 a.m.

Today it was snowing. I knew you were driving. I thought about life without you. I wanted to pull my hair out. And to stop.
Today it was snowing. I knew you were driving. I felt like I was falling through the emptiness of complete darkness. Please, don't take another.
Today it was snowing. I knew you were driving. I need to sleep without pain.

Perhaps the most striking thing about the poem (other than its painful amateurism) is that I actually sent it to Jodi! I could open up to her like nobody else, could lay bare everything to her. She was my rock, a constant source of emotional support, once writing to me during law school about how she'd bought a sunflower, about how captivating it was, "its blazing petals give way to an intricately patterned center that is dark but dusted with pollen. It has the uncanny quality of a vortex. I stare at it and can imagine myself being sucked in and transported to some other world—someplace beautiful, with waterfalls, mountains, springs, and wildflowers—a world where I can sleep by your side and where you awaken cognizant not only of the fact that I'm only inches away from you, but also of the fact that you cannot remember the last time you had a nightmare."

After dating for eleven years, Jodi, who'd long opposed getting married since marriage was "a male-created institution designed to subjugate women," had a change of heart. "I think my grandmother and your grandparents would really like each other," she said to me one night as we walked to dinner. We were on the Taft Bridge in Washington and had stopped to gaze down at Rock Creek as it meandered some one hundred feet below us through the gaping Rock Creek Gorge. I wasn't sure what she was getting at and must've looked confused. "Maybe getting married wouldn't be the worst idea in the world," she said by way of explanation, still staring down at the creek, as if she was contemplating taking not just the proverbial plunge but an actual one. And that was that. There was no getting down on one knee, no presentation of a ring, no asking her father for her hand. There may have been a brief kiss, a squeeze of the hand. We did eventually get each other engagement gifts, though—I got Jodi a gold sun face pendant to symbolize the light she brought to my life, and she gave me an antique pocket watch, explaining that she wanted to spend the rest of her time with me.

I made several weekend trips from Washington to New York to hash out wedding plans with my mother since the ceremony was going to be held at our house in Westhampton. One night as we ate dinner at the kitchen table, Chinese food boxes forming a not-so-great wall across the table, my mother asked if she could invite one of her good friends to the wedding. Although Jodi and I were limiting the wedding to immediate family and a few close friends, I told her of course she could. Without my father there, she was definitely entitled to some support.

"Actually, I've been wanting to talk to you about the guest list," I said, sensing an opening. "I want to invite Aunt Wendy's friends."

My mother's jaw dropped like she was some freakish cartoon character come to life. "Her friends? Are you talking about Warren and Carole?"

"Yes," I said, although until that moment I hadn't known their names. Just to be sure I added, "You know, the married couple?"

"Yes, I know who they are! Have you lost your mind? Why would you do that?"

It was a fair question; I'd never even met them. Maybe it was because I wasn't all that happy as a lawyer, and Aunt Wendy and her admonishment to follow my heart, delivered in the kitchen after my father's funeral, loomed in my subconscious. Maybe after my father's death I felt a need to draw closer to family. Maybe it was Jodi's lefty political sensibilities rubbing off on me. Whatever the reason, the seething emotion accompanying my mother's response annoyed me.

"It seems like the right thing to do," I replied. "Aunt Wendy's a member of our family, you know."

My mother shot me a look that was equal parts confused, hurt, and furious. She slammed her fork down on her plate. "I am well aware of that," she said, enunciating each word slowly and clearly.

I knew I'd screwed up. She took a deep breath. "I am quite aware that Wendy is a member of the family. You know how I know? For one thing, it was me who always bailed her out of jail. Did you know Wendy spent time in jail?"

I shook my head, incredulous both that Aunt Wendy had been to jail and that I was just now finding out about it. Yet another mystery of Aunt Wendy's past revealed.

"Well, she has. She got pulled over once for speeding and of course she had pot in the car. And then to top it off, she resisted arrest. Called the cop a pig and said he had no right to search her car. They took her straight to jail. I had to drive up there in a snowstorm with an infant and a two-year-old, go to the county jail, pushing the stroller through the snow. So, yes, I'm well aware that Wendy is a member of my family."

"Okay, relax, Mom. I didn't mean it that way."

I was actually impressed by Aunt Wendy sticking it to the police. Just looking at her in her sun dress and hippie sandals you'd never know she was such a badass. Joe Strummer would've been ecstatic! Knowing my mother's long-standing antipathy to Aunt Wendy's eccentricities, I figured I should keep any admiration I felt for my wayward aunt to myself and so suppressed the urge to ask about the other times she'd been thrown in jail. "I'm only saying it doesn't seem like such a big deal to invite her friends," I offered meekly.

"Do you want your grandparents to attend your wedding? Because they won't if those two are there."

I hadn't anticipated that angle. "That seems a bit extreme, doesn't it?" I asked.

"Matthew," my mother said, her use of my full name signaling some dark family secret was about to be communicated, that and the fact her eyes narrowed down to slits. "My mother once considered hiring a private detective to kidnap Wendy and take her to Florida, like she was in a cult or something. So yes, I'd say it's an extreme situation."

"You can't be serious."

"I'm dead serious. My father was able to talk her out of it, thank God."

"Wow, I'll need to think through all that," I said.

"While you're thinking about it, think about whether you're really doing this for Wendy or just to make a political statement."

True to family form, I didn't think all that hard about standing up for Aunt Wendy. I dropped it without a second thought. And so Aunt Wendy attended my wedding alone. As she would Rob's wedding a year later.

My capitulation, so swift and complete, still eats at me. It seems like I should've pushed a little harder, maybe at least asked my grandparents directly if inviting Aunt Wendy's friends was a deal-breaker for them. Sure, it would've been an awkward conversation, especially since I'd not once spoken to them about Wendy's situation—I wasn't even sure they knew I knew about it. But I have no doubt my relationship with my grandparents would've survived the conversation.

We were all adults, after all. While I could argue cases to juries and intimidating, black-robed federal judges, I was apparently too squeamish to argue Wendy's case to my own family.

Confronted with my mother's righteous anger and my own surrender, I wondered where my mother's disregard for her sister came from—a disregard that was instilled in me as a kid through osmosis and that as an adult I disdained in my mother and in myself but was too weak to overcome.

I used to assume, somewhat uncharitably, that my mother's beef with Wendy was the product of classism—that maybe Wendy reminded my mother of their humble suburban Long Island roots, and that she felt ashamed or embarrassed by Wendy as she tried to fit in with the city's upper crust. But more recently I've come to think my mother may simply have been jealous of Wendy. Jealous as a kid of my grandparents' perceived favoritism towards Wendy, with Grandma Toby telling my mother that because she was tall and "willowy," she could wear inexpensive clothes from the department store sale rack, but because Wendy was short, she needed more fashionable outfits from the designer stores; or my grandparents' paying more attention to Wendy because Wendy needed help, both academically and socially, while my mother made her way just fine and was given a freedom that she experienced not so much as freedom but as neglect; or my grandparents' willingness to give Wendy a pass, often at my mother's expense. When Wendy did poorly in school, Grandma Toby blamed my mother and her good grades. "What do you expect?" my grandmother asked my mother. "Wendy knows she can't compete with you."

And jealous as an adult of Wendy's ability to live life on her own terms—and to do so apparently quite happily—while my mother remained mired, as my father put it in his letter to Rob and me, "in a difficult marital situation which was not what she'd bargained for." That my mother never came first—either in her own family as a kid or in our family as an adult—may have caused her to resent Wendy's ability to live freely in her own skin.

At bottom, I don't think my mother could ever really understand or accept the privileged status her parents bestowed on Wendy. It was my mother who as a girl never got in trouble, graduated from an Ivy League university, and checked all the boxes of a "successful" traditional life—getting married, having kids, achieving social status—while Wendy was a fixture in the principal's office (mostly for smoking and bad grades), dropped out of community college, and lived a life her own parents perceived as scandalous. Yet my mother felt it was she who could never win—even as an adult my grandmother would give her a hard time for not being a good cook, her not-so-subtle way of ridiculing my mother's Upper East Side lifestyle.

The whole deal makes me sad for my mother. On top of which, understanding the fault lines that at times destabilized my mother's relationship with her sister makes me think it wasn't just Aunt Wendy who deserved a better shake from me—my mother did, too. I was quick to blame her for everything, to think the worst of her, whether it was her yelling at my father or rolling her eyes at Wendy or dispatching her interior decorator to Paris to scour the nooks and crannies of the Left Bank in search of a sconce that would render perfect justice to the antique armoire across the living room. I judged her harshly while not wasting a second assessing my father's chronic truancy. For playing the role of father, however inexpertly, I bestowed on him a permanent hall pass, freeing him to do as he pleased. Or maybe it was simply his absence that earned him that pass. He was out of sight, if not out of mind, while my mother was constantly present. And that virtue proved her downfall—as is often the case. The absent one can do no wrong, while the one before us, within earshot, becomes the target of our anger, our frustrations, even when that anger and those frustrations are with the absent one. My mother's reward for her unconditional love, for her unwavering attentiveness and interest in me, was my scorn. She deserved better from me.

Aunt Wendy arrived in Westhampton a couple of days before the wedding. After she got settled, we grabbed some Busch longnecks, our beer of choice out there, and strolled to the end of our dock, waiting for dusk to fall. She lit a cigarette.

"You don't smoke, do you?" Aunt Wendy asked.

"No," I replied, stifling an impulse to joke that maybe I should start since being a nonsmoker didn't save my father from getting lung cancer.

"That's good," she said as she took a deep drag. "So I hear you're moving to Oakland after your honeymoon. That's so great!"

"Yeah, Jodi got into the sociology PhD program at Berkeley. She's pretty psyched to give up the lawyering thing and go back to school. She's always been more of a cerebral type anyway."

"Good for her. And for both of you. I've always had a crazy notion about moving to California myself. Up north, to Ukiah. I had a friend a lifetime ago from there. He showed me pictures once. It looks so beautiful, the rolling hills, the ocean." She stared straight ahead out to the bay, as if in some kind of trance. A swan family, two white adults and five brownish-grey cygnets, swam silently by the dock heading for their nest in the nearby wetlands.

Breaking free of her trance, she turned to me. "Transitions can be pretty tough, though. Particularly big ones. Just hang in and turn to each other, especially when things aren't so cool. It's worth it."

"Well, I'm assuming the Dead will be all over Bay Area radio, so that should help," I said smiling.

Aunt Wendy grinned at my awkward deflection of her heartfelt advice. "I can't even listen to the radio anymore," she said. "It's so corporate. I just keep a bunch of tapes in my car."

Maybe I felt bad about making light of Aunt Wendy's concern for my upcoming transition to California, or, who knows, maybe it was the swans, but I decided to bring up the wedding invite brouhaha.

"Hey, I just want you to know that Jodi and I wanted to invite Warren and Carole to the wedding." Although I was looking straight ahead, out at the water, I could see in the corner of my eye she'd turned to look at me. "We really did. But Mom told me that Grandma and Grandpa would freak out. I feel like maybe I should've pushed back on that."

Aunt Wendy put her arm around my shoulders, squeezed me close to her, and kissed my cheek. "That means a lot to me. You have no idea how much." She took a deep breath and stared at the swans bobbing in the slight wake of a distant boat. "But you did the right thing. My parents have never been hip to my situation. They have a very traditional understanding of love and aren't capable of seeing my relationship as something beautiful. Everybody has their limitations and that's one of theirs. I've gotten used to it. I do wish they could see in Warren and Carole what I see but I wouldn't trade my relationship for their approval. You can't live your life on somebody else's terms." She took another puff of her cigarette. "I appreciate your letting me know," she said turning back to face the bay.

One day about a year after we moved to Oakland, I came home from work and dropped my keys and loose change in the ceramic dish on the stand by the door, as I did every day. Except this time it struck me, as I heard the metals resonate against each other, that I had created a brand new sound, a melodious cacophony all my own.

My father had his own telltale symphony of sounds when he came home from work each night. First, it was the key turning in the lock, next was the shuffle of his feet as he made his way across the marble floor to the closet, finally the sound of the closet door opening would tell me that my father was home. I'd get excited whenever I heard this succession of sounds—it wouldn't be long before my father would make his way down the long hall to my room, quietly knock on the door, come in, rub my shoulders, and ask if I wanted to sit with him at the kitchen table while he ate his dinner, which had been left in the oven on "keep warm."

I smiled to myself, recognizing that I now had my own sound, one that on this day summoned our chow/shar-pei mix, Baxter, to the front door with a stuffed platypus toy in his mouth—his canine way of welcoming me home. After trying unsuccessfully to wrestle the platypus out of Baxter's mouth, I went through the day's batch of junk mail: credit card solicitations, coupon circulars, magazines about gardening and other activities I had no interest in. I took the entire pile to the recycling bin preparing to toss it all when a small, padded envelope fell out onto the floor. I recognized Aunt Wendy's loopy script on the front of it.

"What's that?" Jodi asked as she took a turn trying to extricate the platypus from Baxter's vice-like jaw.

"It's from my Aunt Wendy. It kinda feels like it might be a cassette."

"That seems unlikely," Jodi laughed. "Although if anybody still listens to tapes, it'd be your aunt."

It was indeed a tape, a mix tape, accompanied by liner notes. "I hope you still have a tape player somewhere in your possession," Aunt Wendy wrote. "My request—play these songs REAL LOUD!"

I rolled my eyes. Really? Still sending mix tapes?

Her letter urged me to listen closely to one track in particular, Wilco's "California Stars." Notwithstanding the eye rolling, I was curious to listen to the tape—she usually included some hidden gems on them. I wandered into the living room and loaded the tape into my still-functioning cassette deck. "California Stars" was the first song. I stood there taking in the lyrics:

I'd give my life to lay my head tonight on a bed of California stars
I'd like to dream my troubles all away on a bed of California stars
I'd give this world just to dream a dream with you on our bed of California stars

The California theme seemed a rather hokey way to acknowledge my move out West, and I had an urge to hit the fast-forward button. But instead, I plugged in my headphones, lay down on the couch, and closed my eyes. As I continued to listen, I remembered Aunt Wendy telling me of her crazy dream to move to Ukiah, that small, unremarkable farm town in Northern California. I also remembered her commenting on some photographs my mother had sent her of Jodi and me hiking in the California hills: "Matt, you never looked so good!" she wrote in a note shortly after we moved to California. "You both look absolutely wonderful!! But, Matt, you look the most changed and absolutely beautiful! Jodi, you always looked happy and pretty—but Matt! I love it."

And then it hit me—I was living her dream and she was ecstatic for me. I'd broken free of the East Coast's shackles, something she could never do, as much as she wanted to. It was as if I'd summited a mountain and suddenly saw the view to the other side, catching my first real glimpse of Aunt Wendy. I imagined "California Stars" as a portal to her bruised psyche, laying bare how music carved a safe space for her, sheltering her from her family's rejection, with California a real-world Promised Land, a place of unconditional love, acceptance, and transformation. I was proof to her of the existence of that Promised Land.

The more I listened to the song, the more I sensed not just Aunt Wendy's aspirations in "California Stars," but my own. I, too, conceptualized California as a far-flung refuge from the East Coast's frenzied pace, unbridled ambition, and bad weather, and on a deeper level, from my father's lost battle with cancer. Ten years had passed, but my mind was still filled with indelible images of oxygen tanks, breathing tubes, and chemotherapy bags. And indelible sounds, too. Of shuffling bedroom slippers, of vomit splashing in the toilet, of an unfamiliar temper.

To me California represented a realm of immortality—a literal, physical safe space. And, as I imagine it did for Aunt Wendy, music also provided an emotional safe space, one that kept me afloat and helped me breathe when the waves of depression invariably rolled in. In the aftermath of my father's death, I'd disappear for hours listening to music, my ears aching from the pinch of the headphones, or playing a single chord on my guitar, over and over again.

Music allowed me to block out the world and retreat into myself. Those moments of internal retreat were moments of exquisite surrender, of luxuriating in the truth. Music was a place where I didn't have to say "I'm okay" when people asked how I was doing. It was a place where I could feel real emotion—grief, anger, sadness; passion, love, joy—the emotions that I'd stowed away in full lockdown as I tried to propel myself forward.

Still, even as I felt Aunt Wendy's kindred spirit present within me, I maintained my childish distance, unable to express my stirrings of connection to her, my burgeoning sense of closeness, of love. The most I could muster, my lone acknowledgement of Aunt Wendy's efforts to connect with me, was to add her to our holiday card distribution list.

In the years following my father's death, I came to believe that communing with the majesty of unsullied nature—internalizing its stillness—could offer moments of peace, a reprieve from the eternal heaviness of simply being and offer a seminal connection to life. I believed that it could stop the world from wildly spinning and keep me bound to it. And so every vacation I took had to have an outdoor element to it, but it couldn't be just any outdoor activity. Boarding some well-appointed tour bus that ferried sightseers to this waterfall or that lake so everyone could take the same photos of the same scenery wouldn't cut it. No, all vacations had to involve excursions into the wilderness, the more remote the better. Backpacking through the Pyrenees Mountains of Spain, trekking across Iceland, suffering a long and horrifyingly turbulent eleven-hour flight from Paris to Réunion Island, a small speck of a French protectorate floating in the Indian Ocean, to scale its epic mountains.

One time, Jodi and I went trekking through the Dolomites in northern Italy, staying in spartan mountain huts—communal rooms packed with bunk beds and horse blankets—each perched around 7,000 feet. One afternoon, we descended from a high pass to a hut situated on a bluff at the end of a long meadow strewn with wildflowers of every color imaginable, the mountains forming a picture-postcard backdrop at the opposite end of the meadow. I sat on the back deck by myself, feeling the late afternoon sunshine caressing my face, drinking in the stillness, the only sounds the periodic ringing of a distant cow bell and the wind. We were alone there except for an older couple who looked to be in their mid-fifties.

As dusk settled in and shadows imperceptibly crept up the face of the mountain peaks, I watched as the husband set out for a stroll in the meadow. The man's gait was somehow both meandering and purposeful. As he made his way slowly toward the far edge of the meadow, I thought *that could be my father.* He wore a light grey Adidas windbreaker like the one my father often wore jogging and had a salt-and-pepper beard probably grown just for the vacation, as my father used to do. He looked exactly how I imagined my father would look had he lived into his late fifties, an age he would've been at that very moment.

My favorite picture of my father is an image I took on a trip to Kenya. It's a black-and-white photo and my father stands in profile in a field of wildflowers, much like the field outside the hut. He wears a pair of heavily creased, beat-up jeans, a plain grey crew neck sweatshirt, and improbably, a trucker baseball hat, the kind with a puffy synthetic material up front and mesh in the back. His salt-and-pepper hair, uncharacteristically long, tumbles out from under the trucker cap, covering the nape of his neck down to the collar of the sweatshirt. The sandpaper stubble of what will later become a full-blown beard is spread all over his face. I doubt anyone from his law firm would have recognized him in such a pedestrian outfit.

His hands are tucked in the back pockets of his jeans, a camera strap holding his 35mm Leica draped over his right shoulder, binoculars hanging low around his neck. The dark sunglasses he wears offer a hint of counterpoint to his thin, yet genuine smile, his veiled gaze locked on some distant horizon. He has no idea I'm taking his picture; I'm standing far away and using a telephoto lens. What he was looking at, what caused him to smile that beautiful smile, is forever lost in the haze of the past. Maybe it was a giraffe's awkward gait. Maybe monkeys playing in the treetops. Or maybe the deep dark colors of sunrise giving way to the flat light of day. It was my father, or at least my fantasy of my father: relaxed, happy, fully present, and alive, yet eyes forever fixed on the horizon. It's the image I carry with me everywhere—in my wallet and in the dreamy recesses of memory.

As I found myself momentarily lost in the uncanny resemblance between the image of my father and the older man meandering through the meadow, the wife emerged from the hut and started out along a low dirt road beneath the meadow, looking for her husband. I felt a sudden sense of urgency, fearful she'd miss him. I thought to call out to her, to tell her to walk in the meadow, that he was just right there above her. But she eventually located him and scrambled up the small hill to join him, stumbling slightly. I could now barely make them out in the dim light but saw that they embraced, her arm draped around his neck. They wandered back through the meadow arm in arm, sharing this seemingly profound moment of intimacy as the first stars began to twinkle above the Dolomiti.

Had the couple's son snapped a picture of his parents at that precise moment, looking back through the years perhaps he'd come to see it as the image that defined them, defined their relationship for him. I have a different image of my parents, one that immediately came to mind as I watched the husband and wife walking in the meadow, a photograph I'd taken of my parents many years earlier while on vacation. Like the photo of my father, I shot it at a distance and in black and white. They, too, are strolling in a meadow, although not arm in arm. My father, in mid-stride, leads the way. He's wearing a jean jacket and khaki shorts, hands stuffed down in his pockets, his gaze downward, as if studying the ground. Several yards behind him, my mother brings up the rear. She's wearing a plain white T-shirt and dark pants, her arms crossed at her chest, head also bent down as if staring at the ground.

This photograph is the quintessential image I hold of my parents. Together, but forever isolated in their respective internal worlds, my mother unable to get my father to slow down, to walk with her, with us.

From time to time I study that photograph and am reminded just how much it has in common with my favorite work of art, a painting I periodically revisit at the National Gallery of Art in Washington. "The Tragedy" from Picasso's blue period depicts husband and wife standing on a beach by the seashore. They are dressed in long, baggy garments, their shoulders hunched up, perhaps to combat some manner of cold, be it the wind or perhaps some internal chill. The husband's arms are crossed at his chest, just like my mother's in the photograph. The two of them stare down at the ground, just like my parents, their heads bent to the task. A small boy stands at their side, clapping his hands, trying to make the most of being at the beach with his downcast and distracted parents. Or perhaps he's trying to draw their attention to him, to get them to focus on him. Or maybe the boy is attempting to intervene, to mediate, to resolve the conflict. Whatever the boy's intention, the parents' gaze is forever removed from him. He can't make it better.

The older couple returned from their walk in the meadow and disappeared into the hut. "Are you okay?" I heard Jodi ask. She'd sat down next to me on the back deck of the hut. I felt her hand on my leg. "Are you crying?"

I quickly tried to compose myself, wiping away the tear moving down my cheek as nonchalantly as I could, telling her I was fine, then suggesting we take a walk in the meadow. A song fluttered through my mind, "Without Letting Go" by Laurie Sargent, about a woman concerned her boyfriend hasn't let go emotionally of his prior girlfriend, that he "said goodbye without letting go." "I ain't gonna settle for half a man / Who just keeps on looking back," she vows. I wondered if I was only half a man to Jodi because I kept looking back, because I'd said goodbye to my father without letting go.

Retracing the older couple's steps, we reached the end of the meadow and looked out across the valley to the dark, brooding mountains beyond.

"That was an incredible day," Jodi said looking up at the stars. "Brutal hiking, but incredible."

"It was," I replied. "We've earned our dinner tonight."

"And the best bottle of wine they've got."

"I wouldn't get too psyched for the wine," I cautioned. "It's hard to imagine the hut keepers have a solid wine program."

"Come on, it's Italy! Hey, what was going on back there? I figured you'd be on Cloud Nine here, out in the middle of nowhere, the breathtaking scenery, your gorgeous wife by your side."

"I am happy," I replied.

Jodi frowned. "It seems like you're somewhere else."

"I was just, you know, thinking about my dad a little."

Jodi put her arms around me and kissed my cheek. "You think he would've liked this place?"

"I do."

We started to head back to the hut for dinner, for that bottle of wine.

"I'm very happy," Jodi said, squeezing my hand. "All I want is for you to be happy."

I squeezed her hand back and thought about that day in Alaska sitting above Ernie's Creek, that overwhelming desire to experience beauty, to absorb it, the recognition of its preciousness and fleetingness, the tentative faith that nature's cold stark beauty will provide meaning and peace—and the devastating suspicion it cannot.

Since my time in Alaska, I'd incrementally grown aware, through moments of sadness both fully conscious and nearly imperceptible, that death's reach can penetrate even the healthiest, youngest, luckiest people in the world. At some unknown point it became clear that death had taken up residence inside me, biding its time. I came to understand that my singular task in life was to dislodge its hold over me. But how?

For years, an ever-expanding melancholy had wrapped its tendrils around me, slowly choking the very life from me, starving me of energy, of passion, of joy, slowly asphyxiating the essential within me. I returned often to that cliché that life is short. Too often, perhaps. Was that the root cause of the heaviness I felt bearing down on me, forcing me to be forever on the move? But going where? Searching for what? The feeling of the imminency of something precious being lost was a merciless taskmaster. Time is wasting, time is precious, don't stop, can't stop, every moment not spent in reverie, breathing in "life," a moment of regret, time you want back but can't have, some dim-witted dog forever chasing its tail, to similar effect and purposelessness.

Jodi could sense this darkness that resided within me, this aimless searching, and did her best to exorcise it, to get me to slow down and live in the moment. But the darkness wasn't something that could be expunged. It was buried too deep. After Joe Strummer's older brother committed suicide when Joe was seventeen, he told a friend they could no longer walk down streets, that they needed to run. "We'll be old when we can't run down streets," he said. "It'll be the end of us if we walk." I tirelessly ran down the long and winding internal streets of my mind, afraid of the same dire consequences should I ever stop, forever searching for the next remote wilderness, the next empty enclave, hoping against hope that finding it, being present in it, would bring peace. But I soon came to understand that exotic vacations, including treks through the mountains of Italy, are just that; they bring no lasting peace. The heaviness traveled with me, like a second shadow. It boarded the airplane with me, it spoke every language in the world.

18

WHAT IT MEANS TO BE A FATHER

Long before I ever thought of becoming a lawyer, I wanted to be a daddy. At least that's what I told my kindergarten teacher. I'd created a picture book, one of those archetypal disjunctive works of art produced by five-year-olds the world over, comprised of colorful stick figures with captions transcribed by the teacher from the kid's dictation. The last drawing in the book, appearing after portraits of my mother lying in bed, my father going to work, Rob going to school, and my guinea pig Charlotte standing erect with a generous toothy grin, is an abstract expressionist work of what appears to be a figure in a robe-type garment of purple, black, and yellow and lacking a nose, eyes, mouth, or limbs. The caption I dictated reads, "I want to be a daddy when I grow up. This is me being a daddy." Apparently, I understood from a young age that fatherhood is an undertaking more spiritual than physical!

One month before our son Jed was born, I turned thirty-five, an occasion Jodi marked with a birthday note: "I cannot wait for the first moment our son lays eyes on you," she wrote. "I know he will immediately fall as deeply and hopelessly in love with you as I am."

It didn't quite happen that way. Jodi delivered Jed cesarian style and somehow the doctor nicked Jed's face with the scalpel which put the boy, bleeding from his left cheek, in an even fouler mood than he would've been in anyway after being unceremoniously plucked from the warm comfort of the womb. There were a lot of tears shed as I held him, my head darting back and forth from Jed to Jodi (who was being stitched up a few feet away), as if I were watching Borg-McEnroe at Wimbledon, circa 1980. Jed looked up at me in my ratty old "I Love Central Park" T-shirt, scrunched his nose, and just kept screaming, no doubt sensing my own paralyzing fear or maybe wondering why I hadn't picked out a nicer outfit for the occasion. Whatever was going through his little brain, I didn't have the sense he'd immediately fallen deeply and hopelessly in love with me.

Truth be told, I intentionally wore that ratty old "I Love Central Park" T-shirt for Jed's arrival—I wanted to feel New York in the room with me. I'm not sure why that was. Maybe having a child born in California solidified my status as a "former" New Yorker, made it seem real that I was never going back—not that I wanted to—and I felt a need to assert my identity. That could be, although I also wonder if it was more about wanting my father in the room with me, wanting to feel his presence, and wanting Jed to feel it, too. In many ways, I'd come to identify my father with New York, the two mixed together as one in my mind. The skyscrapers where he worked, Central Park where he jogged, Mount Sinai Hospital where he died. But more than all that, New York was where our lives intersected, where I had a father. Maybe wearing that T-shirt was a way for my father to experience his son becoming a daddy, and for my son to look up at his father and feel the presence of his grandfather.

Order was eventually restored; Jed was shuttled off somewhere for some minor plastic surgery and Jodi was taken to a recovery room. The task of alerting our families to Jed's arrival fell on me in the hospital hallway. Of course, everyone was overjoyed, although my Grandma Toby had some feedback on the name we'd chosen.

"Jedidiah?" she sighed, exasperated. "Matthew, why would you do that to him? That's the name that will go on his birth certificate, you know." I told my grandmother I understood how the naming process worked and gently reminded her that her daughter's name was "Phylis" with one 'l' due to a spelling error on my mother's birth certificate, so maybe she wasn't the best authority on the subject. My mother had a similar reaction to the name, although she thoughtfully waited to tell me so in person at Jed's bris a week later. Although it was lost on both my grandmother and mother, we picked the name because we wanted our son to have the same initials as my father—JHF—a tradition many Jews employ to honor a deceased relative. Plus, "Jedidiah" was God's pet name for King Solomon—not a bad role model we figured, what with his legendary wisdom and all (and disregarding his seven hundred wives and three hundred concubines).

"It's hard to look into his eyes and not believe there's a God, isn't it?" asked my mother-in-law, Marlene, when I reached her on the phone. I demurred since, notwithstanding our naming Jed after a towering figure in the Jewish faith, my belief in God, never all that strong, waned considerably after my father died. That a faded old T-shirt could conjure my dead father into the birthing room and make manifest the transcendence of the paternal chain? Sure, I could get behind that concept. But the existence of God? Seemed like a stretch.

After I'd made all the calls, I went outside to steal a quick breath of air. I looked up at the sky, filled with gray rain clouds, felt the rain drops land on my face and trickle down my cheeks like tears, and said to myself, "How about that, Pops?"

The night Jodi and I brought Jed home from the hospital, as we stood at the changing table, I half-jokingly suggested we'd made the biggest mistake of our lives. The kid just wouldn't stop screaming. Baxter forgot all his months of baby-arrival training—our blasting a CD of baby cries and gurgles while we held a plastic doll wrapped in a blanket and walked around the house in mindless circles as if it were a psychiatric ward apparently failed to make a lasting impression on his canine sensibilities. He kept barking at the baby, which just made Jed cry even more, which made Baxter bark even more, the two of them locked in a descending loop of frantic despair. On top of that, both sets of grandparents would be showing up in a couple of days to judge our fitness as parents and provide hours of unsolicited advice. We needed to get our shit together—fast.

The first parenting innovation I worked out was to sing to Jed when he couldn't fall asleep, starting that first night with the Grateful Dead's "Brokedown Palace." Because it worked so well, I figured I'd stick with the bedtime lullaby thing for a while, at least for a few more months. What I couldn't have known then was that I'd continue to sing to him nearly every night not for a few more months, but for the next *fourteen years*, the ritual ending only when Jed started staying up later than me. When he was a toddler, when he was the pitching star of his little league baseball team, and even after he became an acne-riddled baritone, he would still ask for a song before going to bed. It didn't matter if he was angry about some parental slight or so tired that his eyelids went up and down in long, slow blinks, Jed would still ask for a song before going to bed. And I obliged, squeezing myself beside him in his twin bed, both of us under the covers, taking a moment before singing to talk about whatever was on his mind—a strong dislike of Hebrew school, nerves before a piano recital, a love of toasted almond ice cream.

I don't know why he insisted on a song every night well into his teens. It could've been a form of manipulation, a simple effort to stay up later, which could explain why he'd often complain if I picked a short song or gave a rushed rendition. Or maybe through the years he just continued to find comfort in the shared ritual. I know I did.

The playlist remained nearly constant, but our relationship to the songs evolved. If I could offer one piece of unsolicited advice to new parents, it'd be to think through your song selection with an eye to when that partially formed newborn cooing in your arms weighs a hundred pounds and can beat you at chess—they may one day ask you about the lyrics.

Jimmy Buffett's "He Went to Paris" was a staple from the start. I love the song's quiet contemplative tone and thought its straightforward story-like structure would make it a good lullaby. That the story the song tells is horrific ("The war took his baby, bombs killed his lady and left him with only one eye / His body was battered, his whole world was shattered and all he could do was just cry") didn't give me pause because this was long before Jed could understand language. It never crossed my mind I might still be singing it to him after he finished his algebra homework. "He Went to Paris" spawned several late-night conversations about World War II, the Nazis, and our Jewish heritage.

Likewise, Springsteen's "Racing in the Street" had once seemed like a natural lullaby. It's a beautiful, piano-driven song best enjoyed in a dark room at the end of a long day. But some of the lyrics can, it turns out, be unsettling to prepubescent ears. "What does it mean to give up living and die little by little, piece by piece?" Jed asked when he was eight. A perhaps age-inappropriate conversation followed about the hardship, struggle, and grief inherent in life and the need for resilience. Jed absorbed the explanation with a healthy sense of detachment, but I still wonder at my choice to expose him to Springsteen's dark vision at such a young age. In my defense, I also sang Springsteen's "Thunder Road," which I hoped would have a more uplifting effect, and it appears it did—Jed came home from his first "away" sleepover when he was five reporting that the experience reminded him of "Thunder Road," what with "the boy and the girl leaving home to go off on an adventure to find new places."

About the time Jed turned four, I added the Grateful Dead's "Scarlet Begonias" to the rotation. I thought its whimsical lyrics might capture his imagination, but it was a miscalculation. Like most children that age, Jed was a literal thinker. The lyric "The sky was yellow and the sun was blue" infuriated him. "That makes no sense," he fumed, wider awake than ever. The lyrics to the song's bridge didn't help ease his mind, either. The line, "Well I ain't often right, but I've never been wrong" left him more puzzled. "How can that be?" he asked. After dozens more listenings spanning several years, one night he offered a possible explanation: "Maybe he never speaks." Temporarily stunned into silence by the profundity offered by my young son, I eventually replied, "That could be."

The final song I added to the repertoire before the ritual fell prey to the march of time was Springsteen's "No Surrender." Jed was struggling with the decision of where to go to high school, and I thought the song's line about learning more from music than school might provide a helpful perspective and relax him some. "That's pretty funny," he said as he absorbed the lyric and a few nights later requested I sing "Surrender." Not immediately putting together that he meant "No Surrender," I instead broke into "Surrender" by Cheap

Trick, wondering how Jed knew the song and also if he was trying to send a subtle message, as reflected in the song's chorus, that he thought his parents were a little weird. "That was good, but I meant the Springsteen song about skipping school," he politely admonished. He ultimately decided to attend the less academically rigorous high school, explaining his decision simply: "I think I'll be happier." I sometimes wonder if Springsteen's rebellious wisdom tipped the scales.

But the song I returned to more than any other was "Brokedown Palace." I'd wager I've sung it more times than Jerry Garcia ever did. A few years ago I attended the funeral of a colleague and was stunned to learn that he too had a ritual of singing that song with his son. The son spoke at the funeral about his father's last few days in hospice, how he got into bed with his father and together they sang "Brokedown Palace" for the last time. Driving home from the funeral I cued it up on the car stereo and as the windshield wipers pushed aside the rain, as I listened to Jerry's smooth, soulful voice singing "Fare you well, fare you well / I love you more than words can tell," it struck me that while I sang that song to Jed, I also sang it to my father. Always did.

"Brokedown Palace" has an honored place as the first track of a multi-CD set I created shortly after bringing Jed home from the hospital. Jodi asked me to put together some music for her middle-of-the-night feeding sessions. Every night after work for two or three weeks I secluded myself in the dormer attic and meticulously combed through my CD collection in search of tracks that might soothe the boy while also helping Jodi soldier on through the night.

This was during the Middle Ages of music, after the demise of cassettes and vinyl but before the advent of online streaming and playlists. Which is to say it took a while to burn the CDs. I spent several hours a night up there but I absolutely relished the exercise. It not only forced me to engage again with my passion for music, a passion expressed only intermittently during the prior ten years in my role as a working stiff, but even more importantly, to *recognize* it as a passion, to understand its seminal role in who I am and embrace it, not run from it.

I could've burned one or two CDs and called it a day. That's all Jodi requested. But no, I burned fifteen CDs, nearly twenty hours of music, all painstakingly curated, each selection pored over and debated like I was filling out a March Madness bracket with a ten-million-dollar pot. How do you pick just one or two songs from Dylan's *Blood on the Tracks*? Although that entire album by itself technically fulfilled the letter of Jodi's assignment, including every song wouldn't have met its spirit since the CDs were supposed to be a "mix." (I landed on "Simple Twist of Fate" and "Shelter From the Storm.")

And so, yes, the project was about much more than throwing together a few mixes. It was an acknowledgement of a dormant passion, a long overdue bear hug of an embrace of that passion, and an effort to share that essential part of me with my son.

And not just all that—on some level it felt like my first opportunity to help shape who my son would be. Of course, like any self-respecting new father, who I wanted my son to be was, well, me. Not sure what the over-under is on realizing how stupid and damaging that innate desire is, but it's likely measured in years not weeks from the birth of said kid and so I hadn't yet had that epiphany. Through the music on those CDs, I hoped to form Jed's musical tastes, subliminally offer him a solid foundation in rock 'n' roll, and, I dared imagine, immunize him against pop. I loaded up those CDs with Dylan, Springsteen, the Allman Brothers, the Grateful Dead, and the Velvet Underground.

I had some initial doubts the strategy would take. Early on, Jodi told me Jed seemed disturbed by Dylan's harmonica solo at the end of "It's All Over Now, Baby Blue." Apparently, the high pitch of the harmonica bothered the baby and caused him to twitch and fuss. She said she'd had to skip the track. It was a crushing blow. I treasure that solo. It's precisely the wailing, piercing pitch, its haunting, other-worldly quality that makes it remarkable. That Jed, even at three weeks, couldn't recognize its dark beauty concerned me.

But the long-game strategy did eventually bear fruit. When he was nine years old, Jed drafted a document entitled, "My Altime Favrite Top Ten Songs" (his spelling has since improved). Written in chicken scratch at number one is "Thunder Road." Four other Springsteen tunes made the cut as well—"Born to Run" (Number 2), "Darkness on the Edge of Town" (Number 4), "Jungleland" (Number 6) and "Atlantic City" (Number 10). "Sweet Jane" charted at Number 8, which, of course, is ridiculously low, but that just proves nobody's perfect, not even my son. Jed could one day become a Supreme Court Justice or Nobel laureate, but I will never be prouder of him than when he handed me that list.

Jodi was at an academic conference the first time I had to take care of Jed by myself. He was a few months old and I was changing his diaper up on the changing table. Bored by the ritual, he reached over the side, grabbed a plastic bottle of lotion from out of a cubby, and put it in his mouth. I didn't take it away; I figured it was as good a way as any to keep him occupied while I took care of his business.

A few minutes later I held his freshly-diapered body in one arm while I puttered around the kitchen with the other. Jed seemed relatively content, fascinated no doubt at how deftly his dad unloaded the dishwasher with one hand. Then out of nowhere, he projectile vomited all over the floor. Burst after burst of colorless vomit. It seemed to go on forever, like the Drums/Space interlude at a Dead show. I panicked. Why the fuck was he throwing up? I thought he might be dying on me. Then I saw a small piece of plastic floating in one of the pools of vomit. Apparently, the bottle of lotion Jed put in his mouth still had shrink-wrap on it, and his brand new teeth had gnawed off a piece that lodged in his throat.

Just as I figured out what had happened, Baxter came bounding into the kitchen and started to lap up the vomit. The phone rang and the console announced it was Jodi on the line. Obviously, I should've let it go to voicemail while I gained control of the battlefield, but I wasn't thinking straight.

"How's everything going?" Jodi asked. She sounded anxious.

"Great," I said as I cradled the phone against my right shoulder, held Jed, who was crying hysterically, in my left arm, and gently kicked Baxter out of the kitchen with my right foot, paw prints of vomit trailing behind him all the way to the living room.

"Is Jed okay? He sounds inconsolable."

"He's just hungry. I'm getting something together for him."

Baxter then came back looking for seconds. This time I kicked him a little harder than the ASPCA might've abided. He whined and retreated from the kitchen.

"What's wrong with Baxter?" Jodi asked. "That's a weird noise he's making."

"Oh, he just sees a squirrel on the back deck. It's all good."

I was pretty upset that I'd let Jed chew on that plastic bottle. Definitely not a great parenting move. But on the other hand, I was ecstatic he didn't die on me. That was a real concern of mine in those days. Not just that he might die from rolling over in his crib and suffocating or from choking on a small toy (or piece of shrink wrap) but from some dread disease. Like cancer. Or that I would. For me, fatherhood brought with it a paranoid fear of the unthinkable coming to pass. Of course, it also brought unimaginable joy and a kind of all-encompassing love I'd never experienced before. The fear, though, could be overwhelming.

In navigating the path of fatherhood, it was interesting, and comforting, to learn that some of my musical heroes had a similar experience of fatherhood. In reflecting on becoming a parent, Springsteen told his biographer, "When that world of love comes rushing in, a world of fear comes with it." "You are not *safe*," he writes in his memoir, "love and risk are everywhere."

Chris Cornell had a similar take on becoming a father. The Soundgarden tune "Bones of Birds" was inspired by the stress, the fear, the sense of powerlessness Cornell felt as he watched his kids grow up and lose their innocence, a natural process for sure, but one that's always associated, he explains, with something bad happening, something they weren't expecting, with loss. When asked if he was a good father, Chris replied, "I maybe almost overdo it I think in terms of the attentiveness and the fear."

The challenge of parenthood, Springsteen says, is to walk through that world of fear so you can live in the world of love.

For me it was easier said than done.

When Jed was an infant, I'd often take hikes in the East Bay hills, toting him in a Baby Bjorn, his tiny form spread-eagled like Barry Manilow on the cover of *Barry Manilow Live*, while Baxter sprinted through the open fields in quest of a fresh cow pie to roll in. There was one route I often took that led to panoramic views of the San Francisco Bay, the Golden Gate Bridge, and the Marin Headlands. I started to bring a bandana whenever we went up there because I'd inevitably start bawling. It took maybe forty-five seconds up at that vista point, looking out at the deep blue water with the sunlight sparkling on it like fireworks, for me to start choking up. I mostly thought about my father, about how I wished he could have met Jed. But also about how I didn't want to die on Jed and leave him to grow up without a father.

That first night singing "Brokedown Palace," I had committed to being present for Jed as much as possible while I was around. And so I rescheduled meetings and dropped everything I could to make sure I caught all of his activities. Bob Dylan's son, Jacob, once told an interviewer that his father never missed a single one of his Little League games, that he kept every home run ball he ever hit. Well, I can do Bob one better: not only did I catch every one of Jed's Little League games, I also sat through every excruciating T-ball game when he was four. And not just that. I watched a soccer ball occasionally interrupt a bunch of quasi-oblivious six-year-olds running past each other on cold, windswept fields. I suffered through his school's winter *and* spring concerts, the screech of violins and cellos played by talentless elementary school kids nearly driving me mad. But I was there.

At least physically.

At times, even now, fifteen years after Jed was born, I catch myself drifting, not being emotionally present for him, that same distance I felt from my father having seemingly seeped into my own fatherly bones. Sometimes Jed will be well into a monologue before I'll realize that he's talking to me, my mind off somewhere else. Or I'll struggle to formulate questions that might draw him out more, settling instead for my own silence.

For reasons that are still a touch opaque to me, Jed has become an avid golfer. He started taking lessons when he was seven or so, inspired by my father-in-law who is himself an obsessive golfer and introduced Jed to the sport. I never got into golf as a kid. I took a few lessons when I'd visit Grandpa Dave in Florida, but after he witnessed me inadvertently let go of his five iron during a wicked follow through, the club sailing up, up, and away and finally lodging in the high canopy of a giant palm tree where it would rest comfortably for the next six months, he stopped taking me for lessons. My game suffered greatly.

But because Jed was into it, I started to play again. I figured it would allow for some good quality time. And it has. One day as I was preparing to take my second shot on number eleven, he asked how my lesson earlier that day had gone.

"It was okay," I reported. "Jay told me I need to relax my swing more, that I'm too wound up. The problem is, that's hard for me. I'm sort of a control freak. It's hard for me to just let go in the day-to-day. You've probably noticed that about me, eh?"

"No, not really," Jed replied nonchalantly. "But maybe that means if you get better at golf, you'll get better at life." Having dispensed that Confucian piece of wisdom, he turned and ambled off down the fairway.

Another time, when I was pouting about how horribly I was playing, telling Jed I thought I had a psychological barrier to becoming a good golfer, that a part of me rebelled at identifying as a "country club" type, Jed laughed and said, "Well, that just means you should want to be a good golfer because most country club golfers suck."

But for every interaction like that, there are a dozen missed opportunities, instances when I should be immersed in the moment, marveling at the transcendent beauty of sauntering down a fairway on a gloriously sunny day with my son—my son!—who will be going off to college in just two years. I should be luxuriating in those fleeting moments that will soon be even rarer, but instead I'm far away in my own world, anxious about the next shot, my body tense (despite Jay's instruction to relax more), my mind held captive by some issue at work or other inconsequential pablum as I trudge off in search of an errant ball, Jed trailing far behind me, head down, casually swinging a club in front of him, back and forth, back and forth, as he strolls alone. I know I should hang back with him, just be with him, even if it's in silence. Why can't I walk with my son? Why can't I just be with him?

At times I wonder if my inability to engage fully with Jed is infecting him with the sadness that I carry around at having lost my father. I also wonder, did Grandpa Dave, who lost his father at eight years old, infect my father with his sadness? And did my father, who yearned for more closeness with his father, infect me with his sadness *even before* he died? Is that when the heaviness set in?

Sometime around when Jed was three years old, I was on an airplane traveling for work, reading *The History of Love* by Nicole Krauss, periodically gazing out the window at an unbroken sea of clouds. Suddenly it occurred to me that I used to be just like my son, full of wonder and excitement and innocence, capable of laughing with abandon. And I realized that I am envious of my son; that I want to feel his lightness; that while there are times when he transmits it to me, like magic, through a touch or a look or in words, he will not be a perfect distillation of happiness, a personification of lightness, forever; that I can't rely on him for it; that it'd be unfair of me to burden him so; that I need to find lightness without him.

And then I read this: "Perhaps that is what it means to be a father—to teach your child to live without you."

Is that what I'm doing on the golf course, in the moments of emotional distance? Teaching Jed to live without me? Is it a loving gesture—a misplaced effort to cushion him from the loss of his innocence, to inoculate him against inevitable sadness, by training him not to be emotionally dependent on his father? Or am I in some twisted way seeking to foster closeness by nurturing in Jed an absence like the one I live with? Or maybe I turn away from Jed because close contact is too painful, because when I'm with him, I feel not just the pain of having lost my father, but Jed's pain of losing me one day. Maybe the depth of that pain is unbearable.

One thing is certain, though: My father taught me to live without him—not by dying, but by not being around when he was alive. I too want Jed to learn to live without me—but not that way.

19

RELEASE ME

I was living in Washington, DC, when I learned that Murphy had died. Cancer. Forty-two years old. Six years younger than my dad. I got a call early evening from an old high school friend still living in New York. He figured I'd want to know.

I couldn't sleep that night. Around 2:00 a.m. I got out of bed and went downstairs, wandering aimlessly until coming to rest in the dining room where I kept the stereo. I dug up the old tape Murphy had made for me of Tommy Keene's *Songs from the Film,* his exquisite calligraphy like print adorning the cassette jacket, still unsmudged nearly thirty years later.

I loaded the tape into my Sony tape deck, affixed my headphones, and closed my eyes, traveling back in time. Listening to that record, now firmly rooted in midlife, I felt transported to the time just before Murphy and I fell irretrievably under the sway of the Replacements and other edgier bands, a realm of naivety and adolescent innocence. I smiled at the thought of our childish love of catchy pop tunes. "I'll never find someone like you," Tommy sings in "As Life Goes By." "How does it feel to be alone again?"

Murphy's funeral was a few days later, but I didn't go. It was during the week, and I would've had to take time off from work to get up to New York, I told myself. There'd be child-care issues to deal with, I told myself. I wasn't expected to attend, I told myself.

In an early Clash tune, Joe Strummer describes hanging out in his garage with a bullshit detector. If such a device had been deployed to my house in the days before Murphy's funeral, it would've alerted with the frequency of a drug-sniffing dog working a Grateful Dead concert. I rationalized, deflected, and defended, groping for excuses to avoid going. But the bottom line was simple: I was self-conscious about mourning my childhood best friend. All his lifelong friends and his bandmates would be at the funeral. Would I be imposing on their grief? Would they resent my staking a claim to being in mourning as well? Would they have been right to feel that way? Was my grief fraudulent? I'd rejected Murphy and his damn-the-torpedoes rock 'n' roll spirit. They hadn't.

Of course, all that was ridiculous. I had every right to grieve for Murphy. During the most formative period of my life we were inseparable friends, sharing the sweetness of boyhood and the struggles of adolescence.

But that feeling of being a fraud was a familiar one. I'd felt it years earlier the day Jerry Garcia died. As if I didn't have a right to mourn his death, like I wasn't a "real" fan.

I was in Charlottesville clerking for the Judge and was ambling down the pedestrian mall that spooled out from the courthouse, heading to my go-to sandwich shop for lunch. A crowd of tie-dyed, mostly college-aged people—the men sporting tangles of excessive facial hair, the women proudly flashing similarly impressive underarm hair—had congregated about halfway down the mall in front of an old movie theater. Some of them had formed a Hacky Sack circle and were kicking away. Others sat on the sidewalk hugging. A boom box played "Ripple," one of the Dead's classic tunes. I was confused by the scene since I'd never come across a group of Deadheads hanging out on the mall before. Then I saw someone had written on the sidewalk in pink chalk, "R.I.P. Jerry."

I stood there feeling completely alone—despite the community of fellow mourners gathered right in front of me. Even though I used to perform Dead tunes at talent shows, quoted the Dead on my senior yearbook page in high school, and had seen the band more than a dozen times, I believed I wasn't a member of that tribe. I was clean-shaven in a suit and tie and had never once played Hacky Sack. Not that I wanted to be part of their tribe. I was only three years removed from describing Alex in my Alaska journal as a "Deadhead scumbag" and not much had changed in my mainstream outlook.

On some level I felt legit, with just as much a right to mourn as any Deadhead. I mean, could any of these jokers play even one Dead tune on guitar? But on a deeper level I understood I didn't quite measure up. I'd never followed the Dead around the country or tripped on acid or even danced around in a circle with my hands flailing above me at a show. I would stand there stoically bobbing my head and tapping my right foot, occasionally bending over at the waist to absorb a particularly transcendent guitar riff. In my mind, this crowd was connected with Garcia and his music on a different level, a more passionate level, and I was an interloper. I felt like I didn't really belong there, like I was a fraud for mourning Jerry. And so instead of communing with the mourners on the mall, I took my sandwich to go, went home, and swapped out my fancy silk Salvatore Ferragamo tie for one from the collection Jerry had recently launched—it was an abstract earth-tone design with stripes of different thicknesses. I'd never actually worn it because I didn't think it looked professional. But nobody back at the office seemed to notice the switch.

The fact is, I never took the whole rock 'n' roll setup seriously. Even as a kid, it seemed kind of juvenile to me. Like a lot of my peers, I was way too deeply programmed by the expectations of the Upper East Side, where it felt like everybody was on the fast track to work in the corporate world. For our senior yearbook, my classmates pegged my future career as "Corporate Caesar." That seemed about right to me at the time. Not that I had any particular interest in becoming a corporate Caesar (whatever that even means). I just assumed I'd end up working in the corporate world. And maybe I assumed as much, maybe I even wanted it, in part because I didn't want to be shunned like Aunt Wendy, didn't want my parents, or anyone else, rolling their eyes at me. No, I wanted to be thought of as a "serious" person, like my father. Music wasn't properly considered an animating principle of one's life—that is, if one were a "serious" person. And somewhere along the daisy chain of years, apparently that's what I became.

I did want to be good at guitar. I did want to be able to play like my heroes. But at the end of the day, I didn't view playing guitar as all that important to my life. I had a primal instinct that just as no NBA players claw their way to greatness from the mean streets of Manhattan's Upper East Side, neither do rock stars. Not enough angst. Not enough fire in the belly among the precious Jewish kids of the one percent. I didn't know then that Mick Jagger grew up comfortably in British suburbia, attended the London School of Economics, and majored in the outlandishly subversive subjects of accounting and finance! Or that Lou Reed's pops was a tax accountant and member of a country club; Reed's biographer Howard Sounes described Lou as a "conventional middle-class teen." Or that Leonard Cohen grew up a rich kid in one of Montreal's most socially connected families.

Or that both Reed and Cohen were Jewish (Lou's dad changed the family name to Reed from Rabinowitz). Or that Joey Ramone was Jewish, born Jeffrey Hyman, or that his bandmate Tommy Ramone, née Tamás Erdélyi, was a Hungarian Jew whose parents survived the Holocaust. My mind wasn't wired to allow for any of that.

And I can't even blame my parents for it. They were both supportive of my interest in guitar. Unlike some other parents, they didn't think rock 'n' roll was the devil's music, that it would lead me straight to Hell, or worse, to a non-Ivy League college. Sure, there was the occasional busting into my room ordering me to turn it down, but that's only because the sonic-induced gyrations of our turn-of-the-century dining room chandelier spooked them. There was no express disapproval, no declaring that I couldn't or shouldn't pursue music. I attached that ball and chain to myself. Willingly, if unconsciously.

Looking back, one strategy I applied for avoiding that world was to tell myself I wasn't talented enough for it, that I didn't have the chops like my buddy Eric did. But it's funny—every few years I'll dust off my dual cassette deck and throw in the tape of Eric's and my performance at that school talent show, the one where I screwed up the bridge to "Scarlet Begonias." When I listen to it now, I notice something else about that gig—how could I have missed it? It's not my flawed performance that catches my ear, it's Eric's—he screwed up just as bad as I did during my solo on "Uncle John's Band." In fact, he got so mixed up, he briefly stopped playing all together while he gathered himself; I kept going, soloing over nothing. And to think that all these years, the only thing I remembered was that I screwed up. That second fiddle mentality had taken root in my head. In my mind, there was *no way* Eric could have screwed up—he was a freaking guitar prodigy. He dedicated himself to his craft. He took it seriously.

Listening to the tape again refreshed my recollection of two other things. After I took my solo in "Scarlet Begonias," you can hear my mother on the tape chuckling, "Look, he's trying not to smile, he's trying not to smile!" She was right. A smile would've suggested I believed I belonged anywhere near the stage with Eric, or worse yet, that I was actually enjoying myself. And the second thing I remembered was I played my solos at half the volume of Eric's, like I didn't want anyone to actually hear them. That emotional state, that lack of confidence, is transformed into aural form on the tape.

After my solo on "Uncle John's Band," Rob comments, "Wow, he's pretty good." I cracked a huge smile when I heard Rob say that and as I listened to the tape again, I had to agree. My solos were solid. They weren't nearly as fast or as technical as Eric's, but they possessed a delicate and tender quality. Certainly not as emotional as Jerry Garcia's playing, but not bad for a teenager. As a kid, though, I heard them as thin, amateurish, basically fraudulent. I didn't believe I had any talent.

I also wonder if in addition to the cultural expectations of my family and upbringing, I never took music seriously because Murphy somehow made me think I didn't belong in that world. That I'd be excommunicated, labeled a fraud. Between his drug and alcohol use, the jet-black hair streaming past his shoulders, the black bolo tie and Peter Buck vest, plus the "who gives a shit" attitude, topped off by being in a real rock 'n' roll band, Murphy had pretty much achieved an authentic rock 'n' roll ethos. And maybe I thought you couldn't really be passionate about music without those clichéd trappings, none of which I had and some of which, like the heavy drug use, downright freaked me out. Sure, I loved music. Sure, I spent most of my free time listening to it, playing it, buying it, and watching it. But not once did I believe it was a realm I could truly inhabit.

What's interesting to me now is that while I saw Murphy as an authentic rock 'n' roll god, nobody else at school bought into that. In our senior yearbook, the editors' forecast Murphy's future occupation not as the second coming of Keith Moon, but as *Delivery Boy.* Murphy ended up toiling away in the corporate media world working at Court TV, for crying out loud. What's clear to me now is my friend was just another awkward teenager, like the rest of us, getting drunk at unchaperoned parties and trying to figure out who he was. Murphy's immersion in the rock 'n' roll lifestyle didn't make his passion for music more legitimate than mine; it didn't make him a more "authentic" person than me. But back then that baseline truth was lost on me. Why? Why did I rate Murphy's love of music as more genuine than mine? I guess because unlike with me, there was no apparent compromise in his posturing. He lived it right down to the clothes he wore. My own sense of identity never found firm footing in that ethos. What I might be willing to fight for was wildly unclear to me in high school. There were competing currents pulling me in opposite directions, my father's way versus Aunt Wendy's, the result being I never really committed to anything and my internal life remained a captive to my external life. I told myself I wasn't like Murphy who saw the river roaring by him, dove into it with conviction, and was swept away. Not even close. I dipped my toe in, felt its force, and retreated to the safety of the riverbank.

Any time I stepped off what I considered to be the mainstream professional path, or even thought about stepping off, I felt like a fraud. That was true about music. But it was also true about the outdoors.

When Jed was ten, Jodi, who by then had become a law professor, had earned a six-month sabbatical and we decided to spend it in Chile. I took a leave of absence from work, and we traveled around

South America as Jed's school schedule allowed. One of our most ambitious excursions was a five-day backpacking trip through the Atacama Desert in northern Chile. Because the area is so remote, we traveled with a guide, a lean, dark-haired Chileno named Yasu who possessed the calm demeanor and quiet wisdom of someone much older than his thirty-one years.

At 7,900 feet, the Atacama is the highest desert in the world and the scenery is beyond breathtaking, supernatural in its strange beauty, from striated green, yellow, and red mountains to fluorescent orange sunsets over a lunar landscape of plateaus and valleys to salt flats inhabited by flocks of bright pink flamingoes to one of the largest geyser fields in the world. The area includes the highest plateau outside Tibet, and for four nights we beheld the darkest night sky on earth, one that each evening spawned a veritable planetarium. We encountered hardly another soul the entire time.

And yet far more impressive to me than the physical place was Yasu's knowledge of it. Every aspect of it. The geology, the astrology myths, the history of the Inca Empire that once flourished there, the meaning of the cave art we passed, the life cycles of the fauna, the names and distinguishing features of every living thing in the desert. There was no question he couldn't answer.

Yasu possessed a Zen-like ease about him, made possible by his self-confidence and comprehensive understanding of this enigmatic realm. With little bits of information, he shared that he led a complicated life, divorced with a young son, but he seemed at peace in the Atacama, his cares far away. He spoke of it as his refuge from the empty promise of everyday life, a place that made sense, one that he yearned for the minute he returned to civilization.

After I met Yasu, I felt that old familiar ache that started with Murphy and reappeared in a thousand variations through the years—like I was a fraud. Like I was only a slightly more ambitious member of the tourist herd taking selfies at the Grand Canyon. I had no real commitment, no passion. What act of commitment, what irrational leap of faith would it take for me to be completely at ease in nature, like Yasu?

As we flew home from the Atacama, I dialed up Soundgarden's *Superunknown* on my iPod and scrolled to the third track, "Fell on Black Days." I needed to hear a specific lyric, words that had been spinning ceaselessly in my head for days: "I'm only faking when I get it right."

Faking it. Was that what I was doing? Because I wasn't authentically committed to being an outdoorsman like Yasu? Oh, I had all the regalia to look the part with my expensive gear and moisture-wicking layers, but I knew in my heart that an essential something was missing. Meeting Yasu kneecapped the inner myth of the mountains as my sanctuary. Like so many incarnations of this cycle in the past, suddenly I felt like an idiot for having ever believed in my ability to escape my lesser self. The downward spiral of depression returned in full flower, transforming an activity I cherished into a vehicle for self-loathing.

A few days later, with Jed at school and Jodi out running errands, I cranked up Pearl Jam's "Release" through my headphones. I sat on the couch, absorbing that ethereal opening riff built around an open D chord, rocking back and forth, back and forth while the drums gently emerged from the darkness of the riff's sonic depths. As Vedder defiantly declares that he'll hold the pain and then offers up his grief-stricken bellow to ride out the first chorus, I felt my open hands that had been slapping my knees in time turn to fists and begin pounding my thighs, as if trying to summon a physical pain to match the emotional pain of Vedder's lyrics. When the final chorus arrived,

I was no longer sitting on the couch, but standing, screaming along to Vedder's repeated command of "Release me! Release me!" my head bent down as if in prayer, my body swaying in front of the stereo, lost in the amorphous lament.

As the ferocious wave of music subsided and the last rippled chord retreated to the depths, I dropped to my knees, exhausted. And then suddenly, for the first time, I realized who it was I'd been screaming at all those years as I communed with that song. It was so simple, so obvious, and yet elusive. I wasn't screaming at some external force, at some malevolent mystical presence pinning me down. No, I was screaming at myself, demanding to be freed from the unrelenting insecurity and anger that crippled my attempts at authenticity and thus at any real happiness. And not just that: I was screaming it for my father—not *at* my father, but *as* my father. In that instant of perfect clarity conjured by the music, he was inside me, imploring me, begging me, "Son, please, I'm okay. Live your life. Release me from this role I'm playing in your tortured psyche." That simple lyric, "Release me!" shouted repeatedly, with furious defiance, was able to penetrate the walls of self-loathing blanketing me. I sat down on the couch and sobbed.

Eddie Vedder once told an audience that "Release" is a song of healing: "It's not gonna lessen the blow of any kind of tragedy but at loud volumes or alone . . . it just helps you get through, because you can't get around it, you don't get over it, you don't get under it, you gotta get through it." That is certainly true of a son who loses his father too soon—there's no getting around it, no getting under it, and definitely no getting over it. There's just getting through it. The trick is to acknowledge the hole that's left behind—a hole that will never be filled—without falling into it, without leading a life swallowed up by sadness, guilt, or a false sense of loyalty to the father, to pain.

Pearl Jam had given me the keys to release the darkness, not permanently but long enough to recognize what I was doing to myself, to temper the self-flagellation, to tether me when I felt as if I was floating away, like Bowie's ill-fated astronaut on a spacewalk, miles above the earth.

Looking back, I wonder if my obsession with Pearl Jam and Soundgarden was a way to vent my rage not just at myself, but at my father. Rage for not being around when I was a kid, for sure. But also rage for an even more primordial reason: for dying on me.

As irrational as it is, there's a part of me, buried way down in there, that's furious at him for abandoning me. That thinks he had agency in the whole thing. That it was the choices he made that killed him. That his work killed him. That New York and its filthy air killed him. That if he'd wanted to, he could've stuck around. That it's his fucking fault he was MIA when I graduated from college; his fucking fault he was MIA when I graduated from law school; his fucking fault my wedding day was equal parts joy and grief; his fucking fault we never took an Outward Bound trip together; his fucking fault my mother has grown old alone; his fucking fault his grandson knows him only as some guy in a black and white photograph; his fucking fault I never got to see him seeing me as an adult, approving of my life, of me; his fucking fault I don't know who he is.

And not just all that.

It's his fucking fault I never made a move on a girl in high school. That's right—*his* fucking fault. My father taught me to suppress my desires, like my wish to be with him, so I wouldn't be disappointed when that wish inevitably went unfulfilled. That's why instead of honoring my desire for Julie that night on the washing machine, I instead berated myself for feeling it, putting on not just any album, but fucking *Nebraska*, a record that critic Sean Murphy astutely describes as “a belly flop into the abyss,” an album that “carries with it death, despair and the electric chair—and that’s just on the opening song.” Thanks, Pops.

And yet my desire to be with him couldn’t be fully extinguished, metastasizing into pushing girls away, unable to give up on my true object of desire. On top of which, by working like a crazed person, by not prioritizing his family, my father sent me the same subtle message that Springsteen writes in his memoir his father sent him, “that a woman, a family, weakens you, makes you feel exposed and vulnerable.” That explains the paper I wrote in college, ostensibly on Hemingway, arguing that men entangled in relationships with women led tragic lives, that only by steering clear of such relationships could a man achieve self-actualization. Getting an A+ on that paper sure as shit didn’t help since it just served to further convince me of the essential truth of the thesis, but it was really all my father’s fault.

As a parent myself now, and with the benefit of time, all these realizations combine with another one, the most important one: like most fathers, like me, my father did the best he knew how. No parent can know the subtle ways their actions will affect their kids. I’m quite certain if my father had an inkling that he might’ve contributed to my insecurities, he would’ve tried to do something about it. If I knew Jed was having emotional difficulties, I’d do whatever I could—including trying to change my own behavior—to help him navigate them. I believe my father would’ve done the same for me.

Of course I feel some guilt about blaming my father for his own tragic and incomprehensible death, to say nothing of my stunted emotional life. In fact, my guilt could be at the root of why I never seriously considered living my life like all the free-spirited outdoor types I idolized—like Bill, like Bob, like Yasu. I wonder if that guilt has expressed itself in my life through self-negation, through telling myself I can't be like those guys, that I don't have the passion, the authenticity—that I need to stay in my lane of self-imposed constraints.

Looking back, what saddens me, what infuriates me, isn't that I never became a rock star or an Outward Bound instructor; it's that I never allowed myself to *imagine* becoming those things—it's that I never allowed myself to dream.

20

A FATHER'S MOST PRECIOUS GIFT: HIMSELF

One afternoon when Jed was nine, we went to a party thrown by the parents of one of his friends. The kids were out splashing in the pool while the adults gorged on tacos and margaritas. The hostess, Lisa, asked me what I'd been up to and I mentioned having just gotten back from San Antonio where, among other things, I'd seen a fantastic new band called Heartless Bastards.

Lisa then made the mistake of asking what the band sounded like, inadvertently launching me into a breathless ten-minute exposition on the myriad components of the band's sonic substructure. "A lot of their songs are built around heavy metal power chords softened slightly by a grunge sensibility and an almost psychedelic overlay," I explained. "Think Neil Young's 'Cortez the Killer' off the *Live Rust* album," I helpfully added. I droned on for quite a while in this vein, describing how one tune mixed bluegrass elements with the African American field holler tradition while another initially presented with a mild country twang that harkened to the Rolling Stones' "Dead Flowers" but then exploded into a full-fledged rock tune concluding in a stellar dissonant cacophony that would've made Lou Reed proud.

Lisa looked at me with a blank stare. I figured I was boring her. Based on the bubble gum pop coming from her house sound system I gathered she wasn't a rock fan. She certainly had no idea what the hell the *Live Rust* version of "Cortez the Killer" sounded like. But, hey, she'd asked. When I'd finished describing songs and bands Lisa likely had zero interest in, she muttered, "Wow."

"Yeah," I agreed, "they were pretty awesome."

"No, I mean you talk so passionately about music." She put her margarita down on the kitchen counter and grabbed my arm. "You should write a music blog."

"Hah, that's funny," I snickered. Not only was I a Luddite who could barely place an order on Amazon, the idea of writing about music seemed silly. Who does that? Nobody I knew. Plus, I had no time to write a music blog. I was a busy lawyer, currently embroiled in knock-down, drag-out litigation for PG&E over the deregulation of California's natural gas market. I immediately dismissed the idea. Sort of like when Bob suggested I blow off the NYU job fair and climb Mount Shasta with him. For a variety of reasons it was never going to happen.

"Seriously," Lisa continued. "You'd be great at it."

I thanked Lisa, told her I'd think about it, and went in search of another margarita.

But unlike Bob's invitation to climb Mount Shasta that I summarily dismissed, Lisa's music blog idea continued to percolate in my head over the next few weeks. *You love writing. You love music. Why not write about music?*

Upon reflection, I had to admit there were stupider ideas floating around out there. And so one weekend afternoon while Jodi was at the farmers' market and Jed was playing video games at a friend's house, I blasted the Heartless Bastards through every room in the house, grabbed my laptop, and wrote a short essay about the San Antonio show. It was the best afternoon I'd experienced in a long, long while. I smiled for three hours straight, giggling at times like I was stoned.

I basked in the glow of that afternoon for several weeks, listening exclusively to the Heartless Bastards while commuting to and from work, and then decided to take the plunge. The biggest hurdle to starting the blog was, of course, convincing myself I had the requisite chops. Every time I thought about launching the blog, I got that same slightly nauseated feeling I had walking out of Sam Ash with my Gibson. I didn't believe I was legit enough to pull it off; once again I was convinced that I was a fraud. Several of my friends knew way more about music than I did and went to shows almost weekly, but they weren't bloggers. Why did I think I could be—or should be? But I kept thinking of that glorious afternoon spent writing about the Heartless Bastards as I blasted the band's music all through the house. *Fuck it*, I thought, *let's do this!*

Each weekend for a few months straight, I set aside a couple of hours to gin up enough content to get the site up and running. When the time came to launch the blog, I drafted an email announcement to everyone I knew who might be interested in it. I kept the cursor hovering over the send button for so long my wrist began to ache. I actually had to let go of the mouse and roll out my neck and shoulders as if I'd just finished a set of heavy back squats. I had to laugh, realizing I was far more nervous about this side hustle than I was about cross-examining witnesses in federal court.

I imagined I felt like Springsteen as he wrestled with the release of *Born To Run* in 1975 and famously threw the finished master recording in a swimming pool, thoroughly unconvinced of the album's greatness. Same thing with my blog email—sort of. But like Bruce, I finally let it go—mustered all my courage and hit send.

To my utter bewilderment, the launch went well. People seemed to enjoy the post and the idea of the blog. I felt like how a baby bird must feel when it first leaves the nest and is stunned to learn it can fly. I'd half assumed I'd come crashing down under the weight of my own perceived fraudulence. But no, I was flying! Soaring, in fact, through a wide-open sky of possibility, excitement, and aliveness.

From that moment on, my earbuds became like a teenager's retainer—taken out only for meals. I was always on the hunt for new bands to write about. Jodi was a little puzzled by my change of behavior but warmed to my nascent obsession, particularly as I introduced her to new artists that fit her groove. After she heard the soaring vocals of Shovels & Rope's Cary Ann Hearst, she became a full-throated supporter of the project.

One of the first bands I discovered in my new role as rock music blogger was not a rock-based band at all, but the country act Florida Georgia Line. Their first album, *Here's To the Good Times*, exploded my preconceptions about the genre, penetrating my rock 'n' roll sensibilities with its catchy riffs and power chords, making me want to rent a convertible and drive top-down to SEC country for a football tailgate. Any music that makes you feel that way is worth listening to even if it inadvertently raises existential questions about who you are. But it was the band's lyrics that closed the deal. The album is filled with highly practical, sagely delivered advice ("When you don't get paid 'til next week but you need some drinkin' cash / Find that coffee can stash and tip it back"); heartfelt appreciations of life's little necessities ("Here's to the ice you float your beer in"); and dreams ("I'm gassin' up the Chevy / I'm gonna pick her up at six /

I hope she's gonna wear them jeans with the tear / That her mama never fixed").

I listened, fully engaged, this despite the fact I was never a fan of country music, at least not the contemporary Garth Brooks variety. I admire Johnny Cash and Willie Nelson as much as the next guy, which is to say quite a bit, and I've been a lifelong fan of Ry Cooder, who's sort of country-adjacent, but I just never could get my head around Nashville country's goody-goody twang, finely buffed edges, and overt religiosity. Florida Georgia Line dragged me kicking and screaming over to the other side.

And I, in turn, brought Jed. Between the ages of ten and eleven, his favorite lyric, sung full-throated every time, was from that first Florida Georgia Line record: "This brand-new Chevy with a lift kit / Would look a hell of a lot better with you up in it." He loved that line from the very first even though he had no idea what a "lift kit" was and had to ask me. For about the next two years, every time we happened upon a truck with a lift kit, we gave each other knowing smiles and nodded like idiots. "These guys are real poets," he told me once as we listened to the record start to finish yet again. "Bob Dylan has nothing on them," he added in all seriousness. He continued to maintain that position even after Dylan was named a Nobel laureate. I had only myself to blame.

Jed and I really wanted to catch a Florida Georgia Line concert but we were going to be out of town when they came through the Bay Area. So I jumped on their website and saw they were playing down in Irvine in southern California on a Saturday night later in the tour. I grabbed us tickets. I figured it would be fun to fly down there together and make a big event of it.

We were pumped for the concert, but a few weeks before the show the band released a new album. As I listened to it on my commute to work, my heart sank. It was terrible. Gone were the power chords, catchy riffs, and cheesy lyrics. Well, that last one isn't quite right; the lyrics were still cheesy, just not in the usual amusing, down-home way. They were now dripping with saccharine-sweet earnestness, the lead singer oddly declaring, ad nauseum, the holiness—yes, the holiness—of his current love interest in the first single, the aptly titled, if distractedly acronym-ed, "H.O.L.Y." (I think it stands for high on loving you). The distance between Florida Georgia Line and the Nobel Prize ceremony in Stockholm seemed to have widened significantly.

I suspected the band would promote the new album hard at the concert, so I warned Jed to temper his expectations. We'd imagined a night filled with songs from *Here's To the Good Times* and now I seriously doubted we'd get it. Jed took my blistering record review in stride and said he was still excited for the show. And because he was, so was I.

We flew down the Saturday afternoon of the show, checked into our hotel near the Orange County/John Wayne airport, grabbed a bite to eat at the hotel restaurant, and jumped in a cab to the Irvine Meadows Amphitheater.

"Learn from your mistakes," Jed remarked matter-of-factly as we walked past a wildly inebriated young woman throwing up in the bushes on the way to our seats.

"That's good advice," I replied, proud of his wildly precocious ten-year-old acuity but suddenly questioning my own parental judgment in taking him to the concert. There were more whiskey bars than Porta Potties spread across the concert grounds; even so, the lines for whiskey dwarfed those for the bathroom. We hadn't even gotten through the gate from the parking lot when the first of many obscenities was dropped by the supercharged revelers whom Jed and

I bookended in age by several years in both directions. I'd never seen so many women wearing skimpy denim cutoff shorts and cowboy boots; fortunately, the eroticism of the scene was lost on Jed, who simply, astutely observed: "There are a lot more girls here than boys."

During the show I saw Jed bobbing along, head swaying, getting into it. But every so often he'd look over at me somewhat sheepishly to see how I was reacting to the music, no doubt because I'd mocked the new record. I could tell he felt he needed my permission to enjoy the music.

About halfway through the concert, the lights went down and a white grand piano was wheeled onstage for "H.O.L.Y." After dedicating the tune to his wife, the lead singer proceeded to croon about how loving her makes him so unbelievably high. "It doesn't sound like Florida Georgia Line, but it's pretty good stuff," Jed said to me almost apologetically.

I thought for a moment about making some critical comment, but then to my great surprise found myself saying, "You know what, that's exactly right." Jed looked at me and cracked a thin smile.

It struck me that while the new record wasn't what I'd expected, divorced from those expectations and judged simply on its merits (sappy lyrics aside), it was for the most part, as Jed said, pretty good stuff. I love my wife, too; so on that level I could relate to the message. And I happen to like piano-centric music—in fact, some of Springsteen's best is piano-based. So what's wrong with Florida Georgia Line losing the twangy guitars and reverb and trying to express adult emotions? Absolutely nothing.

With his simple observation, Jed made it possible for me to experience the music in a different way and enjoy it for what it was rather than dislike it for what it wasn't. I have him to thank for reversing our roles and modeling a healthier, mind-expanding perspective for me. And I have the blog to thank for bringing Florida Georgia Line into our lives.

Each weekend, and sometimes after work, I'd carve out time to write, not wanting to let too much time pass between blog posts. Keeping a schedule required significant effort, but I enjoyed it. I mostly blogged about new bands that had a classic rock sensibility, but I also wrote personal pieces about the confluence of music and parenting in my life, beginning with an essay about the CDs I burned for Jed's late night feeding sessions. Based on the feedback I received from my select group of followers, the personal essays seemed to resonate the most and so I kept at them. An essay about the songs I sang to Jed at bedtime was published by *The Washington Post*; another about the Florida Georgia Line concert was published by *The New York Times*; a third about my regret at not forcing Jed to attend a Who concert with me was published in a literary journal. Having my work appear in such high-profile and respected publications was thrilling; it also provided a tremendous morale boost—I felt as if I could pull off the writing thing, that I had something of interest to say, and that maybe, just maybe, I wasn't a complete fraud.

One of my essays, which proved consequential in the parenting realm, was accepted by the local San Francisco NPR affiliate, KQED, and I got to read it on the radio during the morning commute. The essay, which I submitted just before Christmas one year, described how I found myself flailing around for holiday gifts; how music used to be my go-to gift, but no more because the Streaming Age had taken away my ability to give music as a gift; how to this day, the best gift I ever received was the first three albums by The Clash, which Murphy gave me for my bar mitzvah. Such was the power of that gift, I wrote, that long before I had a son, or even a girlfriend, I fantasized about presenting my unborn child at his bar mitzvah with mint copies of every classic Rolling Stones album: "Here son, now you are a man." But the digital age, I concluded, had killed that dream. My son, who was about to become a bar mitzvah, would not be receiving vinyl from me.

While I did receive some positive feedback on the piece, in general the response was unkind, especially from a bunch of burnt-out Bay Area hippies. One wrote on the KQED blog, "I could not possibly disagree more with your assessment." He said he'd bought his kids a turntable and some vinyl and they loved it. "It sounds to me like you just threw in the towel and gave up, while some of us continue to do our part in keeping the medium alive with the next generation." Another guy said he "cringed" when he heard me reading the piece on the radio. And somebody somehow got my work number and left a nasty message on my voicemail saying I was a disgrace. Over vinyl!

It took me a couple of days to digest all the criticism and put it behind me. But put it behind me I did. Although those muckrakers had dangled the delicious bait of self-doubt in front of me, I refused to take it—for the most part. While they didn't make me question the whole writing enterprise, I did eventually realize that the guy who scolded me to suck it up and get my son a turntable and vinyl might have a point. And so I decided to move forward with the plan for Jed's bar mitzvah gift.

Why? It's a fair question given that Jed's passion for music doesn't match mine. It's not even close. He doesn't lock himself in his room for hours on end to listen to music. Other than Florida Georgia Line and U2, he's shown little interest in going to concerts—he actually considered skipping Springsteen on Broadway in favor of a fancy dinner out with his grandmother. With all due respect to my mother, seriously?

But still, I decided to forge ahead with the plan. Put simply, I viewed the gift as a way to give my son a piece of me, a piece of what makes his dad tick, to have and hold forever. I never received a gift like that from my father, never really got a piece of him, never really knew him.

I did, however, temper the plan somewhat. Because Jed wasn't much of a Stones fan, I didn't get him every classic Rolling Stones album from *Beggars Banquet* to *Some Girls* as the original scheme called for. I exercised the restraint of an ascetic and limited myself to *Exile on Main Street* and *Sticky Fingers*. Instead I bought him several Springsteen and U2 records (with Florida Georgia Line's *Here's To the Good Times* thrown in for good measure) since those were his favorite artists. I also bought him a turntable, tuner, and speakers.

The turntable had a beautiful walnut finish and a sleek modern design with some old school touches, including a manual belt to change the platter speed from 33 RPMs to 45 RPMs. The tuner had a working VU meter and four odd-shaped mad science–type bulbs that protruded from the top with tiny filaments that glowed when the tuner was turned on. For speakers, I got him top-of-the-line bookcase speakers, easier to transport from place to place than floor speakers, I figured.

The night before Jed's bar mitzvah, Jodi and I wrapped his gifts and laid them out on the dining room table so he could open them first thing in the morning. My gift consisted of four separate boxes, one each for the turntable, tuner, speakers, and records. Jodi's gift to Jed was a large, modern black-and-white photographic dreamscape of cloud formations. Jed once claimed to be interested in photography and Jodi had called his bluff. She's also a modern art buff and wanted to give Jed a piece of herself as I did.

When Jed got up the next day, Jodi and I told him to shake the cobwebs and head downstairs since there wasn't a lot of time to spare;

we all had to get ready for the service. Jed scampered downstairs still in his PJs and seemed excited about the number of large, gift-wrapped boxes strewn across the dining room table. I felt bad about that since I knew he wasn't that into music and would likely be disappointed after he tore into them. Maybe not getting-a-lump-of-coal-in-your-stocking bummed, but still, he wouldn't be psyched.

I told Jed it would make the most sense to open the box that housed the turntable first. He tore into the wrapping paper and when he saw what it was, his brow got all furrowed. I had included a note explaining why I'd given him the gift, which he read, but it didn't seem to register much with him.

"Thanks," he said weakly, trying but not able to hide his disappointment.

He went through the motions of opening the other boxes with the speakers, tuner, and records. He looked through the albums without expression. It was a total dud, as expected. Jed then opened Jodi's gift and had much the same reaction. He put on a brave face, thanked Jodi, and went upstairs, leaving everything on the dining room table.

That night after Jed brushed his teeth, he called out from the bathroom, as he always did, "I'm ready!" It was time for his song. I went upstairs and climbed into bed with him. Told him what a great job he'd done with the whole bar mitzvah thing, the preparation and execution. How proud of him I was. "Thanks, Papa," Jed whispered as he pulled the covers up to his neck. There was a brief silence and then he said, "You know, I think we should put the turntable in the basement." We had a large basement with a TV, X-Box, and pool table. My guitars and the piano were also down there. "I don't really have space for it in my room."

"That's fine," I said even though there was a bookshelf in his room that with a little rearranging could have accommodated it. "Jed, I know you think my gift's a little strange. It's not something you need or want or have expressed great interest in."

"Yeah, to be honest I was sort of hoping for Madden 19."

"I know it. But I really wanted to give you something different to mark this amazing milestone, not just something I'd get you for a random birthday. I don't want you to feel any pressure to use it constantly or even at all, though. You can tuck it away for safekeeping and I won't be offended. Just know that if you ever want to find a little piece of your Pops, one day at college or wherever, that you have it in this gift."

Jed looked at me as if he knew I was speaking English but couldn't quite puzzle out what I was saying. I gave him a pat on the knee. "Let's sing."

Of course I chose "Brokedown Palace." As I sang, I thought about my inaugural rendition our first night together, incredulous at the young man Jed had become. When I finished, Jed looked up at the ceiling. "Maybe tomorrow I can set it up."

"That sounds good." I kissed him goodnight, got out of his bed, and walked over to the door. "I love you more than words can tell," I whispered, "and I wish you a lifetime of pursuing your deepest passions."

Jed never did get around to setting up the turntable. I offered to help him but he kept brushing me off. So the whole system—turntable, tuner, and speakers—remained in their boxes in the basement.

After several weeks, I gave in and set everything up myself. I tested the system by spinning "Sweet Jane." It sounded so good, so bright and full, I felt like the guy in the classic Maxell cassette ad, sitting low in that high armed chair, whose hair, tie, and martini glass are literally blown back by the sheer force of the music. Even the occasional cracks and pops of the vinyl didn't detract but added texture and urgency as the VU meter bounced along to those four sublime chords. I organized the albums alphabetically by artist and chronologically within each artist. Then I broke down all the cardboard boxes, turned out the basement light, and shut the door behind me.

It'd be there if he ever wanted it.

21

HAIL, HAIL ROCK 'N' ROLL

I'm standing on the floor of the hallowed Warfield Theater in San Francisco, a venue drenched in rock history, where the Grateful Dead and Bob Dylan each played more than twenty times, where the likes of The Clash and U2 and the Allman Brothers Band once performed. But on this night, I'm waiting not for one of the towering colossi of rock to take the stage, but for Lucero, a road-weary and, judging from the size of the crowd, under-appreciated band from Memphis.

I've recently blogged about Lucero and am fired up for the concert, not just because I've of late become obsessed with their hard-charging sound—and with their self-pitying lyrics about heartbreak that somehow resonate with me even though I haven't been dumped by a girl since 1987—but also because this morning I quit my job at PG&E. Having at long last stepped off the corporate treadmill, I'm feeling light and free—and ready to rock.

As I wait for Lucero, I take a long pull of my beer, number three of the night, and look around at the sparse crowd. We all look pretty much the same—mostly guys in our forties, thinning hair, dressed drably in either "business casual" attire having come straight from work or some combination of denim and dark flannel, sipping beers, talking quietly or not at all to the people we're with. The advanced age demographic and lack of sartorial panache are to be expected; Lucero released their first record more than fifteen years ago and aren't exactly what you'd call young and hip, what with their dad jeans and white T-shirts. It's all earth tones in the place—no hint of an accent color to be found, except for the faint blue glow emanating from behind the liquor bottles at the bar.

I'm not paying much attention to the music being played over the sound system—it's mostly 1960s-era Rolling Stones, some Bonnie Raitt. But then like a slap in the face, the opening distortion-riddled power chords of the Sex Pistols' "God Save The Queen"—that initial jolt of G-sharp immediately sliding up to an A repeated four more times, the last three at an accelerated clip, sounding like a door being kicked in, a soul-quenching cacophony that causes a certain stripe of teenager the world over to feel they've been called to arms, suddenly alive for the first time—blares from the speakers. I'm a bit confused since Lucero's brand of rock has more country to it than punk. But as Johnny Rotten continues his snarling diatribe against the British monarchy, the choice starts to make more sense to me—if you listen closely enough, you can detect an undercurrent of punk in Lucero's strafing guitars, if not in their lovesick lyrics.

Hearing the Sex Pistols causes my mind, well lubricated by beer, to wander back through time to when I'm twelve years old.

On a cold and grey New York winter day, I was at the Crazy Eddie on Third Avenue flipping through record bins. I'd ducked into the store to keep warm before meeting friends at a movie theater a few blocks away and was hanging out way in the back, mostly trying to get away from the freezing wind that blew in every time the front door opened. In front of the S bin, I unzipped my overstuffed Michelin Man parka and rifled through the records, most of which were by artists I'd never heard of: Shalamar, Carly Simon, Status Quo. I wasn't really even shopping, just trying to blend in as best I could with the adult customers, not wanting to draw attention to myself.

Keeping my head down, I shuffled through the records with the speed and rhythm of an assembly line worker. I kept flipping until I landed on the Sex Pistols' *Never Mind The Bollocks, Here's The Sex Pistols*. What did twelve-year-old me know about the Sex Pistols? Not much, other than they seemed . . . well, kind of scary. They wore studded black leather jackets, had crazy hair dyed in odd colors, and always seemed to be flipping someone the bird—three affectations we most definitely did not have in common. I was vaguely aware that the Sex Pistols played "punk" music, whatever that meant, and I was curious about them, in part because of their name, wondering if it really referred to a guy's dick. If so, that was pretty damn cool. Seemed like that probably broke some type of rule. I definitely liked the *idea* of breaking rules. I took the album out of the bin and checked out its salmon-colored cover and block letter graphics. "Sex Pistols" was written across the bottom half of the cover in letters of all different sizes, a mix of capitals and lower-case.

As I inspected the album art, a store clerk in a ratty, short-sleeved-despite-it-being-freezing-outside Led Zeppelin T-shirt came up behind me and said something that even tonight at the Lucero show, decades later, I still hear softly buzzing in my ears, like tinnitus. He said, "That album will change your life."

He spoke with the authority of Moses imparting the Ten Commandments, but my only thought then was, *Huh*? If I listen to the record, will I suddenly get the urge to ditch my overstuffed parka and score a studded black leather jacket? Will I want to dye my hair orange? Will the record rewire my brain so that whenever my parents ask how school is I'll tell them to fuck off? I wasn't quite sure any of that would be a good thing.

But still, this dude's crazy-ass prediction fascinated me. Maybe he knew something about my life. Did he see some potential in me that I didn't? Some coolness lurking underneath that lame parka? Suppose I bought the record, you know, just to see if my life changed a little? Not that I had any particular issues with my life. But if this guy thought it could be taken up a notch, I was listening.

I dug around in my pockets to see how much money I could scrape together. Sadly, I didn't have enough for both the movie and the album. Not wanting to stand up my friends and figuring I could come back and buy the record some other time, I explained to the clerk that I was on my way to a movie and didn't have enough for both.

"You'll never remember the name of that movie," he said, sounding as certain about it as Lexington Avenue running downtown.

He turned away, leaving me feeling like a musical poser, a private school kid who just didn't get it.

Feeling like maybe I'd screwed up big-time, like I'd let down not just the Crazy Eddie dude but in some weird way I didn't quite get, myself too, I put the album back in the bin, zipped up my overstuffed parka, and headed off to the movie, the name of which I now can't remember.

Interesting, I think as the last notes of "God Save The Queen" fade from the Warfield's sound system. Did that Sex Pistols record, which I did eventually buy—and played continuously for weeks and intermittently for decades—change my life? Did music?

As I ponder that question, I think back to my meeting that morning with my boss, Peter, a meeting that *has* changed my life, reflecting on what caused me to take the leap. Peter was stunned and saddened when I broke the news of my imminent departure, asked if there was anything he could do to change my mind—suppose I was allowed to work from home some or have more say in the cases I was assigned? I thanked him but said no, there was nothing.

"What are you going to do next?" Peter asked. "Have you got something lined up?"

"No, I'm just going to take some time for now," I replied. "Think things through a bit. And work on a writing project I've been kicking around."

"I feel like this is my fault, that I loaded you up too much," he said.

I liked Peter and told him that wasn't it, which was only half true. I certainly did feel burned out, having busted my ass for going on a full year with late nights and weekends spent working more the rule than the exception. But it wasn't just the amount of work—it was also the work itself. The last year I'd been diving deep on an issue that, well, let's just say it didn't inspire much passion: the allocation of above-market power contract costs as between customers of traditional utilities and municipal cooperatives. Not that what I'd been working on prior to that—haggling with ratepayer advocacy groups over proposed capital projects and rates of return—was particularly stimulating either. Yet somehow I'd been at the company doing this type of work for twelve years—twelve freaking years! And although I didn't admit it to Peter, unlike some scandal-ridden politician who claims to be stepping down to spend more time with his family, I truly did want to spend more time with mine, particularly with Jed. It'd been months since I'd been able to drive him to school, a task I held sacred, the two of us listening to sports talk radio, strategizing about our respective fantasy football lineups, or rocking out to our favorite station—Springsteen's E Street Radio on SiriusXM. I was no longer a fixture at Jed's basketball and soccer games, and couldn't break out of work early now and then to play golf with him after school. And over the course of his recent bar mitzvah weekend, with the entire family and loads of friends having travelled in for the festivities, I had to carve out time away to finalize a brief that was due the following Monday.

My mind wanders to a passage from Springsteen's sacred text in which he describes the dilemma of his middle child who as a baby was prone to tantrums, in large part because Bruce wasn't around much, until Bruce hits upon the idea of spending time with the boy each night during his midnight bottle feedings. Problem solved—no more tantrums. "My commitment had been all he was really looking for," Bruce writes. Growing up, I didn't feel my father ever committed to me. And so from day one, I decided I was going to commit to Jed. Lately, I'd felt that commitment wavering.

As I take another pull of beer and contemplate the improbable emotional tangents swirling around the Sex Pistols, Springsteen, fatherhood, and my career, I notice that Lucero has wandered out. They're a very unassuming band—no pyrotechnics to welcome them to the stage, no fog machine, not even a PA announcement. They just appear. And start playing. The guitars are loud, freight-train loud, which is welcome, most welcome. I've come to revere the life-affirming call to human sentience of extremely loud live music, that feeling of aliveness and bliss it transmits as its energy pulsates through one's body at 120 decibels, akin to that of sex, a feeling that can't be conveyed through a smartphone.

The staccato riff around which Lucero's first song is built uncoils like a snake and I can feel its benign venom circulating in my blood, causing me involuntarily to nod my head in time to the music as my gaze drifts up to the ceiling. I notice some of my beer has spilled, having been sloshed around by my swaying body, and so I rest it on the floor. Suddenly the chorus wells up, the serpentine riff is gone, replaced by power chords. The lead singer howls, "Even though I left so long ago / I got someone waiting back at home." Some combination of that lyric and the generous amount of beer I've consumed makes me think of my father, dead now for almost thirty years. I wonder, is that what I've been doing all this time? Waiting for my father to come back, to come home? Is that how I ended up in a job I find soulless and deadening? Because I think it'll bring him back?

My focus returns to the stage as the singer sings, "Somehow we both got lost / And you tell me that I can't change." More questions flood my mind. How did I get so lost? Was my father lost, too? Who told me I can't change? Did he tell me? Did I tell myself? Can I change if he didn't? Have I already changed? Did I change today?

The music is lifting me ever higher and I feel like I'm soaring over a majestic mountain chain. Then in mid-flight I hear the opening notes and gentle guitar strum of my favorite Lucero tune, "Here at the Starlite." I glance over at the bar and see there's no line, so I dart over there for one last beer. "Here at the Starlite" is a gargantuan seven-and-a-half-minute tune that starts as a slow-burner and crescendos at the chorus which hits like a tidal wave of sound, taking the song skyward as it gains velocity, depth, and bad intentions, like a falcon, head down, wings dropped beginning its murderous free fall. The singer croons, "Memories too close to home / For something that's never coming back," the tidal wave of the chorus rising and crashing over me. The lyric pierces me, causes me to take a hefty gulp of beer, and it finally dawns on me why I'm drawn to Lucero's achy-breaky lyrics: I, too, am filled with heartbreak for my lost love—not some girl, but my father. And like the girl in all the band's songs, he ain't coming back. Which sucks. But the good news is, I'm no longer waiting for him. I'm moving on, avoiding his fate by not being him.

By the end of the concert, I'm euphoric. I'm where I want to be, where I need to be, standing on this hallowed ground, communing with this music, embracing it, letting it work its life-affirming magic on me. I think back on how music has sustained me throughout my life, how it's brought me, at long last, here, to a place where I'm truly alive.

And I think back to that hipster clerk at the Crazy Eddie all those years ago trying to sell me on the life-altering power of the Sex Pistols. Although music didn't change my life, maybe, just maybe, it saved it.

OAKLAND, CALIFORNIA
2009

About a year after Jed was born, a letter arrived from Aunt Wendy. But this time, there was no accompanying mix tape, nor any of the typical Aunt Wendy lightness. Instead, she wrote that she might be facing surgery soon, that a large mass on her pancreas would probably need to be removed.

"Now that you have a son," the letter continued, "I want to say something to you." She urged me to give my son the freedom to be whatever and whomever he wanted. It was the only way for him to be happy, she wrote. When a child doesn't meet your expectations in life, it's scary, but it's okay, she advised, admonishing me to recognize the difference between discipline and the imposition of my own desires. "Please, what really matters in life isn't how much money or power you have—if your son goes for those, fine. But if he doesn't that's also fine. Happiness comes from being truthful to yourself. The more I listen to Bob Dylan's words, the more meaning I get out of them. And these words have been ringing out since I was a teenager."

The letter ended with a plea: "Please, see your son for who he is. Love him as he is. Embrace him for who he is. I want you to know I have always cared about you. But my family's inability to accept me kept us very apart. I am very sorry. Please don't do this to your son."

Three years passed. Other than an off-the-shelf Hallmark get-well card, I didn't reach out to Aunt Wendy. I assumed if there was reason to be concerned, my mother would tell me. And eventually, she did. But by then, Aunt Wendy was slipping away. Too detached to call, I instead wrote her a letter.

I told her about that magical night in high school when I first heard "Tangled Up In Blue," how it opened up a whole new world to me and how she solved for me the riddle of its identity. The letter was my way of telling Aunt Wendy, albeit somewhat indirectly, perhaps too indirectly, that our brief interactions, measured in hours over my lifetime, added up to way more than the sum of their parts, to something fundamental, that they had helped shape the person I became. I felt an urgent need to acknowledge, at long last, the connection I now realized Aunt Wendy had tried her entire life to nurture. It felt like the most important letter I'd ever written. I fantasized it might have some magical healing power, if not sufficient to cure her, then at least potent enough to mend the hole in her heart produced by her family's dismissiveness—by my dismissiveness. I imagined her reading my letter, smiling, and feeling a little less alone.

But before the letter reached the hospital, my Aunt Wendy died. It was returned to me unopened. I stood in the hallway just staring at that envelope, unable to move. Eventually I sat down on the living room couch and stared out the window, watching the cars go by.

I already knew Aunt Wendy had died—my mother had told me a few days before. She said she'd gone to visit Aunt Wendy at the hospital three weeks prior. As she approached the entrance to the Sloan Kettering Cancer Center, she saw an old woman in a wheelchair sitting just beyond the doorway. She was wrapped in blankets even though it was a hot July day and was smoking a cigarette. As my mother got closer, she smelled pot and saw that the old woman was actually smoking a joint. And then she saw it wasn't an old woman at all but her fifty-eight-year-old sister.

"I couldn't believe it was her," my mother told me. "If I hadn't been there to see her, I would never have recognized her, she was so small and frail."

My mother and Aunt Wendy hadn't spoken in five years, the result of some fight I knew little about. But they reconciled that day at the hospital. My mother told Aunt Wendy she loved her. And Aunt Wendy told my mother the same.

Warren, one of Aunt Wendy's "friends," called my mother to tell her Aunt Wendy had died. He said there wouldn't be a funeral, that Aunt Wendy had asked to be cremated and that they planned to scatter her ashes in a private ceremony. He didn't say where. I guess he figured it didn't matter to my mother, and she didn't ask, so maybe he was right about that. But I would've liked to know.

Although I knew Aunt Wendy had died, I still thought my letter had made it to her in time. Without thinking, I got up from the couch, put on my headphones and cued up "Tangled Up In Blue." I knew every lyric to that song by heart, had listened to it hundreds of times, but the last line struck me like I was hearing it for the first time: "We always did feel the same, we just saw it from a different point of view."

I thought back to Aunt Wendy's invocation of Dylan's "Hurricane" at the seder many years before and realized I'd never gotten back to her with my thoughts about the song, as she'd asked me to. If I had, I would've told her I listened to the song that night after the seder, with my headphones on, the vinyl of her old album cracking violently from the microscopic dust and dirt layered in its grooves. I would've told her she was right, that the song, a passionate call to social justice, did in fact rock. And I would've told her I loved it.

I thought about when she sent me that tape of Van Morrison covering Dylan's "It's All Over Now, Baby Blue." I wished I'd thanked her for it, wished I'd told her that as much as I liked Van Morrison's version, I still thought Dylan's acoustic live version from *Biograph* was the gold standard, with its haunting, piercing harmonica solos that sounded like cries signaling the end of the world.

I thought about the mix tape she sent me when Jodi and I first moved to California, the one with "California Stars" on it. I wished I'd told her how much I appreciated her sending it, how it helped me understand her—and myself—better, helping me to know all that we shared.

Above all, I wished I'd treated Aunt Wendy as she'd treated me—like family.

Aunt Wendy believed in the power of music to provide meaning and purpose and fulfillment. As a boy, I had a fledgling belief in all that, too. I felt that power percolating deep within me. But I couldn't find a viable outlet to give it expression. Aunt Wendy could and did. The courage she showed in giving herself over to music, in displaying openly her passion, helped chip away over time at the internal wall I'd constructed to keep the power of music at bay, to keep it in its confined lane. As a kid, I thought our points of view were so far apart, we couldn't possibly feel the same. But we did. I just didn't know it.

Rereading the letter I wrote to Aunt Wendy now, more than a decade later, it feels inadequate. There's so much I didn't try to tell her because I didn't yet know it.

I didn't tell her I'd started to write about music and sensed her presence every time I sat down at the computer, encouraging me to feel, to free myself, to know it's okay.

I didn't tell her about my decision to quit my job at PG&E, how I was afraid I was becoming my father, my ever-increasing and passionless work stealing all my energy, all my time; didn't tell her how thrilling it felt after I left to have emotional space for Jed—and for myself—or how that weighty decision was made to feel light by reflecting on the courage she displayed in living her life.

I didn't tell her she'd helped me to live my admittedly conventional life on my own terms. Whether it was my decision to light out for the Alaska wilderness, leave the East Coast for California, quit my corporate law firm job to work as an environmental attorney at the Justice Department, take an extended break from work to travel around South America, or ultimately to quit the law to dedicate myself full-time to writing about my father and my son—and her—I didn't tell Aunt Wendy that through her example, she unwittingly helped me overcome my family's resistance and chart my own path.

I didn't tell her I've embraced her challenge, born of a lifetime of rejection, to treat my son with unconditional love. That I aspire to it every day. That nothing he could choose to do, and nothing that he is, could ever make me not love him.

And I didn't tell her I love her and am sorry for my complicity in her rejection.

My family and I relegated Aunt Wendy's voice to a whisper. Only as an adult have I made out its words.

The night my letter to Aunt Wendy was returned to me unopened, I got into Jed's bed and told him I'd be singing him a new song, a song by a guy named Bob Dylan called "Tangled Up in Blue." Jed took the news in stride—he was only about four-and-a-half at the time and wouldn't express intense preferences for particular songs for another few years. As I sang to him, both of us lying on our backs looking up at the ceiling, I stole a few quick side glances and noticed his little brow furrowing periodically, perhaps trying to follow the narrative of it and definitely not falling off to sleep.

When I finished, he looked at me a little funny and said, "That's a lot of words. How can you remember them all?"

"I've listened to the song lots," I explained. "Eventually, the words just got stuck in my head."

He considered my answer, seemed satisfied with it, and then said, "What's the song about, anyway?"

I turned to my son, kissed him on the forehead, and said, "Everything."

ACKNOWLEDGMENTS

I'd like to thank Lisa Algert, who unwittingly started me down the road to becoming an author by outlandishly suggesting I start a music blog; Hilary Zaid, for her invaluable feedback on the manuscript, for schooling me on the publishing world, and, above all, for encouraging me to do something more with my writing; Jodi Fodor, editor extraordinaire, for conceiving of the book's structure, and for her countless suggestions that helped put my voice on the page; Andrew Harlem, for discovering the veins to mine and equipping me to follow them to the depths; Adair Lara for helping me get the project off the ground; Nancy Davis Kho for her helpful comments on the manuscript; Erica Silverman, for suggesting I turn my essays into a memoir, for admonishing me to stop "jumping from stone to stone" and instead plunge deep, and for believing in the project before it was a project; and Pam Friedman, who encouraged me to find, inhabit, and nurture the deepest, darkest spaces within me.

Thank you to my wife, Jodi, for putting up with my inward turn dictated by the project, for tolerating the countless dour renditions of "Sweet Jane" wafting up from the windowless basement office, and for helping me see the beauty in life always.

And, of course, Jed, thank you for accompanying me on this journey, for enriching it beyond my wildest imaginings, and for allowing me to tell a part of it. I love you more than words can tell.

About the Author

photo credit: Laurie Bishop

Matt Fogelson is a writer and former lawyer whose true passion is music, primarily of the classic rock variety. His Substack, *Fine Tuning*, blends personal storytelling with a love for the music that makes sense of life, centering on new artists and the intersection of music and parenting. His work has appeared in *The New York Times*, *The Washington Post*, *Scary Mommy*, and NPR. Matt resides in Oakland, California.

PERMISSIONS

The author would like to thank the artistic creators and rights holders of the following songs and literary works for granting permission to reproduce excerpts of their copyrighted material in this book:

BROKEDOWN PALACE
Words by ROBERT HUNTER Music by JERRY GARCIA
© 1971 (Renewed) ICE NINE PUBLISHING CO., INC.
All Rights Reserved
Used By Permission of ALFRED MUSIC

DARK STAR
Words by ROBERT HUNTER Music by JERRY GARCIA, MICKEY HART, BILL KREUTZMANN, PHIL LESH, RON McKERNAN and BOB WEIR
© 1971 (Renewed) ICE NINE PUBLISHING CO., INC.
All Rights Reserved
Used By Permission of ALFRED MUSIC

SCARLET BEGONIAS
Words by ROBERT HUNTER Music by JERRY GARCIA
© 1974 (Renewed) ICE NINE PUBLISHING CO., INC.
All Rights Reserved
Used By Permission of ALFRED MUSIC

FROM A BUICK 6

Words and Music by BOB DYLAN

IT'S ALL OVER NOW, BABY BLUE

Words and Music by BOB DYLAN

LIKE A ROLLING STONE

Words and Music by BOB DYLAN

SWEETHEART LIKE YOU

Words and Music by BOB DYLAN

TANGLED UP IN BLUE

Words and Music by BOB DYLAN

TIGHT CONNECTION TO MY HEART (HAS ANYONE SEEN MY LOVE)

Words and Music by BOB DYLAN

UP TO ME

Words and Music by BOB DYLAN

BLACK

Words by EDDIE VEDDER Music by STONE GOSSARD

ONCE

Words by EDDIE VEDDER Music by STONE GOSSARD

RELEASE

Words by EDDIE VEDDER Music by EDDIE VEDDER, STONE GOSSARD, JEFF AMENT, MIKE McCREADY, AND DAVE KRUSEN

FELL ON BLACK DAYS

Words and Music by CHRIS CORNELL

FRESH TENDRILS

Words by CHRIS CORNELL Music by MATT CAMERON

MAILMAN

Words by CHRIS CORNELL Music by MATT CAMERON

THE DAY I TRIED TO LIVE

Words and Music by CHRIS CORNELL

BEFORE WE DISAPPEAR

Words and Music by CHRIS CORNELL

CRUISE

Words and Music by CHASE RICE, TYLER HUBBARD, BRIAN KELLY, JOEY MOI AND JESSE RICE

PUBLISHING, ROUND HILL WORKS, BIG LOUD MOUNTAIN, DEEP FRIED DREAMS, BIG RED TOE MUSIC AND ARTIST REVOLUTION PUBLISHING
All Rights on behalf of SONY MUSIC PUBLISHING (US) LLC and DACK JANIELS PUBLISHING Administered by Sony Music Publishing (US) LLC, 424 Church Street, Suite 1200, Nashville, TN 37219
All Rights on behalf of BIG LOUD MOUNTAIN, DEEP FRIED DREAMS and BIG RED TOE MUSIC Administered by Round Hill Works
All Rights on behalf of ARTIST REVOLUTION PUBLISHING Administered by Anthem Entertainment
All Rights Reserved – International Copyright Secured – Used by Permission
Reprinted by Permission of Hal Leonard LLC

HERE'S TO THE GOOD TIMES
Words and Music by RODNEY CLAWSON, CHRIS TOMPKINS and LYNN HUTTON
Copyright © 2012 ROUND HILL WORKS, BIG RED TOE MUSIC, BIG LOUD SONGS, SPIRIT CATALOGUE HOLDINGS, S.A.R.L., HOUSE OF SEA GAYLE MUSIC and SHADES OF NEON
All Rights for BIG RED TOE MUSIC and BIG LOUD SONGS Administered by Round Hill Works
All Rights for SPIRIT CATALOGUE HOLDINGS, S.A.R.L., Administered by Spirit Two Nashville
All Rights for HOUSE OF SEA GAYLE MUSIC and SHADES OF NEON Administered by Clearbox Rights
All Rights Reserved – Used by Permission
Reprinted by Permission of Hal Leonard LLC

ROUND HERE
Words and Music by THOMAS RHETT, CHRIS TOMPKINS and RODNEY CLAWSON
Copyright © 2011, 2012 EMI BLACKWOOD MUSIC INC., CRICKET ON THE LINE MUSIC, BIG LOUD SONGS, ANGEL RIVER SONGS, BIG RED TOE MUSIC and AMARILLO SKY SONGS

All Rights for CRICKET ON THE LINE MUSIC Controlled and Administered by EMI BLACKWOOD MUSIC INC.
All Rights for BIG LOUD SONGS, ANGEL RIVER SONGS, BIG RED TOE MUSIC and AMARILLO SKY SONGS Administered by BIG LOUD BUCKS
All Rights Reserved – International Copyright Secured – Used by Permission
Reprinted by Permission of Hal Leonard LLC

TIP IT BACK
Words and Music by TYLER REED HUBBARD, BRIAN KELLEY AND RODNEY CLAWSON
Copyright © 2012 ROUND HILL WORKS, BIG LOUD MOUNTAIN and BIG RED TOE (BMI)
All Rights Reserved – Used by Permission

REAL MEN
Words and Music by JOE JACKSON
© 1982 POKAZUKA LTD.
Used by Permission - All Rights Reserved

AS LIFE GOES BY
Words and Music by THOMAS CLAY KEENE
©1986 by DePAUL MUSIC
Used by Permission - All Rights Reserved

AMONG THE GHOSTS
Words and Music by BENJAMIN NICHOLS
© 2018 EMPTY ROAD MUSIC (BMI), ADMINISTERED BY KOBALT MUSIC PUBLISHING LTD
Used by Permission - All Rights Reserved

HERE AT THE STARLITE
Words and Music by BENJAMIN NICHOLS
© 2002 EMPTY ROAD MUSIC (BMI), ADMINISTERED BY KOBALT MUSIC PUBLISHING LTD
Used by Permission - All Rights Reserved

SWEET LITTLE THING

Words and Music by BENJAMIN NICHOLS

WITHOUT LETTING GO

Words and Music by LAURIE SARGENT

CALIFORNIA STARS

By WOODY GUTHRIE

HE WENT TO PARIS

Words and Music by JIMMY BUFFETT

DEATH OR GLORY

Words and Music by

JOE STRUMMER and MICK JONES

THE HISTORY OF LOVE

BORN TO RUN

MURPHY'S LAW, VOL. ONE